Nonverbal Sex Differences

Nonverbal
Sex Differences

ACCURACY OF COMMUNICATION
AND EXPRESSIVE STYLE

JUDITH A. HALL

THE JOHNS HOPKINS UNIVERSITY PRESS
Baltimore and London

© 1984 The Johns Hopkins University Press
All rights reserved
Printed in the United States of America

The Johns Hopkins University Press, Baltimore, Maryland 21218
The Johns Hopkins Press Ltd., London

Originally published, 1984
Johns Hopkins Paperbacks edition, 1990

Library of Congress Cataloging-in-Publication Data
Hall, Judith A.
    Nonverbal sex differences.

    Bibliography: pp. 163–200.
    Includes index.
    1. Nonverbal communication (Psychology)
2. Sex differences (Psychology)   I. Title.
BF637.C45H28   1984   155.3′3   84–47957
ISBN 0-8018-2440-0 (alk. paper).
ISBN 0-8018-4018-X (pbk.)

for Fred, Jacob, and Rebecca

Contents

List of Tables

Preface

The study of nonverbal communication, a fast-growing enterprise among psychologists, is important to anyone interested in human social behavior. Evidence from anthropology, ethology, and sociology, as well as from psychology, demonstrates that the nature of face-to-face relations depends to a remarkable degree on nonverbal behavior — movements and expressions of the face, eyes, and body, qualities of the voice, and interpersonal touch and spacing. Nonverbal behaviors tell an eloquent, though often subtle and unconscious, story of how we feel about others, the roles we desire to enact from moment to moment, and the cultural expectations we have grown up with. A person's social identity depends significantly on nonverbal behavioral style.

There can be no doubt that our sex — whether we are male or female — and the sex of others with whom we interact are major factors in social perception, in expectations for interpersonal behavior, and in actual interpersonal behavior. It is no wonder, then, that nonverbal behavior and skill also vary predictably as a function of the sex of the people involved. The primary purpose of this book is to document these differences, using quantitative methods to draw together a large research literature, much of which is unknown, or at least unsummarized in systematic fashion. The study of nonverbal sex differences still has far to go, but now, at least, investigators will know the state of current knowledge and may be helped in deciding which issues most deserve their attention.

Though there are many possible explanations for these sex differences, the most ardent statements about them have emphasized the theme of women's oppression. According to the oppression hypothesis, as I call it, male-female nonverbal differences and differential nonverbal treatment of men and women reflect and maintain women's subordinate social position. Nearly every published discussion repeats this position, sometimes in strong advocacy, and sometimes simply as an interesting hypothesis. Since no one has critically examined this interpretation of male-female nonverbal differences, I made it my purpose to give special scrutiny to this hypothesis, as well as to explore and evaluate other possibilities.

It would have been satisfying to be able to endorse a theoretical point of view after studying the evidence and the arguments, but this has not been possible. Certainly the attention paid in this book to theoretical issues and evidence, and the comparatively balanced nature of the discussion, will benefit future investigators. But the fact remains that when asked why these robust sex differences exist, I still have to reply that I do not know.

This book is the product of many years of guidance and support from others. My parents, Elizabeth and Max Hall, fostered my intellect throughout my life, and my father, by his superlative example, taught me the importance of clarity in writing. My brother Clay Hall introduced me to social psychology. And the lessons learned from Robert Rosenthal are almost impossible to count; he helped me to become a psychologist, to think clearly about data, and to be intellectually courageous.

I am grateful also to friends and colleagues who generously provided comments on the chapters: Ross Buck, Bella M. DePaulo, Mary Amanda Dew, Howard S. Friedman, Fred Gordon, Amy G. Halberstadt, Klaus R. Scherer, Deborah S. Stier, and Marylee C. Taylor. Finally, I eagerly acknowledge my debt to the veritable army of investigators on whose research the book is based. Without their efforts we could not document nonverbal sex differences at all.

Nonverbal Sex Differences

1   Goals and Methods

This book is about interpersonal communication via nonverbal cues in human males and females. *Nonverbal* refers to people's communication skills and styles of expression, excluding the actual verbal messages they might be using. Examples are smiling, gazing, and the ability to judge the meanings of nonverbal cues. People have noticed nonverbal sex differences for probably as long as society has existed. Very likely, this awareness is implicit in stereotypes of the sexes — for example, in the stereotypes of women as intuitive and pleasant and of men as insensitive and unexpressive.

Scientifically documented nonverbal sex differences are not hard to find, and are in fact of substantial magnitude compared to many other psychological sex differences. Neither are explanations hard to find; these range from the neurophysiological to the sociological. Writers have suggested that nonverbal sex differences have evolutionary significance, reflect different degrees of specialization of the brain, reflect and perpetuate the domination of women by men in societies around the world, and reflect differences in men's and women's roles and activities.

The first goal of this book is to document the existence and size of sex differences for all the nonverbal skills and behaviors that have been frequently studied. Though there are many studies to summarize, the procedures for doing so are straightforward and the evidence generally allows confident conclusions. The second goal is to evaluate different explanations, both conceptually and in light of theoretically relevant data. The third goal is to compare the size of known nonverbal sex differences to psychological sex differences of other kinds, for example verbal ability, aggression, and a variety of personality traits. These last two goals are, compared to the first, more difficult to carry out and lead to less-definite conclusions. The theoretical issues cannot yet be resolved by recourse to empirical data, and indeed may never be, for reasons made amply clear throughout the book. The comparisons of nonverbal to other sex differences yield provocative but still tentative results, because the list of behaviors studied is not exhaustive and because of methodological inconsistencies.

When social psychologists began developing ways to describe human social behavior objectively, early in the twentieth century, nonverbal sex differences were among the earliest topics of study (for example, Allport 1924). Though this research was continued throughout the century, the past decade has seen an explosion of research due both to social psychologists' concern with women's issues and sex roles and to the rise of nonverbal studies as a major emphasis within American social psychology.

Research on nonverbal sex differences is important for several reasons. First, it helps satisfy our irresistible curiosity about how men and women behave and why, using rigorous methods that represent a great advance over the more naive and subjective impressions gained from everyday life. At the same time, as almost any investigator would agree, the empirical methods used to study nonverbal behavior may still be quite faulty — unsubtle, for example, or inappropriate to studying the intentions and perceptions of people in ongoing interaction. Second, the study of nonverbal sex differences can illustrate and potentially can help us understand fundamental elements of social life, such as socialization and social roles. Third, such research can have practical applications. Understanding the behavioral tendencies and preferences of each sex could help prevent miscommunication in such interactions as those between doctors and their patients and teachers and their pupils. And finally, such research could have political significance. If differences in how men and women are treated nonverbally or in how they behave nonverbally are factors in maintaining status differences between them, then knowledge of nonverbal sex differences could help provide a recipe for social change.

Though some behaviors to be discussed are clearly nonverbal, such as interpersonal touch, others seem at first glance to be both verbal and nonverbal. For example, people often make errors while speaking — tripping over their tongues and repeating or omitting words. In a sense, these are aspects of verbal behavior because they are part of the stream of words. But they can also have little relation to the literal meaning of the words and may instead reveal aspects of the emotional state or the self-presentational style of the speaker. These are common functions of nonverbal behavior. Therefore, speech disturbances, as well as how much people talk and how fast, are included here as aspects of nonverbal style.

There are exceptions, also, to the statement that our context for study is the forum of interpersonal communication. Some behaviors that are discussed are not necessarily part of communication, in the sense that a person knowingly conveys ideas and feelings to someone else. Instead, some behaviors are indicative of a personal style of expression or movement that may show up even if a person is not interacting with someone, as when studying at a desk or watching a movie. Also, a large amount of research measuring expression and judgment has been conducted in controlled laboratory settings that do not actually involve interpersonal communication, but, rather, responses directed to a camera or judgments of films or tapes. Sometimes one assumes that the behavior would be the same in real face-to-face situations; sometimes the accumulated evidence argues strongly that this is the case (R. Rosenthal et al. 1979).

Our awareness of nonverbal sex differences probably begins early in life. Telling a man from a woman is one of the commonest distinctions we make in everyday life. We can do it on the basis of the slimmest pieces of information. For example, people can identify men from women moving in total darkness, just from looking at tiny lights attached to their bodies. Similarly, when we talk on the telephone, we usually know the sex of the other person after their very first word or two.

This skill, which we rapidly come to take for granted, is based largely on primary and secondary sex characteristics. In everyday situations, the characteristics of height, facial hair, musculature and the like are usually obvious. Other clues are dress style, hair length, and adornments. But some of people's accuracy at telling the sexes apart probably has to do with their implicit knowledge of stylistic behavioral differences, that is, differences in nonverbal behavior. These have been called tertiary sex differences (Birdwhistell 1974). Being a male or female is so important a fact of existence that when our judgment fails — when there just are not enough cues available for us to know the sex of someone — we are truly confused and uncomfortable. Without knowing the sex of someone, we are unable to make a host of important, though probably unconscious, assumptions without which "normal" interaction is seriously impaired.

The idea that we display our role, or present ourselves, via nonverbal behavior has long been accepted. Our bearing, demeanor, and mannerisms can all be put to use to show the world that we are bold, shy, friendly, and so forth. Some of the time, such a constellation of characteristics is part of a total performance in a recognized role such as teacher, boss, friend, or mother. It has also been suggested that "male" and "female" are roles, each with its set of prescribed behaviors. To the extent that people display their sex role, nonverbal behavior takes on great importance as a vehicle for such display. Though it seems generally assumed that the male or female nonverbal display is intended for the opposite sex (for example, Birdwhistell 1974; Henley 1977), the evidence collected in this book raises the possibility that the salient audience may instead be others of one's own sex.

Because so many things seem predictably associated with one sex or the other — from small things like the color of one's socks to large things like rates of mental illness and occupational choice — there has developed a large research enterprise devoted to documenting and explaining the differences, documenting people's beliefs about the sexes, and investigating the impact of sex stereotypes on people's lives. Even the definition of terms such as sex, gender, and sex role has become a matter of scholarly debate (Spence and Helmreich 1978; Tresemer 1977). The definitions used in this book are simple. *Sex* refers to sexual identity: what you would say if asked whether you were a man (male) or a woman (female). *Sex role* refers to society's expectations about appropriate behavior for the sexes and the ways in which those expectations are expressed in behavior.

It is very difficult to explain sex differences. Because maleness and femaleness are complex mixtures of biology, tastes, attitudes, personality traits, and social behavior, investigators' inability to experimentally manipulate these many factors means that there is no certain way to ascertain which factor or factors "cause" a given sex difference. It is easy to speculate on which of these many aspects of maleness and femaleness is a likely causal antecedent for an observed difference in nonverbal behavior, and certain explanations do appear over and over in the literature. But our ways of attempting to demonstrate the origins of a sex difference are indirect and are usually not capable of ruling out all alternate explanations.

By the same token, since there are many differences between the sexes, there can in principle be many explanations. The relationships among nonverbal behaviors are not well established, and it is therefore unwarranted to assume that one explanation is needed for all nonverbal sex differences. For example, women are more sensitive than men to nonverbal cues and they approach others more closely than men do, but these two traits could develop for different reasons.

We need to focus research efforts on explanatory factors. Most studies simply document a sex difference and then speculate as to causes. There are several reasons for this: first, the logical primacy of describing a phenomenon before trying to explain it; second, the difficulty of conducting explanatory research; and third, the fact that many investigators have looked at sex differences for the sake of methodological completeness rather than out of intrinsic interest, and therefore had little reason to explore their determinants.

For whatever reasons, there is an abundance of descriptive research on nonverbal sex differences. Clearly, investigators have frequently been unaware of how much published research is available. For a number of areas covered in this book, there has been no adequate, or even somewhat adequate, review.[1] One reason for both the lack of awareness and the lack

---

1. The most complete review to date is my own (Hall in press), a much condensed and not as exhaustive version of the present summary.

of thorough reviews is that much of the research is extremely recent, though it must also be true that investigators have often done inadequate searches before embarking upon research.

In conducting this review of sex differences, I discovered that, for some topics, the end result was a resounding confirmation of conclusions already reached by other authors. For other topics, I was led to question the validity of conclusions and interpretations offered by previous writers. And finally, the wealth of research permitted me to answer some new questions and to point to others that have not been adequately asked in existing research.

One way that the present book goes beyond previous discussions, aside from including more studies and trying to organize explanatory themes, is in systematically asking about sex differences in more than one way. Although the most obvious way is to ask about the sex of the person who possesses the skill or is producing the behavior of interest, one can also ask about the sex of the recipient or target of the behavior. A question posed in this way would be, "Do people stand closer to women than to men?" There are still other questions about sex differences. Is same-sex communication different from opposite-sex communication? Do men communicating with other men act differently from women communicating with other women? And do men treat women differently than women treat men? Whenever there are enough data, these questions are addressed.

The chapters are organized according to the communication-skill modalities of judging and sending and according to "channels" of behavior. Channels are sources of cues — facial expression, gaze, interaction distance, touch, body movement and position, and voice. Since people communicate through a totality of cues and not through one kind at a time, this division of the book on the basis of channels is arbitrary and sometimes frustrating to efforts at integrating results and explanations. But for summarizing the findings economically and numerically, there was no choice but to organize the chapters in this way.

To summarize studies, I have used statistical procedures. This is partly because no one could summarize, and no one could bear to read about, so many studies if they were handled individually or entirely verbally. But even more importantly, quantitative methods are powerful ways to draw conclusions and to detect trends and relationships in the data. Later sections of this chapter present the overall methods used to summarize research, and other chapters present any additional detail that is relevant to specific topics.

Readers unfamiliar with statistical reviews of literature may be surprised that relatively few studies are identified individually in the text and tables. When specific studies are mentioned, it is often not because they are outstanding in quality or results but rather because they address theoretical issues or because they represent categories of behavior or study designs that are dissimilar to others and therefore cannot easily be pooled with them. Whenever there was a sufficient number of studies on the same basic question, the study characteristics and results were quantified and subjected to statistical analysis.

When a literature is not too large, a reviewer doing such a quantitative review may provide tables showing the numerically coded attributes and results for each study reviewed. But when there are many studies, this is impractical. I have not provided such detailed tables but rather summary tables showing major findings. This is analogous to what the authors of individual studies do when they present statistical analyses and summaries of their data rather than the actual data for each person studied. To help readers locate the literature for each main analysis, however, I have supplied an appendix, which lists all the studies, by authors and years, that contributed data to each major research question.

Necessarily, in a quantitative review of this sort, the emphasis is on overall tests of the hypotheses in question. This unfortunately means that some results of individual studies are not included. For example, sex sometimes interacts statistically with other factors in research designs. Because few studies are similar enough in design to permit quantitative summary of such interaction effects, they sometimes remain hidden in the pages of the original research reports. It is important to acknowledge the simplifying nature of the kinds of analyses presented in this book. Though I have tried to bring to light results that point to possible moderating factors, there are surely relevant results that I have failed to mention.

METHODS EMPLOYED IN SUMMARIZING RESEARCH

Literature Used for Documenting Sex Differences

Persons of all ages are included, from newborns on up, but only if they were described in the original reports as mentally and physically normal or were unselected with regard to mental or physical health (unless I specifically state otherwise). The research methodologies of the studies included were based on systematic observation, objective testing, or computer-assisted analysis of voice recordings.

The study of nonverbal communication tends to branch out into related areas, which have widely varying methodologies. Because of the large number of studies that fall under a strict definition of nonverbal behavior or skill, it was necessary to draw boundaries. For example, because one important function of nonverbal communication is to express emotion, one can easily become interested in the experience of emotion itself. Thus, the study of mood or personality will contain, in principle at least, insights into sex differences that are relevant to nonverbal communication. The finding that women experience somewhat more anxiety than men (or at least admit to it), as shown in chapter 11, could certainly have implications for their nonverbal expressions. But to include studies on topics such as this would open the door too wide for a thorough review of the literature to be feasible.

Similarly, some research methodologies do not fit a strict requirement for systematic observation of nonverbal behavior or testing of nonverbal skill. For example, if classroom observers watch preschool children and rate them on scales of "aggression" and "exhibition," this surely implies something about the nonverbal behavior of the children observed. But to include studies with such methodology would, again, force the inclusion of many additional studies, many of which would be hard to interpret because of the necessity of inferring nonverbal behavior from global ratings. Possibly, a boy and girl could engage in exactly the same behavior, but the boy's behavior might be called "exhibitionistic" and the girl's "aggressive," because of different standards of judgment based on sex stereotypes (Buck 1977).

Further, studies using such global ratings very often cannot separate verbal from nonverbal behavior, and since I have tried to avoid mixing these information sources, this is another reason to exclude such studies. The only significant exception is found in chapter 10, where ratings of voice quality are discussed. Global ratings of the voice are a major, though still problematic, method used by investigators of that channel of communication.

Self-reports, due to questionable validity, are also excluded from the summaries of sex differences, though they are discussed as a separate category when self-rating data are available.[2]

Sources

Every author who summarizes scientific literature is concerned that the published literature is biased in offering mainly statistically significant results, especially those results that support current beliefs. If this bias occurs, one's summary may be an exaggerated or totally erroneous version of the phenomenon of interest. One way to minimize such bias is to

---

2. Other topics excluded from the quantitative summaries of nonverbal behavior are: physiological measures; body self-image; imitation of aggressive models; crowding and density (unless the dependent variable was a nonverbal behavior); empathy; role-taking ability; most research in which nonverbal behavior was role-played; handwriting style; clothing and adornments; subjects' drawings; composite measures that cut across channels (for example, a tension factor that included both nervous laughter and trembling); research using territorial markers of sex; and perceptual skills, such as finding hidden figures and making tone discriminations. Most of these excluded categories are very small. Some are discussed in chapter 11.

include as many unpublished studies as possible — doctoral dissertations, for example — in the belief that null or unpredicted results may be better represented there. In this book, however, I have excluded unpublished data, with only a few exceptions which are identified as such. Unpublished data are excluded for two reasons. First, they are hard to acquire in a systematic way and are often not easily available for general scrutiny. Second, the published literature is not as likely to be biased for sex differences as for other topics. This is because these studies often did not primarily explore sex differences but rather persuasion, or recognition memory, or some other substantive topic. Therefore the nature of sex differences would have been but a minor factor in whether the studies were published. Sometimes sex was entered into statistical analyses just to increase precision, again not because the author was especially interested. The reporting of these incidental analyses of sex is one reason why the literature on nonverbal sex differences is large.

Because sex differences are so often not the main topic of an article, they are often not highlighted in the article's title or abstract. For this reason, literature-search procedures based on titles and journal abstracts are very inadequate. My method therefore was to search the actual contents of forty English-language journals devoted to nonverbal behavior and to social, personality, developmental, cross-cultural, clinical, counseling, and general psychology. For those with a high probability of having relevant results, such as the *Journal of Personality and Social Psychology,* every article was individually examined, back to the earliest volume locally available. For journals with a smaller likelihood of containing anything of interest, I looked at the table of contents of each issue rather than at each article, but with frequent inspection of promising articles. Using this method, I found many results that have never been included in a review of nonverbal sex differences. In addition to this primary search method, I gathered references from bibliographies and from my own reprint files.

What Constitutes a "Study"?

Often it was necessary to decide how to group subjects within studies. In simple cases, a report presented results for one or more independent samples of subjects and did not present results for subgroups within the samples. Here I counted each sample as a separate study. In a more complex case, a report was based on samples that had subgroups, such as older and younger children or experimental and control subjects. Procedures for these cases depended on several factors. My strong preference was to use the entire sample as the "study," with no breakdown by subgroups, in order to increase the stability of the data. This practice was also justified because most of the time the results for the entire sample were more completely reported than for the subgroups. But there were exceptions. Where the data for subgroups were considerably better reported than the data for the sample as a whole, I called each subgroup a study. When the subgroups happened to be the age groups that I sought to examine separately — infants, children, adolescents, and adults — I also used the subgroups as studies. And when the subgroups were racial, ethnic, or cultural groups and the behavior in question was interpersonal distance, I also used the subgroups as studies, for reasons given in chapter 7.

It was also desirable to keep results independent within a data set for a particular nonverbal variable, that is, to make sure that each result was based on an independent sample of subjects. In some instances, therefore, it was necessary to average over repeated observations of a sample or to select the measures that made the most sense, in order not to include the sample more than once. There are only two exceptions to this practice. For expression accuracy, the data set is not entirely independent, due to the occasional measurement of two very distinct kinds of skill on the same sample. And for body movement and position, the data set is not independent for the same reason: investigators often measured several different kinds of movements for a given sample. It seemed foolish to disregard all but one kind, and it also made no sense to average the results over various behaviors in order to arrive at a single result per sample.

Quantitative Methods

With many studies to summarize, one employs categorization and numerical indices. Categorization is used to describe attributes of research design and other features of a study (for example, whether a sample consisted of infants, children, or adults). Numerical indices are used to describe the results themselves. I have used three outcome indices commonly used in quantitative research summaries (see, for example, Eagly and Carli 1981; R. Rosenthal and Rubin 1978). These are direction, effect size, and statistical significance.

Direction is a simple tally of which way the result came out, disregarding effect size and statistical significance. In a study that compares men's and women's accuracy at decoding nonverbal cues, if women score higher than men — even if only by a tiny amount — then the direction variable is coded as favoring women. In a few cases, the difference is actually zero, and in others the authors say "no difference," meaning not that there was literally no difference but rather that there was not a statistically significant difference. Both of these stated outcomes are disregarded in the summaries of direction.

Using the direction index, it is possible to calculate the number of studies favoring one sex or the other over all the available studies, and to test whether the proportion favoring one sex is statistically significantly different from the proportion of .50, expected under the null hypothesis.

It is important to remind readers that there are other comparisons of interest besides male versus female subjects — for example male versus female targets (recipients) of communication. Whenever such other comparisons are made, the same outcome indices can be used, whether they are direction, effect size, or statistical significance.

Effect size is not a new concept, but its use in reviewing literature may be new to some readers. For many years, researchers have sought and employed ways of stating how large a given difference or relationship is. Obviously, it is desirable to know how large a difference is, not just its direction and not just its statistical significance (which is a function of effect size but also of other factors, such as the size of the sample). With the systematic statistical treatment by Jacob Cohen (1969) and recent applications by psychologists (for example, R. Rosenthal and Rubin 1978; M. L. Smith, Glass, and Miller 1980), the concept and calculation of effect size have become known to many research psychologists. Many research summaries employing effect size have been published on topics such as psychotherapy outcome, interpersonal expectancy effects, the effects of educational interventions, and sex differences. (See Glass, McGaw, and Smith 1981, Green and Hall 1984, or Rosenthal 1980 for further explanation of the use of effect sizes in reviewing literature.)

Effect size is an index of difference or relationship that is standardized in some way so as to make comparisons between studies possible. Often, two investigators of the very same topic will employ different measuring instruments or observational techniques, which makes comparison difficult. Or, even if they employ the same techniques, they may discover that their subject samples show different degrees of variability, in which case a direct comparison of differences could be misleading. One effect-size statistic, *d,* standardizes mean differences between two groups according to the amount of variation in the samples (J. Cohen 1969).

A closely related index of effect size is the Pearson product-moment correlation, *r.* When one variable has only two categories, as in male versus female, such a correlation is called a point biserial correlation.[3] This is the index of effect size used in this book. For readers not familiar with this statistic, it has a range from -1.00 to $+1.00$, and when squared it tells how much variation in one variable is accounted for by the other. A negative correlation means that as one variable increases, the other decreases, and a positive correlation means that as one increases, the other also increases. In this book, rs that represent the sizes of sex differences are

3. The relationship between d and point biserial r is: $d = 2r/\sqrt{1 - r^2}$ and $r = d/\sqrt{d^2 + 4}$. For small to moderate values of r (up to about .25), d is essentially $2r$.

always calculated so that a positive value indicates a higher mean for females and a negative value indicates a higher mean for males.[4]

The magnitude of such a correlation can be evaluated both absolutely and relatively. Though chapter 11 addresses at greater length the question of the evaluation of magnitude, some comments are called for here. First, few psychological or behavioral sex differences that do not depend on obvious physiological differences seem to be large in absolute magnitude, that is, in terms of how much variation sex is capable of explaining. Second, nonverbal sex differences seem on the average to be no smaller than, and often larger than, sex differences for other behaviors and traits. A few illustrative, well-established sex differences from other research areas may help set a context for evaluating the magnitudes of nonverbal sex differences: the correlation between sex and amount of conforming in a group is .16 (females more; Eagly and Carli 1981); the correlation between sex and scores on tests of quantitative ability is $-.23$ (males more); and the correlation between sex and scores on tests of verbal ability is .18 (females more; both Hyde 1981). Chapter 11 offers explicit comparisons of nonverbal sex differences with these and other known sex differences.

Once one has calculated effect sizes for a collection of studies, giving each a sign that reflects the direction of the difference observed, one can perform a variety of further statistical tests. One informative procedure, used here, is to correlate the effect-size estimates with other study attributes, such as age group of subjects, over the whole set of studies. If the size of the sex difference for, say, smiling is appreciably associated with some factor such as age, we are led to hypothesize further about why such a relationship exists. Uncovering moderating variables in this way does not in itself test a causal hypothesis but instead points toward areas where further study might be profitable.

Statistical significance is one of the commonest ways of deciding what to make of a research result. It tells, of course, how confident we can be that a sample difference is real, or the probability that it would happen by chance if there were actually no difference in the population from which one has sampled.

Priceless though this statistic is, it has its limits. It tells about the believability of a result but not about its size. A difference between two

---

4. Very infrequently was r actually reported in the studies reviewed. My calculation of r depended on how the data were presented. If only means and standard deviations (SD) were given, I calculated first d (d = [female mean − male mean]/pooled within-sex SD; J. Cohen 1969), then r as in note 3. If t and degrees of freedom (df) were given, I calculated d ($d = 2t/\sqrt{df}$), then r. If F and df were given, I calculated r as in the preceding case, substituting $\sqrt{F}$ for t. If Mann-Whitney U was given, which was extremely rare, I estimated what the corresponding t would have been, and proceeded from there. If only a p-value and df were given, I estimated r using standard tables.

groups could be incredibly small, but if enough people were in the sample, the difference would become statistically significant. Conversely, a difference could be large but, due to small sample size, could fail to reach significance by the conventional $p = .05$ criterion. It is for these reasons that researchers have turned to an estimate of the effect size as an additional, nonredundant piece of information.

Once one knows the p-value of each result in a set, one can summarize them in several ways, two of which are employed here.[5] The first is to count the proportion of results that achieved statistical significance favoring each group. The other is to calculate a combined probability. This is a single new p-value that summarizes all of the individual p-values in the data set, taking into account the directions of the actual differences. Though there are several ways to compute a combined probability (reviewed by R. Rosenthal 1978), only one, called the Stouffer method, is used here.[6] Statistically minded readers will want to know that these combined ps, as well as all other ps, are given in two-tail form and are assumed to have been two-tail in the original studies if an author did not state otherwise.

Though these three indices — direction, effect size, and statistical significance — were the methods of choice for summarizing research results, the data were not always in sufficient quantity or in the correct form to permit the application of all three procedures. Some studies are therefore discussed individually, in a qualitative rather than quantitative way, and this is especially true if their results had particular relevance for theoretical issues.

---

5. In some cases where p was not reported, it was possible to calculate or estimate it from data given. For example, if sample size and effect size were available, t could be calculated and p found in standard tables.

6. The formula for calculating this combined p is: $\Sigma Z / \sqrt{N}$, where Z is the standard normal deviate obtained for the sex difference in each study, which is always given a sign to reflect the direction of the result, and N is the number of Zs under consideration. Combined ps were calculated only for results for which something about significance was known (either Z, exact p, rounded p such as "< .05," or "not significant"). If nothing was known about significance, the result was excluded from the calculation of combined p. Results of "not significant" were translated into Zs if sufficient data were readily available, but if not, they were given Zs of zero; this procedure gives a conservative value of combined p whenever there is a marked trend favoring one group, since those "not significant" results probably do, on the average, favor that group. When results were given in rounded form (for example, "$p < .05$"), I did not calculate an exact Z but used the Z that corresponded to the rounded p. This is conservative because the actual Z would be larger than this.

2   Judgment Accuracy

Surely one of the oldest stereotypes of women is their interpersonal sensitivity. Perhaps because of their nearly universal responsibility for child rearing, women are generally expected to be prosocial and nurturant. The need to decipher children's nonverbal cues of emotion, intention, and need could also spawn the expectation that women are generally responsive and accurate in judging people's emotions.

Cross-cultural research does show that young girls are expected to be nurturant and that they actually do display more nurturance than boys do, though there is considerable variation from country to country (B. Whiting and Edwards 1973; B. B. Whiting and Whiting 1975). Girls are, in particular, socialized to be caretakers of young children starting at an early age in a number of places in the world, though much less so in the United States than in some other places (Whiting and Edwards). Even in some monkeys, juvenile females spend more time carrying and tending infants than do juvenile males (Hrdy 1977). The skills drawn on in child care could indeed contribute to greater interpersonal sensitivity in women.

Stereotype assigns women to the "socioemotional" domain of activity, as distinguished from the "task" or "instrumental" domain associated with men (Broverman et al. 1972; Parsons and Bales 1955; J. E. Williams and Best 1977). The empirical basis for such a claim has been criticized by researchers who document exceptions to such a simplistic dichotomy (for example, Aronoff and Crano 1977; Craddock 1977). Research on self-report, however, definitely shows tendencies for women to exceed men on a cluster of traits variously called socioemotional, expressive, and interpersonally oriented, whereas men exceed women on a cluster called task oriented, instrumental, and agentic, though for both clusters there is considerable overlap between the sexes (see chapter 11 as well as Bem 1974, Spence and Helmreich 1978, and M. C. Taylor and Hall 1982). These clusters are often called "feminine" and "masculine," respectively, though such usage invites overinterpretation due to imprecision and a long tradition in psychology of labeling as feminine or masculine anything that distinguishes the sexes in a statistical sense (Constantinople 1973). Even among elementary school children, these constellations differentiate girls' self-reports from boys' self-reports, though again with much overlap (Hall and Halberstadt 1980). Scales that measure these traits almost invariably include interpersonal sensitivity and awareness of others' feelings among the "feminine" traits. Such a definition of femininity could both reflect and enhance the interpersonal sensitivity of women.

The ancient concept of "women's intuition" is probably part of this same set of beliefs about women, though cast often in an unflattering light (West 1979). Women's intuition connotes interpersonal awareness but also psychic powers and irrational thought. Many writers over the centuries have repeated the idea that men are cognitive and analytical while women are emotional and nonanalytical. Though the idea of women's intuition usually has pejorative connotations, it could actually be based in part on women's greater accuracy at decoding nonverbal cues or on their tendency to reach quicker interpretations of nonverbal cues than men do (Allport 1924; Kirouac and Doré 1983).

Yet another possible source of greater interpersonal sensitivity in women is their disadvantaged status in most societies of the world. Mentioned by English (1972), Weitz (1974), Henley (1977), and others specifically with regard to women's nonverbal skills, this hypothesis states that people who are oppressed have heightened needs and therefore motives to understand subtle interpersonal cues. Such knowledge is hypothesized to aid their efforts at social adaptation. For illustration, a female secretary might notice and interpret every flicker of expression on her male employer's face; such knowledge may tell her how she's doing from moment to moment, how to improve her performance, how to please him better. The boss, on the other hand, might notice little besides her sheer presence or absence and her typing skill; if he believes he does not need to monitor her feelings or opinions, he will not be motivated to do so. As a result of many such experiences, his nonverbal judgment ability may be poorly developed.

Some research does support the status–nonverbal-awareness hypothesis; for example, less-dominant individuals in a group glance more frequently at others than do more-dominant individuals (for example, Anderson and Willis 1976). But whether it is low status in women that accounts for their heightened ability to judge nonverbal cues is a question that requires more evidence than is currently available, as will be seen later.

Several definitions can be imposed on the general term "interpersonal sensitivity." Some have been employed only sporadically in the empirical literature, and not all have to do specifically with nonverbal cues. Knowing what is tactful, for example, is interpersonally sensitive but does not necessarily require an understanding of nonverbal communication. The definitions employed in this chapter are accuracy at decoding nonverbal cues, usually cues of emotion, and accuracy at recognizing faces. The present chapter documents sex differences for these skills, and the next chapter considers in more detail several explanations for women's superiority at both.

ACCURACY AT DECODING NONVERBAL CUES

Demonstration of Sex Differences: The PONS Test

I first became interested in nonverbal sex differences when, as a graduate student working with Robert Rosenthal at Harvard, I joined with him and several others to study people's abilities to judge the meanings of nonverbal expressions of the face, body, and voice. This research, which began in 1971 and culminated in a book in 1979 (R. Rosenthal et al. 1979), was the first serious effort to validate a test of this skill. It was not, by any means, the first effort to measure such skill, for researchers had been asking subjects to judge nonverbal cues since the second decade of this century. But it was the first extensive, systematic effort to use standard test-validation procedures to develop a measuring instrument for decoding skill.

In validating our test, called the Profile of Nonverbal Sensitivity or PONS test, we and our colleagues tested over ten thousand people ranging in age from third grade to middle age. As often as possible, we gathered additional information on these people, such as nationality, mental health, cognitive skills, and, naturally, sex.

The test consisted of a sound motion picture, in black and white, that lasted forty-five minutes. As the test subjects watched and listened, they made judgments which they recorded on a multiple-choice answer sheet. The film contained 220 two-second segments of nonverbal behavior taken from a variety of scenarios, all of which were enacted by a young Caucasian woman. The decision to have an expressor of only one sex, and indeed to have only one individual to do the expression, was defensible on several grounds. But it caused a problem with regard to our understanding of sex differences in people's decoding-skill scores, which I shall return to later.

The scenarios were chosen to reflect everyday life situations and were enacted as spontaneously as possible in front of videotape cameras. The scenarios included both positive and negative emotion and both dominant and submissive demeanor. Examples are talking to a lost child (positive and dominant), criticizing someone for being late (negative and dominant), asking forgiveness (positive and submissive), and talking about one's divorce (negative and submissive).

Each was presented in the film in eleven different channels of visual, auditory, or audiovisual cues. The visual channels were face only, body only (neck to knees), and full figure (face plus body). The auditory channels were electronically filtered speech and randomized-spliced speech. In filtered speech, an electronic device makes the voice sound muffled (and the words incomprehensible, which is the goal) by removing the highest frequencies (Rogers, Scherer, and Rosenthal 1971). The randomized-spliced method (Scherer 1971) makes the words incomprehensible by physically rearranging pieces of an audiotape so that the sequence is scrambled. Both of these methods are described more fully in the book on the PONS test mentioned earlier. In each case, what is accomplished is the rendering of human speech into purely nonverbal elements, such as rhythms, loudness, frequencies, variations in loudness and frequencies — though both content-masking techniques sacrifice some of these nonverbal features.

I have described five nonverbal channels, three visual and two auditory. The remaining six channels consisted of every pairing of the visual with the auditory — face with filtered speech, for example. In each pairing, the nonverbal expressions were always those that belonged together for that scenario; the face from expressing gratitude was never, for example, paired with the voice from ordering food in a restaurant. On the answer sheet, test subjects circled the scenario description that they thought was correct from a choice of two. Accuracy scores were based on the number of items identified correctly.

Now that the PONS test is described, let me proceed to the sex differences. The greatest detail concerning them is contained in the book on the PONS test mentioned earlier. Here I present only the most important and well-replicated results.

We found that females score higher on the PONS than males do. In a sample of 480 U.S. high-school students, which we treated as one of our main normative samples, girls showed higher accuracy on all but one channel (randomized-spliced speech). The difference between boys' and girls' total scores was significant at $p < .001$, and the effect size (r between sex and score) was .23. Though highly significant, this difference between males' and females' scores is only moderate in size. What is "small," "medium," and "large" is, of course, a relative matter. An effect of the size just stated is small when compared to some effects produced by manipulating conditions in a psychological experiment but is large compared to many other psychological sex differences (see chapter 11).

This correlation of .23 means that 5 percent (or .05, the square of .23) of the variation in test scores is explained by sex. The other 95 percent is due to other factors, some of which we know about on the basis of research done with the PONS. Such factors include age, personality, and practice. Another way to state the same relationship is in terms of the effect-size estimate, d (J. Cohen 1969); d in this instance is .47. This effect size tells us that the averages of the boys and girls were .47 standard-deviation units apart. An effect of this size should, according to Cohen, be visible to the naked eye — that is, given enough opportunities for observation, one should be able to detect the presence of such a sex difference without recourse to statistics. Finally, to state the sex difference in yet another way, females' total score was 172.2 out of 220 (78 percent), while males' was 166.2 (76 percent).

Samples of U.S. elementary-school children, junior high-school students, and college students revealed similar sex differences. Though the samples got dramatically more accurate with advancing age, the male–female difference remained more or less the same. To substantiate this finding, twenty-three samples of subjects ranging from third grade to adulthood, a total of 1,048 individuals, were analyzed in an analysis of variance that had sex and age as independent variables. Sex and age were both significantly associated with total scores, with females scoring better by at least two percentage points on every channel. Notably, there was no significant interaction of sex with age, indicating that the magnitude of the sex difference on total score remained fairly constant over the four age groups. The same sort of analysis was performed for just the four elementary-school grades, and again sex and age were individually important contributors to skill, but the age × sex interaction was not significant: the sex difference stayed about the same over the four grades.

Other analyses of the PONS showed that females — both children and adults — were especially good, relative to males, at decoding scenes with negative as opposed to positive emotional content. But females' advantage over males was constant for scenes labeled as dominant and for scenes labeled as submissive.

In samples of students in elementary school, junior high school, and high school, males exhibited slightly more variability in their PONS scores than did females. This phenomenon is not peculiar to the PONS test; on tests of cognitive abilities, males' scores are often more variable (Maccoby and Jacklin 1974). It is important to note, however, that the PONS test has shown good discriminant validity with regard to tests of cognitive skill such as intelligence and achievement tests. In other words, decoding skill as measured by the PONS is not synonymous with, or even closely related to, the kinds of skills measured by standard cognitive tests.

At the time that the book on the PONS was written, 133 samples of subjects had been tested that had at least two members of each sex. Eighty percent (106 samples) showed females to score higher than males, a difference that was highly significant ($p < 10^{-9}$). These 133 samples showed a range of effect sizes (r) that went from $-.44$ to $+.76$, but the median effect size was .20, a figure very close to the .23 found for the U.S. high-school norm group described above.

Some of the 133 samples were not from the United States, which provided the opportunity to examine the cross-cultural generality of the sex difference. Included in the analysis to be described here were 46 samples, with a total of nearly two thousand people from ten nations. These samples were chosen according to the following criteria: that they were not from the United States, that they were tested in or near their native countries, that they were not diagnosed as psychopathological as a group, and that they were of junior high-school age or older. For comparison, six large, diverse, clinically normal samples were chosen from the United States; they were high-school age or older and chosen without reference to their decoding-accuracy scores. The total number of people in these comparison samples was just over a thousand. All of the cross-cultural groups were tested with English-language answer sheets, except for the Israeli, Mexican, and German samples, who used answer sheets translated into their own languages.

Table 2.1 shows the eleven cultural groups, the number of samples in each group, and the average magnitude of the sex differences, stated in terms of the correlation coefficient, r. On the average, these groups showed a difference between males and females of about two percentage points on the total score of the PONS test. These data were subjected to an analysis of variance that tested the effects of nationality on the sex differences. Nationality was a significant contributor to the sex differences, with a p-value of .04, indicating that there was significant variation between national groups. However, it is obvious from table 2.1 that the nations with larger numbers of samples showed fairly homogeneous sex differences, while the nations for which only one or two samples were available showed the extreme differences, that is, either extreme female superiority or actual male superiority in one case. Such a pattern suggests that the more extreme differences, which contributed to the significant culture effect, were partly due to sampling error, that is, unstable estimates of the true sex difference resulting from small samples of subjects. The bottom of table 2.1 shows that the average effect size (r) was .20, a figure which is, again, close to the U.S. normative data and also identical to the median of the entire group of 133 samples described earlier. Samples from the United States show overall sex differences that are neither the largest nor the smallest obtained around the world; instead, they are about average.

The key message from the descriptive cross-cultural data is that the sex difference in overall ability to decode the nonverbal cues of the PONS test is generalizable to at least several other national groups. This conclusion is consistent with the results of most earlier investigators. Dickey and Knower (1941) found Mexican adolescent girls to excel over Mexican

TABLE 2.1. Sex Differences in Decoding Skill (PONS Test)

National group	Number of samples	Mean effect size (r)
Australia	18	.26
Canada	14	.24
United States	6	.16
Israel	3	.22
New Guinea	3	.19
Northern Ireland	2	.03
Mexico	2	.08
New Zealand	1	.41
Hong Kong	1	.37
West Germany	1	− .10
Singapore	1	.40
Mean sex difference (r)		.20
Median sex difference (r)		.22

adolescent boys at judging photos of male and female faces. Ekman and Friesen (1971) found a tendency for New Guinean girls and women to excel over their cohort males in judging photos of male and female facial expressions. Izard (1971) found English, Greek, and French women to be better judges of male and female facial expressions than men from their respective countries. In only one published study was there no advantage for women. This was Frijda's (1953) study, done in Holland, of men and women's abilities to decode the filmed behavior of two women. Frijda found no difference at all between the performance of women and men, though it should also be noted that his sample was small (forty people) compared to the hundreds tested in most of the other cross-national samples.

In further analyzing a subset of the cross-cultural PONS data, R. Rosenthal and DePaulo (1979b) have demonstrated that the major channels of the PONS test show consistent differences in how marked females' decoding advantage is. They examined scores on three channels — face, body, and voice tone — for the largest samples (at least twenty of each sex). Scores for the face channel showed the largest difference, with a median r of .15; the body channel was next, with a median r of .10; and the voice channel showed the smallest sex difference (though still favoring women), with a median r of .08. (The magnitude of the sex difference is smaller on individual channels than on total score because of the decreased reliability of the individual-channel scores caused by their shorter length.) Of the twenty samples examined, sixteen showed this linear trend. Women were, in other words, especially good compared to men when judging facial expressions, and least good, though still slightly better, when judging vocal cues.

Demonstration of Sex Differences: Broader Review of Research

Earlier, I said that the design of the PONS test — the fact that it had only one sex represented as a source of nonverbal expressions — presented a problem. That problem was that we could not be sure that the sex differences we observed were general sex differences in decoding skill. The patterns we found might be true only when people judge a female sender. It was therefore very important to examine the existing literature thoroughly, paying particular attention to the sexes shown in the nonverbal stimuli (for example, films or tapes) that were judged.

It was in searching for earlier results that I became aware of how large the available literature was, and of how poorly acquainted with it were the psychologists who studied nonverbal sex differences, including ourselves up to that point. In the five years preceding the publication of my first review of sex differences in decoding skill (Hall 1978), two major reviews had contained statements, purportedly based on the literature, that there were no such sex differences (Hoffman 1977; Maccoby and Jacklin 1974). Each of these reviewers was considering a definition of interpersonal sensitivity that was consistent with mine but somewhat broader; thus their conclusions of "no difference" were based on more kinds of studies than I am considering here. But the important point is that these reviewers failed to locate the great majority of decoding-skill studies and were therefore misled. And these most recent reviewers are not alone; the literature is full of statements to the effect that there is no, or hardly any, sex difference in decoding skill. Some statements are qualified, but some are dogmatic, such as this quote by Westbrook (1974, p. 388): "The belief about women's greater sensitivity . . . defined as accuracy of judgment [of nonverbal cues] . . . appears to be a cultural myth."

My research produced a very different conclusion (Hall 1978, 1979, 1980). I located seventy-five studies, dating from 1923. Although I included PONS research among these seventy-five, I deliberately included only a few representative samples in order not to flood the data set with results all based on the same testing instrument. In all of the studies, groups of subjects served as judges of nonverbal expressive stimuli that consisted of face, body, or vocal cues, alone or in combination. These cues were presented via drawings, photos, films, videotapes, standard-content speech (where one or more people read standard passages or the alphabet while trying to express various emotions), randomized-spliced speech, or electronically filtered speech (the last two techniques were described earlier in this chapter). The nonverbal behavior captured in these various visual and auditory channels was usually deliberate, or "posed." "Spontaneous" cues were elicited in some studies by exposing expressors to emotion-provoking circumstances, such as pleasant or unpleasant films, and secretly videotaping their nonverbal responses.

With the exception of one study, all of the decoding-skill studies were based on cues that were assumed by the investigators to be truthful or sincere. An additional group of studies, not reviewed here, involves the decoding of cues of deception; they are not included because the stimuli to be judged are not entirely nonverbal. Sex differences for detecting deception have been reviewed, however, by Zuckerman, DePaulo, and Rosenthal (1981), who found that women are slightly better at detecting deception than men are ($r = .08$).

In the seventy-five nonverbal decoding studies in my review, subjects responded to the stimuli most often in a multiple-choice style, choosing among various emotional or situational descriptions. A few other judgment approaches were used, such as pointing to a facial photo after hearing a story; for a list the reader should see Hall (1978).

Since the time the original review was published, I have found fifty additional independent results, this time including only one based on the PONS. The newer group was basically like the first group, but included tasks that were somewhat more varied, such as judging emotions in a chimpanzee's face, judging age or personality traits from nonverbal cues, decoding the meanings of infant cries, and decoding the meaning of proxemic (interpersonal distance) cues.

Table 2.2 displays the results of each review of nonverbal decoding differences. Several ways of describing the results are offered, as explained in chapter 1. The first row considers simply the direction of the difference, regardless of magnitude or statistical significance of the individual studies. For this index, the two sets of studies agree on the finding that females scored higher than males more often than vice versa. The figures of 84 percent and 81 percent for the earlier and later reviews, respectively, are very close to the analogous figure for all 133 samples tested with the PONS test (80 percent).

TABLE 2.2. Sex Differences in Decoding Skill (All Studies)

Index	Analyzed before 1978 (75 studies)	Analyzed after 1978 (50 studies)
Direction of effect (excluding no difference or unknown)	84% (51/61) favor females ($p < 10^{-6}$)	81% (26/32) favor females ($p < .0004$)
Mean effect size (r) [a]	Between .12 (75 studies) and .20 (46 studies)	Between .09 (50 studies) and .25 (18 studies)
Statistical significance (all studies)	31% (23/75) favor females significantly, 1% (1/75) favor males significantly	20% (10/50) favor females significantly, 2% (1/50) favor males significantly
Combined p	$p = 10^{-6}$ (75 studies)	$p = .00006$ (43 studies)

[a] Positive values mean female advantage.

The second row of table 2.2 states the size of the sex difference, in terms of the correlation coefficient, r. Both a lower and an upper value are given, following the practice of Eagly and Carli (1981). The lower value is the average r over all the studies, considering any unknown r to be zero. This procedure is very conservative since, given the strong tendency for females to score higher (row one), it is highly probable that the effect size in those studies where the effect size was not calculable was not, in fact, zero but rather some positive value. The second, or upper, effect size is the average r for only those studies in which r was known, that is, excluding all the unknown results. This figure may be an overestimate of the true sex difference because of the possibility that it represents only the very largest sex differences obtained. This would be the case if authors reported in detail mainly their largest effects, reasoning that readers or journal editors would not be interested in anything else.[1] The effect sizes in table 2.2 are very similar for both the earlier and later literature reviews. In addition, when the earlier review is limited to those studies that did not use the PONS test, the average effect size (r) for those studies where it was known was still .20. Thus, the effects are identical, on the average, whether it is the PONS or some other instrument that is used.

The third row of table 2.2 shows that roughly one-quarter of the studies showed one sex to be significantly more accurate than the other, and this trend is overwhelmingly in favor of the women. To find only one-quarter of the studies to be significant may appear inconclusive until one recalls that by chance alone — that is, if there were no real sex difference — we should expect to find only about 5 percent of the studies to be significant in either direction.

The final row of table 2.2 shows the combined p, or summary p for the entire set of studies under consideration. As is evident, these combined ps are extremely small, and the direction is, again, in favor of greater female decoding skill.

In addition to documenting these summary sex differences, in the 1978 review I also examined several other interesting questions on the basis of the seventy-five decoding studies. These results can be summarized as follows:

1. The sex of the expressors in a study did not make any difference in the direction, magnitude, or p-value of the results. In other words, women remained better judges than men, and by about the same amount, whether they were judging other women or were judging men. This finding puts to

---

1. There is evidence, however, in the case of decoding skill, that this upper value is not an overestimate. Readers will recall that when summarizing the PONS data alone, using all studies and not only the largest or most significant results, we found almost identical sex differences to the upper effect sizes in table 2.2.

rest our uneasiness over the interpretation of sex differences based only on the PONS with its one female sender. In addition, whereas these conclusions are based on a comparison between studies, some earlier investigators had made such comparisons within individual samples of subjects, by employing senders of both sexes and analyzing accuracy separately for each sex of sender. Such internal comparisons have also indicated that sex differences in judging skill did not vary with the sex of the expressor (Dimitrovsky 1964; Dusenbury and Knower 1938; Ekman and Friesen 1971; Gallagher and Shuntich 1981; Gitter, Black, and Mostofsky 1972a, 1972b; Vinacke and Fong 1955).

2. The age of the expressors, whether they were children or adults, had no effect on the sex differences.

3. The age of the subjects themselves also made no difference (whether they were preschool and grade school, junior high school, high school, or college and older). This result is exactly parallel to results described earlier for the PONS test alone: among children, the sex difference is approximately as large and as consistent as it is among older groups.

4. The channels being judged (visual versus auditory) did not make a significant difference in the sex-difference results, though the direction of the trend was consistent with R. Rosenthal and DePaulo's (1979b) conclusions based on the PONS, namely that the visual cues produce larger sex differences than the auditory cues do. In my 1978 review, the average known effect size (r) for the visual cues was .16 (twenty-nine studies), while the average known effect size for auditory cues was .09 (ten studies). The later review of literature showed similar trends, with known effect sizes of .26 (fourteen studies) and .09 (one study), respectively.

In a fascinating later paper, Eagly and Carli (1981) added an additional analysis to this list: how did the authors' sex affect the sex-difference results? In summarizing research on sex differences in persuasion and conformity, these authors found that the higher the proportion of men among the authors, the more susceptible to influence were the women in the study compared to the men. Eagly and Carli then performed the analogous analysis for the earlier set of decoding studies summarized in table 2.2, and found a correlation of $r = -.36$, $p < .02$, between the proportion of male authors and the size of the sex difference. This indicated that the more men there were among the authors of a study, the less accurate were the female subjects, relative to the males. Eagly and Carli suggested that authors may succeed, somehow, in making their own sex look better — with male authors finding women to be more influenceable but less accurate at nonverbal decoding, and vice versa for female authors.

For the later set of decoding studies summarized in table 2.2, I performed a parallel analysis of author sex, using their coding (1 = 50 percent or more of the authors were female, 2 = more than 50 percent were male).

The earlier result was not replicated: the correlation between the proportion of male authors and the size of the sex difference (r) was .17 (seventeen results), a nonsignificant effect in the opposite direction from Eagly and Carli's.

Self-report of Decoding Accuracy

Zuckerman and Larrance (1979) developed a scale for measuring people's perceptions of their own decoding accuracy. Though the scale was reliable, people's perceptions were not actually much correlated with their decoding skill; this was also found by R. Rosenthal et al. (1979) with a different self-report scale. But what is still intriguing is that sex differences in self-reported accuracy were very much like actual sex differences: the correlation between sex and self-reported skill was .22, indicating that women thought themselves more skilled than men thought themselves to be. This figure is closely comparable to the effect sizes shown in table 2.2.

ACCURACY AT RECOGNIZING FACES

The recognition of faces is certainly a nonverbal judgment skill, though not one that necessarily draws on the identification of emotions expressed in the face. Rather, face recognition is the ability to know whether you have seen a particular face before. This skill is most obviously based on remembering facial features but could also include recognition of the expression on a face. It is a skill that has considerable everyday relevance, since one must recognize many faces each day, and forgetting one is embarrassing. However, no one has correlated skill at recognizing faces with skill at decoding facial expressions, so it is not known whether the two skills have anything actually in common. Face recognition is generally studied by cognitive psychologists, not by "nonverbalists"; it is therefore no surprise that the relationship between the two kinds of face-judging skill has not been examined.

Research on face recognition takes a fairly standard form. In infant studies, subjects are shown target faces, which are later paired with novel faces. The proportion of visual attention (fixation) given to the novel stimuli is interpreted as a measure of recognition: the more attention paid to the novel face, the more familiar, and therefore uninteresting, the original target face is presumed to be. In studies of children and older groups, subjects are shown photographs of faces, and later they are shown those photographs imbedded among a set of different faces. Subjects must identify the ones that were seen earlier. Investigators vary the age, sex, or race of the individuals in the photographs, as well as the number of

TABLE 2.3. Sex Differences in Face-Recognition Skill (Adults)

Index	Results (28 studies)
Direction of effect (excluding no difference or unknown)	74% (14/19) favor females ($p = .04$)
Mean effect size (r)[a]	Between .08 (28 studies) and .17 (12 studies)
Statistical significance (all studies)	14% (4/28) favor females significantly, 4% (1/28) favor males significantly
Combined p	$p = .01$ (25 studies)

[a] Positive values mean female advantage.

photographs viewed.[2] The literature also contains some studies that tested face recognition in a different way, by testing how good a person was at associating names to faces. Because of the involvement with verbal material, such studies are not considered in this review of face-recognition skill, though they show females to excel just as the pure face-recognition studies do.[3]

In an earlier writing (Hall 1979), I quoted another author who said that sex differences in face-recognition skill did not exist. This was unfortunate, for it is not so, at least not among adults, where the data show more female accuracy. On the basis of smaller reviews of the literature, Haviland and Malatesta (1981) and McKelvie (1981) reached the same conclusion.

Of the twelve studies on children (over two years of age) and adolescents, one showed a significant difference (favoring girls), and the direction of the sex difference favored girls in 71 percent (5/7) of the studies in which it was reported. The average magnitude of the sex difference (r), known for five studies, was .15; the average magnitude including all unknown results as showing no difference was .06. In one of these studies, a nonsignificant difference favoring girls held up over all four grades tested (grades one, two, three, and six).

2. Studies also use more than one index of recognition accuracy. Sometimes accuracy is defined in terms of "hits," or number of correct judgments, and sometimes in terms of a statistic from signal detection theory known as d-prime, which takes into account the subject's tendency to claim to recognize the faces. If a subject said she recognized every face, then she would appear to be 100 percent correct, but that number would be misleading since she in fact did not differentiate between faces she had and had not seen. D-prime corrects for this.

3. Borges and Vaughn (1977) and Witryol and Kaess (1957) both found women to be significantly better at associating names to faces (mean r between sex and accuracy = .35). Also, J. H. Feldstein (1976) tested preschool children's knowledge of their classmates' names and found girls to be significantly more accurate (r between sex and accuracy = .34).

Results of studies on adults are shown in table 2.3. The pattern is almost identical to that found for children and adolescents, but the differences are significant due to the larger number of studies. Further examination of the literature showed that female faces were not more easily recognized than male faces on the average, but same-sex recognition was better than opposite-sex recognition (a trend that was significant in approximately one-half of the studies that tested for this effect).

Studies on infants showed a very different pattern. Of the sixteen studies located, not any obtained a significant sex difference. The average size of the difference (r), known for only three studies, was $-.04$, indicating that infant boys showed very negligibly more recognition of faces than infant girls. The direction of the sex difference was reported only for these three studies: one favored females, one favored males, and one showed equal performance. It is regrettable that the direction and magnitude are so rarely available. On the basis of the reported data, one must conclude that there is no evidence for a sex difference among infants of around five months on the average, but it is still possible that an interpretable trend could emerge if direction and magnitude were known. Most studies did demonstrate that infants could recognize faces at better than chance levels; so it is not the case that investigators have sought sex differences where there is in fact no demonstrated ability on the part of the infants involved. Existing research suggests, therefore, that sex differences in face recognition develop over the course of childhood.[4]

An important study by Goldstein and Chance (1970), which tested recognition of faces, snowflakes, and inkblots, found that women's recognition superiority was unique to faces. Females' skill thus seems to be part of their developing sense of the saliency of social stimuli and not part of general visual-memory skills.[5]

Following Eagly and Carli (1981), I performed an analysis of the effect of author sex on the size of sex differences for face recognition among children and older groups. These results were perplexing. When only adults are considered, the higher the proportion of male authors, the smaller was the sex difference ($r = -.68$, twelve results, $p < .05$), in keeping with the hypothesis that authors succeed in making their own sex look

---

4. The aggregate results certainly suggest this, and Chance, Turner, and Goldstein (1982) found a significant trend for females' advantage to increase over the age levels of grades one and two, grades five and six, grades seven and eight, and college. One study, however, found a significant tendency for males to become more accurate with age, relative to females, though overall, females were slightly more accurate (ages seven, twelve, and seventeen years, and adults; J. F. Cross, Cross, and Daly 1971).

5. One study tested voice-recognition skill and found men to excel significantly (McGehee 1937). If this is a replicable difference, it would parallel exactly the face–voice difference in men's versus women's scores on decoding skill (this chapter) and for expression accuracy (chapter 4).

good: when male authors predominate, sex differences favoring females are diminished, but when female authors predominate, the superiority of females increases. But when only children are considered, the relationship is completely reversed ($r = .79$, five results, not significant). What makes the results additionally perplexing is the fact that three of the five children's studies and two of the twelve adult studies (including the largest sex difference) were conducted by the same research group (four results in Chance, Turner, and Goldstein 1982; one in Goldstein and Chance 1970). Until more studies come to light, these inconsistent results cannot be interpreted.

SUMMARY

We have seen in this chapter that females are better decoders of nonverbal expressions than are males, and that this result is very consistent and of moderate size. It shows up in a large proportion of the published studies and is present over various ages of the subjects and the sex of the expressors. The main qualifying factor that has been uncovered is the channel of nonverbal communication being judged: though females are reliably better than males in decoding nonverbal cues, their advantage is most pronounced for facial cues, less pronounced for body cues, and least pronounced for vocal cues. We have also seen that females past infancy are somewhat better skilled at recognizing faces than are males in their samples, though the connection between this skill and decoding skill is unknown. One naturally wants to know what might explain these sex differences. Several hypotheses exist and some have been tested, at least for decoding skill. These are the topic of the next chapter.

In all of the remaining chapters, possible explanations for nonverbal sex differences are discussed. Much of this discussion is speculative, since there have been few efforts to test any hypotheses about their origins. For decoding skill, however, the situation is different. In this area, investigators have provided more empirical data bearing on explanations and have systemized their thinking to a considerable degree. The quantity of theoretically relevant research for decoding skill is still limited but is sufficient to merit treatment in a chapter of its own. Though decoding skill is the focus of chapter 3, the explanations that are entertained can be applied to other nonverbal skills and behaviors as well. Chapter 3 serves, therefore, as a theoretical basis for all the later chapters.

3 Explaining Judgment Accuracy

No one knows why women are better than men at decoding emotional expressions and at recognizing faces. Some research has been done to find explanations for women's advantage at decoding nonverbal expressions, but it is far from conclusive. An important point to make here is that our lack of certainty about the sources of these sex differences is not entirely due to limitations in the existing research. To be sure, there are such limitations — samples are small, or a result is not adequately replicated, or a particular construct may not be operationalized in the ideal way — but in addition, researchers who try to explain sex differences come up against an inevitable degree of uncertainty due to the nature of the sex construct itself.

Being a man or a woman means many things all at once. What one would like to do is to isolate which of the countless correlates of sex give rise to a particular sex difference. Usually the universe of possible explanations can be narrowed on the basis of logic, but even then the complexities can be very great. Many direct and indirect influences can exist for almost any sex difference. Since it is impossible to measure all relevant variables, there is no way to completely prove or disprove any hypothesis, though with enough effort one could certainly obtain more support for some hypotheses than for others.

To illustrate the investigator's dilemma using a topic from this book, there is some (albeit mixed) evidence that men touch women with their hands more than vice versa. This has been hypothesized by some writers to be a manifestation of differential status between men and women. But it could also be due to some other factor, for example the possibility that women like being touched more than men do. Thus, women's refraining and men's not refraining from touching the opposite sex could reflect mutual accommodation, not dominance and subordination. That is, the psychology of the situation may center on what each enjoys, not on their relative statuses. But it is also possible that the very fact of differences in the emotional responses of men and women to being touched could reflect a cultural or personal history of status differences, with the more dominant (men) expecting, perhaps unconsciously, that others will keep their hands off them and the less dominant (women) expecting that others have freer access. To tease out causal determinants of such a sex difference is clearly difficult. I would not say that it is impossible, but I would certainly say that it has not been done yet for any nonverbal behavior. The difficulty of untangling causal antecedents of sex differences is one reason why the nature-nurture debate remains very much alive (see, for example, Maccoby and Jacklin 1980 versus Tieger 1980 on sex differences in aggression).

Two proposed explanations can also seem very different if one does not recognize that they may be focusing on different elements in a causal stream, or on different levels of analysis. One hypothesis may emphasize social learning and another brain functioning, but instead of being rival hypotheses they may simply be tapping different aspects of one process: learning causes changes in brain functioning, which in turn cause some behavior that we wish to explain.

The touch example demonstrates this point. A causal stream may begin (at least for heuristic purposes, begin) with women's oppression and end with sex differences in nonverbal communication, but oppression and nonverbal sex differences may not be directly related. Oppression may be a distant cause of sex differences if centuries of oppression have led to certain stereotypes and social practices. But oppression may not be an immediate cause of such sex differences. A particular woman who displays a sex-linked nonverbal behavior may not be at all oppressed, compared to other women or even compared to the men in her environment. Instead, the assumptions and expectations that she shared with her entire culture all her life — assumptions and expectations that may indeed be a product of women's oppression — may have produced her behavior. If her behavior then contributes to the impression that women are easily dominated or compulsively pleasant, then this will surely influence the way she is treated in society, and in turn the way she responds nonverbally. It is easy to see the conceptual complexity that is unavoidable when we talk about determinants of sex differences.

Possible origins of nonverbal sex differences can be catalogued, but as the foregoing makes clear, they could operate either singly or jointly in complex ways. Nonverbal sex differences could be biological in origin, selected for over the course of evolution because they offer adaptive advantages; for example, women's greater sensitivity to nonverbal cues could have an innate basis if it was particularly useful for them in child rearing. Some nonverbal sex differences could follow from biological adaptations but have no adaptive significance in themselves. Women's wide hips, for example, serve a purpose in childbirth, but their effect on women's style of walking is coincidence; anatomically determined behavioral differences may, of course, be exaggerated by social custom, in which case social learning of one sort or another is involved.

Acquisition of nonverbal sex differences by learning can take several forms. One can learn by reward and punishment, by observation, and by "self-socialization," or the internalization of modes of behavior that are consistent with one's self-concept (Kohlberg 1966; Maccoby and Jacklin 1974). An additional mechanism would be via compliance with norms of reciprocity (for example, smiling when smiled at) — learning which, like other kinds of learning, can generalize beyond the circumstances in which it took place. Others' expectations are also powerful elicitors of behavior, mediated via nonverbal cues and responded to nonverbally in ways that are probably outside the awareness of everyone involved (Word, Zanna, and Cooper 1974; R. Rosenthal and Rubin 1978). The out-of-awareness nature of nonverbal behavior is, indeed, one reason why it is seen as a dangerously subtle means of social control (Henley 1977).

Complicating our understanding of ways in which nonverbal sex differences may be acquired is the important distinction between nonverbal behavior with communicative properties and that with sign properties (Wiener et al. 1972). Communication, according to a strict definition, involves a shared code that relates referents to signals and the implicit understanding that communication is taking place (though intentionality is necessarily a difficult criterion to impose; see Wiener et al.). Signs, on the other hand, may mean something to an observer but have no communicative function from the sender's perspective; twiddling my hair, for example, might serve a purpose such as relief of tension, but would be considered outside of the communicative system per se unless I knew it would convey the fact that I was tense and was thus relieving it, and the recipient understood it to be conveyed with this purpose. Though the distinction between communications and signs is extremely difficult to put into practice, some such distinction is highly relevant to our conceptualization of nonverbal sex differences. To take a good example: a woman could smile to communicate her deference or pleasantness, or simply because she feels happy (in which case it has meaning to her but she is not knowingly communicating anything to another and indeed may not even be aware that she is smiling), or because she has an unconscious habit of smiling (in which case it has no meaning for her). In both of the latter cases, though her smile may have much meaning, correct or not, to an observer, she is not in fact making a conscious or even half-conscious statement about herself.

With these possibilities and complexities in mind, let us review progress in explaining sex differences in nonverbal judging skills. As mentioned earlier, though most of the research to be described was concerned with the decoding of nonverbal cues and expressions, several of the hypotheses discussed here apply to other nonverbal sex differences as well. Readers may want to refer back to this chapter at later points in the book.

MASCULINITY AND FEMININITY

Sex stereotypes find women to be "interpersonally sensitive" (see Broverman et al. 1972). Part of being feminine in our society — in stereotype and in self-report — seems to include being oriented toward others in a way that includes sensitivity to their feelings, along with nurturance and an "expressive" style. Masculine traits, on the other hand, in terms of stereotype and self-report, involve personal efficacy, self-assertion, and task accomplishment.

Since sex differences are observed both in nonverbal receiving skills and in these sex-related aspects of personality (see, for example, Spence and Helmreich 1978), it is sensible to ask whether there are within-sex correlations of these sex-role variables and nonverbal skills. The ability to judge nonverbal cues may be characteristic of more "feminine" persons of either sex, when femininity is defined as including the relevant interpersonal motivations and skills. Similarly, we can hypothesize that more "masculine" persons of either sex would be poorer nonverbal receivers. If such relationships were shown to exist, then we would be able to speculate that it is the sex-related personality traits that account for the nonverbal sex differences. Although *femininity* and *masculinity* can be operationally defined in a variety of ways (see Constantinople 1973), most theories and measuring instruments do place social sensitivity, affective expressiveness, and overall socioemotional orientation among "feminine" attributes.

To test these hypotheses, one administers to the same sample of subjects both the appropriate nonverbal receiving tests and the appropriate measures of femininity and masculinity. One correlates the scores within males and females separately, and if there are indeed correlations in the predicted directions, then one examines whether the personality variables might be able to account statistically for the nonverbal sex difference. If accounting for personality made the nonverbal sex differences much smaller, then we would certainly be onto an important possible determinant of the sex difference.

Twelve studies have examined these questions. Eleven of them were reported in one paper by Hall and Halberstadt (1981) and the twelfth was performed by Isenhart (1980). Hall and Halberstadt's eleven samples contained almost 800 individuals in three U.S. cities and represented children, adolescents, college, and postcollege adults. Isenhart's sample was of college age. All but two of the studies employed some form of the PONS test (see chapter 2), an audiovisual test of decoding ability. All of the studies employed one or more measures of ability to decode nonverbal cues conveyed via face, body, or content-free speech and employed one or more measures of masculinity and femininity measured on separate scales.

The use of separate masculinity and femininity scales rather than the kind that is a single continuum that goes from masculinity at one extreme to femininity at the other was prompted by the fact that many authors have recently argued that these constructs are not logical opposites, but are, rather, independent and complementary dimensions (see Bem 1974; Spence and Helmreich 1978). A person can therefore have both masculine and feminine qualities with no implied contradiction. In such scales, the masculinity scale is designed to tap socially desirable "agentic" or self-assertive, instrumental traits, and the femininity scale is designed to tap socially desirable "communal" or socioemotional traits. In eleven of the studies to be discussed, subjects filled in one or more sets of these scales describing themselves; in one study, parents made such judgments for their preschool children.

The hypotheses were for positive correlations, within each sex, between decoding skill and femininity and negative correlations between decoding skill and masculinity. The data did not show this. Almost all the relationships in Hall and Halberstadt (1981) were very weak. Only for adults was there any significant relationship, and this showed, contrary to prediction, that more masculine persons of each sex were the *better* decoders (of face and body cues only, $r = .25$, $p < .01$). An additional significant result showed that the ability to decode face and body cues became relatively more positively correlated with masculinity as the age groups became older, and relatively more negatively correlated with femininity (linear contrast, $p = .004$). Isenhart's study was consistent with these results, showing a correlation of $-.06$ between femininity and decoding skill (the correlation for masculinity was not reported).

Because femininity was not positively associated with decoding skill, nor masculinity negatively associated, the hypothesis that these personality styles might explain sex differences in decoding received no support. The evidence actually suggested that more masculine adults, of either sex, are more skilled in decoding nonverbal cues. An intriguing interpretation of this unexpected result can be made, but one which obviously needs to be tested in future research. It concerns the adaptive uses of nonverbal decoding ability. It may be that the harmonious interpersonal goals of the feminine person (for example, comforting others) can be achieved through prosocial motivation alone, without benefit of superior ability to read other people. The goals of the more masculine person, on the other hand, may involve interpersonal effectiveness — for example, accomplishing joint tasks, being a good leader, or winning in competition – and this kind of effectiveness may require a more-developed ability to judge others' needs, intentions, and feelings. In the absence of more refined research, however, this is speculation.

EMPATHY

Related to the masculinity-femininity hypothesis is the empathy hypothesis. It is treated as a separate hypothesis because empathy is traditionally measured with specific empathy scales and not as a part of the more general concepts of masculinity and femininity. Males and females differ in self-reported empathy: women, more than men, report that they share other people's moods vicariously (see chapter 11). The empathy hypothesis states that women are better decoders than men because an important determinant of decoding skill is the tendency to empathize with other people; in other words, the knowledge of another person's moods is facilitated if one actually shares those moods.

The only two studies bearing on this question were done by me and are reported in Hall (1979). In these studies, I administered forms of the PONS test to college students along with standard empathy scales (three altogether), on which the women did indeed score as more empathic than the men. Items from these scales include "I become nervous if others around me seem to be nervous" and "I am so sensitive to the moods of my friends that I can almost feel what they are feeling." In short, there was no relationship between decoding skill and empathy. The median correlation between the empathy scales and the decoding tests was zero. Thus it does not appear that the trait of empathy is a good candidate for explaining sex differences in decoding skill.

ATTENTION AND PRACTICE

Women may be better decoders of nonverbal cues because the female role is one that prescribes, perhaps even requires, selective attention and exposure to nonverbal cues. Though little research has attempted to test such a hypothesis, indirect evidence does support it.

Women pay more attention to nonverbal information about people than men do. Mazanec and McCall (1976) asked college students to watch films of two people talking and then to write down everything they could remember. Women recalled proportionately more actions; men recalled proportionately more verbal content. Argyle et al. (1970) found that women were more influenced by nonverbal than verbal cues, compared to men, in an experiment in which subjects rated expressors who varied the degree of dominance-submissiveness in their verbal and nonverbal behavior. Zahn (1973, 1975) found the same thing in a comparison of voice with verbal content, in which subjects rated spoken messages on their positivity-negativity. (Savitsky and Izard 1970 and R. Brooks, Brandt, and Wiener 1969, however, did not find that women gave significantly more weight to nonverbal than verbal cues.) If we are persuaded that these attentional patterns do vary between the sexes, then women's greater overall skill in nonverbal decoding could result from the exposure, practice, and opportunities for feedback that are implied.

As documented in chapter 2, women's greatest relative skill lies in decoding the face. Attentional patterns could also account for this differential skill. DePaulo et al. (1978) have shown that although people generally give more attention to visual than vocal cues, and to facial than body cues, women show more pronounced tendencies in this direction than men do. Further, attention given to face and body has been demonstrated to be correlated with skill in decoding these same channels (DiMatteo and Hall 1979).

As will be discussed in chapter 6, women gaze at others' faces in interaction more than men do. Perhaps because of this, they also have been shown to be more accurate at noting occurrences of eye contact in others (Kleck and Nuessle 1968) and to have more apparent knowledge of the relationship of pupil size to mood (S. L. Williams and Hicks 1980). The gazing tendency could contribute to women's facial decoding skill in two ways: one decodes better that which one is paying attention to at the moment, and one gains added knowledge about whatever kinds of cues one habitually attends to.

One study examined the hypothesis that sex differences in gazing could account for sex differences in decoding skill (R. Rosenthal et al. 1979). The number of seconds of eye contact engaged in by each of fifty undergraduate subjects while in a three-minute conversation was measured, and each subject took a shortened version of the PONS test (see chapter 2 for description). The correlation (r) between sex and decoding skill was .31 ($p < .06$). When eye contact was taken into account (using partial correlation), this relationship fell to $r = .24$. Thus, some of the sex difference in decoding skill was accounted for by sex differences in gazing behavior. In this study, only total score on the PONS was analyzed, so it is unknown whether the results differed as a function of visual versus vocal decoding (which they should, logically).

Why women show these attentional patterns requires explanation, of course. Women may simply learn, by direct tuition and by example, that they are supposed to be interpersonally observant. They may find themselves more often as passive observers of others in conversation; this is suggested by studies which find that mixed-sex speaking groups are dominated by men (chapter 10), and also by research that finds that girls spend more time with adults and less with peers than boys do, a situation that should promote less active participation by girls (B. Whiting and Edwards 1973). Women may not only passively attend but also actively seek nonverbal information, especially the cues given by the face. Women may seek cues of approval or disapproval, which do in fact seem to be especially registered on the face (a point to be developed later in this chapter). Or, they may seek cues that indicate how contented others are from moment to moment, as part of a general motive to maintain harmonious relationships.

Finally, specific learning factors could account for sex differences in decoding. One such factor could be differences in exposure to young children, in a setting in which nonverbal decoding is required. There is no question that American girls do more babysitting than their male peers, although in American society, routine care of younger siblings is not as common as it is in some others, as documented by B. B. Whiting and Whiting (1975). In the widely spaced cultures they studied, girls ("child nurses") were given extensive responsibility for the care of younger siblings. Could this kind of experience produce women's advantage in nonverbal decoding?

R. Rosenthal et al. (1979) performed a study suggestive of such an effect. They gave the PONS test to American married couples, matched roughly on age, who did or did not have a child of toddler age. The parents did score somewhat better than the nonparents ($p = .10$), and most of the difference was due to the women. Practice at decoding children's cues did seem to enhance decoding skills, especially among the wives, who in all likelihood spent much more time with the child than did their husbands. Of course, since this study was not an experiment in the strict sense, one cannot be completely sure that it was parenthood that created the difference in skill. Though the result is intriguing, it is not clear why such general practice should lead to differential skill for various channels of cues (for example, face, body, voice). Further, as chapter 2 showed, sex differences in decoding skill occur as early as eight years old in American children. I do not know whether girls of this age have enough greater exposure to younger children to produce the skill difference.

ACCOMMODATION

Women's tendencies to attend preferentially to facial cues and to be relatively better decoders of the face may be caused by the hypothesized female trait of accommodation, according to R. Rosenthal and DePaulo and their colleagues (R. Rosenthal and DePaulo 1979a, 1979b; Blanck et al. 1981). These investigators have tried more systematically than any others to develop a comprehensive theoretical framework for understanding women's and men's nonverbal decoding skills as well as a variety of other skills, traits, and behaviors. In the context of cue decoding, accommodation is proposed to take the form of attending to, and decoding well, only those channels of information that are polite to attend to and decode, and ignoring others. The most polite channel is the face, because the face is highly controllable by the sender and rarely emits unintended or "leaked" information, while other channels are more leaky or inclined to be sources of unintended cues (for arguments supporting the differential leakiness of nonverbal channels, see Ekman and Friesen 1969b, 1974; R. Rosenthal and DePaulo 1979b; DePaulo and Rosenthal 1979; Zuckerman, DePaulo, and Rosenthal 1981).

R. Rosenthal and DePaulo (1979a, 1979b), drawing on existing evidence and theory, arranged five kinds of nonverbal cues according to their "leakiness": face (most controllable, least leaky), body, voice, very brief cues of the face and body (analogous to leaked and quickly corrected displays of emotion), and, finally, cues incorporating interchannel contradiction (considered most leaky due to conflict, hesitancy, deception, or other unusual cognitive or emotional states in the expressor). The authors discovered that women's decoding skills, relative to men's, parallel this ordering: the sex difference is greatest for face and becomes smaller and smaller with each successive channel of the hierarchy. Rosenthal and DePaulo hypothesized that women recognize, consciously or unconsciously, that people will not respond well to having their unintended cues decoded, and therefore women accommodate to others' wishes by showing a polite pattern both for attention (shown for face, body, and voice) and for decoding accuracy.

Rosenthal and DePaulo's hypothesis is consistent with a large amount of data, which they describe in their writings. Some examples of other evidence they cite to support the accommodation hypothesis are that women are better expressors than men and are less concerned with monitoring how they act. It is important, however, to make several points. Rosenthal and DePaulo's argument is based on logic rather than on empirical demonstration. They reason that because the same ordering of channels reflects *both* degrees of leakiness *and* women's advantage in decoding, there might be a connection. That connection they call accommodation. It will be important to ascertain in future research if accommodation is actually the motive responsible for the sex-difference patterns, since there is actually no direct evidence that this is the case.

Rosenthal and DePaulo sought, in their own research, supporting evidence for their interpretation of women as accommodating in their nonverbal judgments. One such piece of evidence seemed to show that women "overlook deception": women were more likely than men to say people were expressing "liking" (in videotapes) when those people were actually describing someone they disliked but in a manner designed to appear *as though* they liked that person; in other words, women apparently saw mainly the overtly expressed, false, message and not the underlying, true, message, even when instructed to judge the underlying feelings. Later, however, DePaulo suggested the alternative interpretation, that people are actually poor at reading underlying messages even when they are trying to do so, and that they read the manifest or intended message despite themselves (DePaulo et al. 1982). If this is correct, then the above result, rather than showing that women overlook deception, instead shows that everyone judges the manifest message and women are much more accurate at doing so (which we know to be true; see chapter 2).

Other evidence against the idea that women overlook deception comes from the authors' review of studies testing ability to detect deception, which found that women were actually better at it than men were, though it was a very small difference (Zuckerman, DePaulo, and Rosenthal 1981).

There is certainly ample evidence from other areas of research to suggest that women are pleasant, by one definition or another. For example, women are more polite than men in the use of language (Jay 1980) and more agreeable in group situations (Strodtbeck and Mann 1956). In some ways they seem to have a more positive outlook than men, at least in terms of public appearances. The term *Pollyanna effect* has been used to describe women's tendency to use more positive words to describe others (Warr 1971; A. J. Lott et al. 1970). Wives in one study tended to interpret their husbands' nonverbal messages in a more positive light than vice versa (Noller 1980a). Possibly indicative of actual accommodation is Weitz's (1976) finding of strong negative correlations between women's nonverbal dominance and warmth and the self-rated dominance and affiliativeness, respectively, of men with whom they were conversing. Accommodation, in the sense of behaving so as to please the other, is not, however, the only interpretation invited by these results. Indeed, one wonders how accommodating it is to behave less warmly when the other has high affiliative needs. Women's behavior in this study may reflect instead their application of nonverbal sensitivity to satisfying their own needs in the situation, such as to avoid mutual escalation of either dominance or intimacy. But even if we accept Weitz's results as indicating female agreeableness, it is still the case that to document women's seeming optimism or agreeableness in other spheres is not to demonstrate that it is women's accommodating nature that motivates their skills in decoding of more-leaky versus less-leaky nonverbal cues.

It is conceivable that women's decoding advantage over men is not as great for more-leaky, as opposed to less-leaky, cues because the more-leaky cues may not constitute as large a proportion of all the nonverbal cues which one must decode daily as the more consistent cues do. The socially smart person may be wise indeed to develop relatively more skill on the more consistent cues, simply because they are the most frequently occurring ones and therefore actually carry more total information, not because of any desire to be socially accommodating. It is also possible that women's and men's enculturated traits and activities give the more-leaky cues less real relevance as far as women are concerned. In competitive and dominance relations, such as are associated with men, leaked nonverbal cues could be of extreme significance because of their potential to indicate such things as vulnerability, the act of concealment, or the other's true motives, feelings, or intentions. Thus the pattern uncovered by Rosenthal and DePaulo could reflect sex differences in practice and exposure to leaky versus nonleaky cues, rather than sex differences in the motive to please others.

Finally, though Rosenthal and DePaulo use the term "eavesdropping" to describe the male pattern of nonverbal decoding skill, it remains to be demonstrated that such a motive is actually involved. It is possible that men's skill pattern may derive from an attentional style in which attention is not directed preferentially to any channels but is instead spread diffusely, a pattern which could reflect men's tendencies to be less attuned to nonverbal communication in general. They may not, in other words, recognize that anything is to be gained or lost by attending more to some cues than to others. Men thus may have no particular need or motive to read leaky cues but may wind up with a relative advantage only because women *are* actively attending to other kinds of cues. If so, then men's relative advantage at decoding leaky cues may have no motive and be put to no particular use, in which case "eavesdropping" may be a misleading term.

OPPRESSION

Though no one has offered a carefully worked out theory of the relationship of social position to nonverbal behavior and skill, a number of authors have stated the hypothesis that women's nonverbal decoding accuracy may be due to the fact that women are permitted to exercise a less than satisfactory degree of social power (for example, English 1972; Weitz 1974; Frieze and Ramsey 1976; Henley 1977). According to this hypothesis, when people are denied such power, they become especially alert to the behaviors and moods of more powerful others and develop more subtle ways of exercising social influence. D. L. Thomas, Franks, and Calonico (1972) have also proposed this as an explanation for the sex difference on a skill called "role-taking" — the ability to see things from another's point of view. The reasoning behind this hypothesis is that in order to please others, a socially weak person needs to be able to detect others' needs, wishes, and moods. As an example, if a person has trouble commanding people's attention in conversation, by virtue of low status, he or she must be attuned to others' nonverbal behavior in order to find and exploit every opportunity for gaining the floor; such a person might become very good at estimating when others are ready to yield the floor and how they would respond to an attempted change of turns. Popular beliefs reflect the adapting-to-oppression hypothesis in the stereotype of traditional wives: they are said to get their own way only by using subtle, often manipulative, but definitely skillful methods, while their unsuspecting (and insensitive) husbands still think they have theirs.

To test this hypothesis it is necessary to define and measure oppression. (I do not accept the argument that since women are, by definition, oppressed, one needs go no further to explain their nonverbal sensitivities.) There are two basic ways to operationalize oppression, first in terms of individuals and second at a structural or aggregate level. The studies to be described below represent both of these levels of analysis.

Testing the oppression hypothesis at the individual level requires measuring the degree of oppression, either subjective or objective, faced by particular individuals and relating that to their nonverbal skills. This is not as easy as it may sound because oppression is a complex idea that can be operationalized in many ways. One could be oppressed by having a job with little autonomy and much arbitrary supervision; or by having a domineering spouse; or by believing that powerful people in general control one's destiny. These are only illustrations of possible definitions we could impose on the word *oppression*. In the research involving individuals to be described below, only one sort of oppression was used: oppression as defined by a woman's taking either a "liberal" or "traditional" role vis-à-vis men. A woman who has a traditional role is considered more oppressed than a woman with a more liberal role, because the traditional role embodies patriarchal values and the concentration of power and privilege in the hands of men. It must be emphasized that this specifically *sex-role* oppression is only one definition that could reasonably be applied.

Structural oppression, as I use the term, refers not to individuals but to whole societies. Though individuals within a given society may vary a great deal in the kinds of oppression named above, nevertheless as a group, the members of that society may differ on some indices of oppression relative to members of a different society. To do such cross-cultural testing of the oppression hypothesis, one relates the average nonverbal decoding skill of individuals within societies to societal-level measures of oppression. This was possible, to a limited extent, for the eleven national groups tested with the PONS test, which were described in chapter 2. Archival sources were consulted for indices of women's status in the eleven countries represented, and these data were related to the magnitude of the sex differences in nonverbal decoding ability in the samples tested from those countries. Performing analyses at a highly aggregated level like this is risky in that there is no way of knowing if the status of women as defined by the archival data actually describes the status of the women who were tested. In our case, there is a reasonable chance that this error was committed, since the archival data describe the country as a whole, whereas our data represent particular regions within the country and particular strata (in particular, our samples were often English-speaking people recruited in a university setting).

Sex-Role "Oppression"

As described in more detail in Hall and Halberstadt (1981), two samples of adults and one sample of children were administered forms of the PONS test along with self-report measures of "attitudes toward women" (Spence, Helmreich, and Stapp 1973). The attitudes-toward-women scales contain statements about men's and women's roles in society with which subjects are asked to state their degree of agreement. Examples are "Swearing and obscenity are more repulsive in the speech of a woman than of a man" and "Sons in a family should be given more encouragement to go to college than daughters." The children's form contains the same items as the adults' form but they are phrased more simply (Hall 1976). For males we would predict no particular relationship between decoding ability and these scales, since it is difficult to see how such a scale could tap any kind of oppression among men. However, among females we would predict that the more traditional (less egalitarian) would be the best decoders, according to the hypothesis stated earlier. This prediction rests on the assumption that traditionality on questions of women's rights and social roles represents acceptance of an ideology of male domination.

For males, the correlations of attitudes-toward-women scores with decoding skill were negligible. For females, however, the correlations were *positive*: mean r for video decoding $= .27$, combined $p = .032$, and mean r for audio decoding $= .27$, combined $p = .027$. This indicates that females with *more* egalitarian, "liberal" views toward women's role were better decoders than more traditional females — exactly the opposite of the original prediction.

Among the adults in these samples, a questionnaire was also administered, in which they were asked to rate (1) their preference for degree of traditionality of their marriage regarding division of labor, wage earning, decision making, and the like, (2) their rating of the actual degree of traditionality of their marriage, and (3) actual division of labor in their marriage. Of special interest were two specific chores that we considered to be of low status and that are typically performed by women — housecleaning and laundry. Thus, we operationalized the concept of oppression in the home in terms of subjects' preferences and perceptions of the traditionality of their marriage and their estimations of their own sex-role-related behavior. Further, since husbands and wives participated together in these studies, we were able to verify subjects' responses in terms of what one spouse said about the other.

In both samples, the home-life measures were not appreciably related to men's decoding skills. For women, though, the results were consistent and interpretable, though the magnitudes were only moderate. Almost every correlation was negative, indicating that greater traditionality was associated with poorer decoding skill. The correlations for auditory skill were larger than for visual skill (for which none was significant). The correlations for auditory skill were: for traditionality preference, mean $r = -.24$, combined $p < .13$; for actual traditionality, mean $r = -.25$, combined $p < .08$; for percent of housecleaning performed, mean $r = -.31$, combined $p < .02$; and for percent of laundry performed, mean $r = -.33$, combined $p < .02$.

Though the bulk of the results found relationships opposite to those predicted, there was one result that fit with the hypothesis. This result was not quite significant and could therefore have occurred by chance. For one of the adult samples, which was given an auditory decoding task in which the sender was male rather than female, the correlation between decoding skill and the traditionality of the marriage was positive ($r = .47$, $p < .10$). This could indicate that oppression as here defined is positively related to women's ability to decode men in particular, but further research is needed before this is more than speculation.

On balance, therefore, the data suggest that the more-liberated, not the less-liberated, woman is a better nonverbal decoder. One can put forth a fascinating after-the-fact interpretation — that only a woman with highly developed interpersonal skills could negotiate a high level of interpersonal equality with her spouse and, conversely, that poor decoding skill helps to perpetuate a woman's disadvantaged position. This interpretation still connects decoding skill to oppression but not in the same way as implied by the original hypothesis.

The oppression hypothesis has been applied, by analogy, to blacks' predicted ability to decode nonverbal cues: because they are oppressed, they should be especially skilled in decoding nonverbal cues, particularly, one would assume, the nonverbal cues of the white majority (Henley 1977). The literature actually shows that blacks and whites differ very little in their decoding skill (Halberstadt, in press). Thus the evidence available so far fails to support the oppression hypothesis for the decoding skills of both women and blacks.

As mentioned earlier, oppression could still have a role in the development of women's nonverbal skills but not in a direct way. It is possible that the historical fact of women's subordinate status could lie behind sex-role prescriptions. Girls and women could learn that as females they ought to be good decoders, not because they are actually oppressed in any sense of the word, but because society prescribes certain roles and behaviors for them. Just as men are expected to know something about football and the insides of car engines (at least in American society), so women may be expected to be good at understanding emotional expression. Though women's oppression may play a part in such sex-role expectations, in that such expectations reflect the earlier extreme circumscription of women's activities (Stone 1979), it would nevertheless be an overstatement to claim that women's nonverbal skill stems from their oppression in any direct sense.

Structural "Oppression"

As described above, the eleven cultural groups tested with the PONS test were employed in an analysis of cross-cultural differences in women's status (see chapter 2 for cross-cultural results). As with oppression at the level of the individual, oppression at the level of the culture can be defined in many different ways. An additional problem in testing the structural hypothesis was that not only were there numerous possible definitions of women's status, but also it was impossible to find appropriate data for all or even most of the cultural groups at hand.

Many library sources were consulted. Only three kinds of indices that seemed to me to indicate women's status were located for all or most of the cultural groups: *educational* (relative enrollment of men and women in higher education; Statistical Yearbook 1974), *occupational* (index of segregation in occupations; Boulding et al. 1976), and *cultural* (number of women's nongovernmental organizations per capita; Boulding et al.). I do not consider these variables to be definitive indices of women's status; they are, rather, merely some indices of women's status out of many that I would ideally have gathered.

It was important that the educational and occupational indices described women's status *relative* to men's; a variable such as the sheer number of women in higher education could indicate general modernization rather than women's position in particular. Both the educational and occupational indices meet this criterion. The third index, women's organizations, is not such a relative index, but it is at least standardized by population and seemed like a plausible indicator of female solidarity and consciousness.

TABLE 3.1. Correlations of Sex Differences in Decoding Skill with Women's Status in Eleven National Groups

National index	Vocal skill	Visual skill
Enrollment in higher education	.28* (.52)	−.21 (−.39)
Segregation in occupations	.02 (−.19)	−.05 (−.04)
Women's organizations per capita	.34** (.67**)	−.07 (.10)

Note: National variables are scored so that higher values indicate more apparent social power or equality for women. Correlations are based on the number of separate samples available from the eleven countries described in chapter 2; correlations in parentheses are based on number of nations represented, aggregating over samples within each.

*$p < .08$.
**$p < .05$.

These three indices were correlated with the decoding-skill sex differences obtained in each sample, calculated by averaging women's scores, averaging men's scores, and then taking the difference, so that higher values indicated a greater margin of female superiority in decoding nonverbal cues.

When the national indices were correlated with sex differences on total decoding score, that is, score over all 220 items of the PONS test, there proved to be no relationship at all. This was true whether I used the raw sex difference or the sex difference standardized in terms of the correlation between sex and skill (r). However, when different channels of the PONS were examined separately, an interesting pattern emerged, though one that was weak, as the correlations in table 3.1 show. Table 3.1 shows the correlations between women's status and the sex differences separately for the auditory and visual (face and body) modalities. Correlations for vocal cues were positive, indicating that less ostensible oppression was associated with greater skill in women, while correlations for visual cues were negative. Only a few of these were significant, however. (In parentheses are shown correlations based not on the fifty-one samples but rather based on the eleven nations. These correlations are larger in magnitude than those based on individual samples, due to the added reliability of the aggregated variables, but are not significant because of the small number of countries represented.) Table 3.1 suggests that women's advantage in vocal decoding is greater when women have higher status, whereas women's advantage in visual decoding may be unchanged or even slightly smaller.

A weak pattern like that of table 3.1 would, under most circumstances, go unnoticed and uninterpreted. However, there are reasons why this pattern attracts my attention, as does the similar pattern described in the preceding section on "oppression" measured at the level of the individual person, where the less "oppressed" (less traditional) women scored higher on *vocal* channels of the PONS test. Table 3.1 shows that women who are less "oppressed" by structural criteria were more skilled relative to men in decoding vocal cues. These patterns are interesting because of the kinds of information that are postulated to be conveyed by vocal versus visual, particularly facial, cues.

Evidence from other studies on nonverbal communication suggests that the face and voice "specialize" in the content of their messages. This evidence, stemming from five studies, is summarized by DePaulo and Rosenthal (1979). The face seems to be a more reliable source of information pertaining to the positivity versus negativity of emotion. This is no surprise when we consider that the presence or absence of a smile is probably a primary source of knowledge about a person's state of happiness. The voice, on the other hand, appears to be a better source of information about dominance versus submission. Loudness may be one source of such cues.

Research also indicates that although people in general pay more attention to the face than the voice when presented with the choice, women show a greater preference for the face than men do (DePaulo et al. 1978). Facial cues may have special relevance to women; this is consistent with their gaze patterns (discussed in chapter 6). As mentioned earlier, it has also been shown that the amount of attention one allocates to the face and body is correlated with accuracy at decoding them (for example, people who attend more to the face are better decoders of the face).

If we accept the hypothesis of cue specialization for the face and voice channels — specialization in positivity-negativity and submission-dominance, respectively — then we can offer an interpretation both for sex differences in patterns of attention and also for the data on sex differences and women's status. Women may pay more attention to the face, relative to men, because they care more about the information on positivity-negativity contained in the face; they may pay special attention to information about how approving or disapproving, or how happy or sad, someone is. Men, on the other hand, may care more about how dominant or submissive the speaker is feeling and thus may attend comparatively more to the voice and show added skill in decoding the voice, relative to women.

Women who are less oppressed — meaning more autonomous — would therefore have less need to attend to the face. This postulated reallocation of attention from the face to the voice among the less-oppressed women could account for their more-developed skill at decoding vocal cues, and the concomitant (though admittedly very weak) tendency for them to be less-accurate decoders of the face.

Another interpretation of the same results for women's status is based on Rosenthal and DePaulo's theory of accommodation. As described earlier, these authors show that the face and voice channels differ in how much control the expressor has over the cues given off. The face is more controllable than the voice, the voice being more likely to convey unintended information on emotion. Rosenthal and DePaulo argue that women's greater accuracy on face cues than on voice cues, compared to men, reflects women's polite reluctance to decode vocal cues which the expressor may not have meant to convey. This interpretation can be applied to the women's status results. Women who are less oppressed have less need to be accommodating, as defined by politely ignoring leaked cues from the voice, and therefore they should be relatively better vocal decoders and possibly worse facial decoders. Though both of these interpretations — based on the channel specialization and accommodation hypotheses — are speculative at this time, they do have the virtue of integrating several sex-difference results in a sensible way.

HEMISPHERIC SPECIALIZATION

The left and right hemispheres of the brain have been shown to have specialized functions. The right hemisphere is specialized for spatial processing and for processing difficult-to-verbalize stimuli (McGee 1979), and, especially relevant to our interest in nonverbal communication, for processing stimuli of emotion such as recognizing emotions in voice tone, identifying facial expressions, and recognizing faces (Safer 1981). The left hemisphere, in contrast, controls language functions and the processing of easy-to-verbalize stimuli to a greater degree (McGee).

Sex differences also exist in hemispheric lateralization, or the degree to which one hemisphere is relatively dominant for various kinds of processing. Males have been shown to have greater right-hemisphere specialization than females in a number of studies (reviewed in McGee 1979). Males also have superior skills in some tasks controlled by the right hemisphere, such as spatial ability (Hyde 1981). Females excel in some skills controlled by the left hemisphere, such as verbal skill (Hyde).

Could it be that the sex differences in nonverbal judgment described in chapter 2 could stem from differences in the sexes' utilization of each hemisphere? Unfortunately the evidence available so far on sex differences in hemispheric specialization and in nonverbal ability falls short of supplying a theoretically coherent picture. The sexes do not seem to differ in their reliance on left versus right hemispheric processing for face-recognition tasks (Safer 1981; A. W. Young and Ellis 1976). Therefore the sex differences in accuracy in performing such tasks would not seem to be accountable in terms of differential lateralization. For identification of facial expressions, there is a hemispheric-processing sex difference, males showing more involvement of the right hemisphere than females (Safer). But males are poorer than females at decoding, even though such cues seem to be processed more by the right hemisphere than by the left. Safer offered a possible answer to this paradox by suggesting that decoding of nonverbal cues involves a mixture of nonverbal *and* verbal information processing: recognition is a right-hemisphere process but labeling expressions is a left-hemisphere (verbal) process.

In Safer's study, facial photographs were exposed at high speeds to either the left or right hemisphere, and subjects then stated whether the face thus seen was "same" or "different" with regard to a face shown earlier to both hemispheres. Men's accuracy in identifying expressions presented to the left hemisphere was poor. Women were significantly more accurate than males at distinguishing the expressions overall but mainly because of their distinctly better performance at judging facial expressions presented to the left hemisphere. Consistent with these results, males showed more right-hemisphere lateralization than females, that is, a greater tendency for the right hemisphere to do the processing. In this kind of task, then, right-hemisphere lateralization seems not to promote accuracy; instead, bilateral processing of the sort shown by females seems to.

In interpreting these results, Safer raised the possibility that in females the cerebral hemispheres communicate with each other more effectively than in males, leading to superior integration of verbal and nonverbal codes (that is, information stored in the left and right hemispheres, respectively) and in turn to superior nonverbal-judging skills. Consistent with this suggestion, a study of brain anatomy has found that the bundle of nerve fibers that connects the two hemispheres, the corpus callosum, is indeed bulkier in women than men, which could facilitate transfer and integration of information between the two hemispheres (De LaCoste-Utamsing and Holloway 1982).

But Safer also acknowledged that the direction of causation is unclear. Sex differences in hemispheric specialization could produce sex differences in nonverbal skills, but the path of causation could also be reversed. Indeed, skilled musicians show a different pattern of hemispheric processing of melodies than do naive listeners (Bever and Chiarello 1974), suggesting that training and expertise can change hemispheric information-processing patterns. Interestingly, the trained musicians' relative lack of hemispheric specialization for processing melodies is similar to that shown by women in Safer's study for judging facial expressions. Music and nonverbal communication may be similar in that the development of expert understanding may produce a high degree of integration of verbal and nonverbal knowledge — the ability to describe music in words and the ability to label emotional expressions. Thus, differences in hemispheric processing could be the result and not the cause of nonverbal sex differences.

CONCLUSIONS

Six possible explanations for sex differences in nonverbal judgment accuracy have been discussed. Though treated as distinct operationally, they are not necessarily distinct conceptually. Empathy, for example, could be considered an aspect of femininity; accommodation could be considered an aspect of oppression; oppression could be the causal antecedent of femininity; and accommodation could be the antecedent of differential practice and attention. Disentangling one possible cause from another and establishing a causal chain are not easy when experimental control is lacking, when the constructs are hard to measure, and when no one study has measured more than one or two of the relevant constructs at once.

None of the explanations is entirely satisfactory, yet. The most promising seem to be practice/attention and accommodation, though in both cases more research is definitely needed. All we know for certain is that somehow women become more adept at judging of nonverbal expressions and at recognizing faces.

Though nothing exactly definable as decoding skills has been measured in infants, one line of research has found newborn females to be more responsive (by crying more) than newborn males to the sound of another infant's cries (see chapter 11). This could mean that girls are born with a predisposition to be responsive to nonverbal cues, which could set the stage for superior acquisition of knowledge about them. But it is too soon for this to be more than an interesting suggestion. Though inborn dispositions cannot be ruled out either logically or on the basis of any existing data, they are not discussed at any length in this book. Haviland and Malatesta (1981) have offered a delineation of social-learning, biological, and interactive models for the development of nonverbal sex differences in infancy and beyond. There is no reason why biological adaptation could not result in a human female who is predisposed to develop nonverbal skills and other nonverbal behaviors conducive to maximizing reproductive success, both in attracting mates and ensuring the survival of offspring. But at this time, given that social, nonbiological causes are easier to study, make good a priori sense, and are subject to amelioration if that seems called for, it seems much more profitable to concentrate on them.

4　Expression Accuracy

Complementary to skill at judging nonverbal cues is skill at expressing oneself via nonverbal cues, often called encoding or sending skill. In this chapter the term *expression accuracy* describes skills in expressing emotion or other meanings via face, body, and voice, as well as a different but related kind of sending for which the term *skill* seems inappropriate. This is the transparency of one's face, body, or voice when one is experiencing emotion but not consciously trying to communicate anything to anyone. Investigators have often called this "spontaneous sending," in contrast to "posed sending" where one is deliberately trying to look or sound in a way that conveys specific meanings. A person who is accurate at spontaneous sending has a face, for example, that reflects current moods or thoughts, even if that person is unaware of it.

Spontaneous sending has mainly been studied in the face, and only rarely have other cue channels been examined. It is harder to achieve spontaneous expression via the voice since, by definition, one always knows if one is talking and presumably has some intent when doing so. A small number of investigators have succeeded in designing studies that seem to capture spontaneous vocal expression, however. Cunningham (1977), for example, induced feelings of elation or depression in subjects, without their realizing the investigator's purposes, and then asked them to read passages of prose; presumably, the induced emotion was registered in their voices without their knowledge.

One could justifiably point out that "real-life" expression — ordinary interpersonal communication — is neither entirely posed nor entirely spontaneous in the senses described above. The posed and spontaneous expressions measured in laboratory studies are pure extremes, neither of which is probably very important in actual interaction. What our face, body, and voice do is most often a mixture of the planned and the unplanned, not one or the other. Some nonverbal behaviors — for example, nonverbal cues that regulate the flow of conversation — are used for a purpose but are not planned. They are so well learned as ways of regulating turn taking that no conscious attention need be given to them. They are not spontaneous; they are automatic.

Further, the pace of interpersonal interaction proceeds too fast for much conscious advance planning of nonverbal behavior, and it is also believed by many investigators that one cannot in fact control one's displays fully, even if one were to try. Even the face, which is often considered to be the most controllable nonverbal channel (see chapter 3), is probably capable of "leaking" cues of emotion against one's will. Of course, the nondeliberate production of cues of emotion need not mean that we are trying to conceal or disguise our feelings. A person may express genuine feelings of happiness, for example, without consciously planning to, but also without any particular desire to conceal them.

Why, then, in our research do we not test a more real-life kind of expression? The reason is methodological. It has always been a challenge to those studying communication skills to achieve some degree of certainty about what is being felt or communicated. True, we could videotape people interacting in "real" situations, but how would we be sure of what they were feeling? Some such certainty is necessary if we are to measure the accuracy with which they express themselves. This problem of establishing a criterion has been solved, provisionally, in several ways (further discussed in R. Rosenthal et al. 1979).

One way is to use the consensus of experts or naive judges — that is, whatever they say is being expressed is what is being expressed. This approach has not been used very often because of its obvious deficiency in establishing any objective criterion of the true message. When nonverbal expressions are judged out of context, or are short or frozen (as in a photograph), both of which are often the case in research situations, expressions can be highly misleading. For example, a person who is weeping can actually appear to be laughing under such circumstances.

Most research has employed the posed or the spontaneous approaches outlined above. In each case, one has a somewhat objective, though not infallible, criterion by which to assess accuracy. In posed sending, the criterion is that which the expressor was trying to send; since this is always determined by the investigator and known to the expressor, there is generally no confusion about what it is. In spontaneous expression, people are put into situations that elicit emotion, as in Cunningham's study, or as in Buck's slide-viewing paradigm (Buck 1979) in which expressors view color slides of varying content during which a hidden camera videotapes their facial expressions. In neither case is the expressor conscious of expressing emotion, but the investigator is able to assess what they were expressing by reference to the eliciting circumstances (that is, if the stimulus was a gory accident scene, an accurate facial response would register some kind of disgust or horror).

But for both posed and spontaneous sending, who is to decide how well the expressions match the criterion? This too is a methodological difficulty. Most investigators have chosen to rely on the judgments of impartial decoders, such as a group of college students who do not know the expressors. Thus, a sender's accuracy at expression would be defined by the proportion of judges who are able correctly to identify those expressions in terms of the criteria established by the investigator. For example, on a particular posed item in which an expressor was asked to convey anger via the face, that expressor's accuracy score would be the proportion of judges who said his or her face conveyed anger. This is a form of consensual judgment but not one in which the setting of the criterion itself is left to consensus. Rather, it seems intuitively correct to define expression "accuracy" in terms of how well one is judged by others. It makes especially good sense when those accuracy scores are to be used comparatively — to compare one expressor with another or one kind of expressor with another kind, as when men and women are compared.

Because a person's expression accuracy is defined in terms of judges' accuracy, the process of obtaining expression-accuracy scores is more laborious than it is for many other kinds of nonverbal measurement. To measure decoding skill, for example, one must obtain or prepare a set of stimuli to be judged, which can be a big job, but once it is done the process of testing and scoring individuals is easy: just sit them down in a group, have them judge the photos, films, or tapes, and then score each answer as right or wrong according to preestablished scoring criteria. Once the initial effort of preparing testing materials is done, the materials can be used repeatedly by future researchers who also want to test decoding skill.

But testing expression skill generally has the following steps: (1) Bring subjects individually into the laboratory and record their nonverbal behavior while they are posing expressions, or if spontaneous expressions are desired, while they are (for example) watching slides or films. (2) Take the nonverbal recordings of these individuals and make out of them a set of stimuli (slides, tapes, and so on) that will be judged by another group of subjects. (Sometimes these judges are the expressors themselves, in which case one produces both encoding and decoding scores for the same individuals.) Putting together this set of stimuli can be very time-consuming and must be done anew by each investigator who measures expression accuracy; previous investigators' efforts cannot be applied with a new group of expressors because, of course, the expressors are different. Stimulus materials can easily involve hundreds of nonverbal clips to assemble, often in a random ordering. (3) Recruit a group of judges and test their ability to decode these expressions (as described above for measuring decoding skill). (4) Score the data by expressor rather than by decoder; that is, calculate the accuracy of each expressor, averaging over judges, instead of calculating the accuracy of each decoder, averaging over expressors. And all this is *just* to calculate expression-accuracy scores — most of the time, an investigator wants other data as well, such as personality scales, questionnaires, or observations of the expressors' behavior in other contexts.

Considering the labor involved, it is no surprise that studies of expression accuracy are not as numerous as are studies of decoding accuracy. Though in my sex-differences reviews (chapter 2) I located 125 studies of decoding skill in which decoder sex was a factor of interest, I found less than fifty analogous studies of expression accuracy. Also, fewer correlates have been established between expression accuracy and other skills and attributes than is the case for decoding skill. Finally, it comes as no surprise that fewer individuals are tested in a typical encoding study (Hall 1980).

One fact that has been ascertained is that posed-expression skill and expression of the spontaneous kind described earlier are positively related. The correlations between these two kinds of accuracy range from about .30 to about .50 (Zuckerman et al. 1976; Cunningham 1977; Fujita, Harper, and Wiens 1980; Buck 1975). Thus, a man (for example) whose face reveals sadness as he watches a sad film is also likely to be good at expressing sadness in his face if he is deliberately trying to do so. Though neither kind of accuracy is exactly what we see in everyday life, as discussed above, nevertheless they are related to a strong enough degree that we can conclude that neither is an entirely unique or bizarre kind of expression accuracy.

DEMONSTRATION OF SEX DIFFERENCES

As with the review of the decoding literature described in chapter 2, my review of the expression-accuracy literature was done in two phases, an earlier and a later. The earlier consisted of studies I located prior to 1977 (Hall 1979, 1980), and the later consisted of studies I located subsequently. The first group had twenty-six results (from twenty-two separate samples of expressors), and the second group had twenty-three results (from seventeen separate samples).

Both groups included both children and adults as expressors, both audio and video channels of expression, and both posed and spontaneously elicited expressions. To be included, a study had to measure ability or accuracy at encoding nonverbal cues via facial expression, body movement, or content-free voice-tone cues; had to employ the decoding accuracy of a group of decoders as the criterion of encoding accuracy (in most studies the exact same group of decoders judged both male and female senders); and had to report some findings relevant to the encoding accuracy of male versus female encoders. A study was included even if its encoding group consisted of just one male and one female. Clearly the inclusion of such studies could introduce some error into the data, due to the fact that a single male and a single female expressor could differ in many ways besides their sex. With larger groups of expressors, one is somewhat more confident that any apparent male-female difference is due to the encoders' sex and not to irrelevant variables. Most studies had many more than two encoders, fortunately; many had more than ten, and some had fifty or more.

In these studies, groups of 2 to over 200 judges viewed and/or listened to the nonverbal stimuli either "live" or prerecorded on still film, movie film, videotape, or audiotape. They were asked to make judgments, multiple-choice or checklist style, of the emotional or other meaning of the expression, of the degree of friendliness in the expression, of the truth or falsehood of the vocal expressions, of the pleasantness of the sender's feelings, or of the nature of the stimuli that elicited the facial expressions. The first three kinds of dependent variables were employed in studies of posed affects, and the last two were employed in studies using spontaneous-affect displays. In the studies employing spontaneous expressions, the experimenters surreptitiously recorded encoders' faces while they were viewing affectively arousing visual material on slides, videotape, or in person. Methods of voice content-masking were randomized-spliced and electronically filtered speech (see chapter 2) and standard-content speech, in which speakers recite meaningless or affectively ambiguous material, varying the expression to suit the intended emotion. In all studies, the judgments of the decoding subjects were scored for accuracy and those mean scores, computed separately for each encoder, were the sending-accuracy scores examined in this review.

As with the sex-difference results summarized in chapter 2, the expression-accuracy sex differences were quantified in the following ways: direction of outcome (which sex was more accurate, if either was), effect size measured in terms of the correlation (r) between sex (coded 0 = male, 1 = female) and expression accuracy, and significance level.

Table 4.1 summarizes the overall results for both groups of studies.[1] In

---

1. As mentioned in chapter 1, these analyses include some nonindependent studies — that is, the same group of subjects sometimes contributes more than one result (due to scores being computed in different scoring categories, such as posed versus spontaneous). This could lead to misleading p-values. But the nonindependent results were not always in the same direction within a sample, and there were not many nonindependent results altogether, making such bias not likely to be very great.

TABLE 4.1. Sex Differences in Expression Accuracy (All Studies)

Index	Analyzed before 1977 (26 results)	Analyzed after 1977 (23 results)
Direction of effect (excluding no difference or unknown)	71% (15/21) favor females ($p = .05$)	59% (10/17) favor females (not significant)
Mean effect size (r)[a]	Between .25 (26 results) and .31 (20 results)	Between .12 (23 results) and .18 (15 results)
Statistical significance (all studies)	31% (8/26) favor females significantly, 4% (1/26) favor males significantly	30% (7/23) favor females significantly, 9% (2/23) favor males significantly
Combined p	$p = .007$ (26 results)	$p = .002$ (22 results)

[a] Positive values mean female advantage.

both, females were better expressors — that is, their expressions were more accurately judged by the decoders whose performance served as the criterion. More studies showed superior female expression than superior male expression, though this difference in proportions was not great for the later-reviewed studies. The effect sizes (r) were consistently in favor of women (for both the very conservative hypothetical lower estimate based on all studies and for the higher estimate based on known effect sizes; see chapter 2). And both indices of statistical significance showed that this sex difference was reliable.[2]

Because of the relatively small number of studies in the two groups summarized in table 4.1, certain analyses were conducted treating all of the results as one group.[3] These analyses showed that adult samples showed somewhat larger sex differences for visual (chiefly facial) expression than did child samples; there were no vocal results for children, so for voice this comparison could not be made. This difference was not significant, but it was not trivial: the correlation between age (coded 0 = child, 1 = adult) with the magnitude of the sex difference (expressed as the correlation between sex and accuracy) was .38 (eighteen results). Most of this age effect was due to one study that found preschool boys' spontaneous facial expressions to be much more easily judged than preschool girls'. Interestingly, Buck (1977) found dramatic decreases in preschool boys' spontaneous facial expression accuracy from age four years to six years (cross-

2. Without one unusually large result showing male superiority for preschool children, the lower and upper effect sizes (r) for the later-reviewed studies are .18 and .26 respectively.

3. For these analyses, each sample was entered only once, eliminating the nonindependence mentioned in footnote 1. When a sample produced two sex differences — for example, for both posed and spontaneous expression — the effect sizes (r) were averaged to produce a single result.

sectional finding), but no comparable decrease for girls. This suggests that socialization pressure or modeling induces boys during this period to reduce expression of emotion via the face.

Whether cues were visual or vocal showed a significant difference. The correlation between channel (coded 0 = vocal, 1 = visual) and the size of the sex difference (r) was .37 (thirty results), $p < .05$: there was a larger sex difference for visual cues than for vocal cues. Indeed, vocal cues showed no sex difference on the average. The overall sex effect (r) for visual cues was .34 (eighteen results), compared to − .02 (twelve results) for voice; this visual-vocal difference was strongly apparent in both the studies reviewed earlier and those reviewed later. The vocal-cue results were, however, highly variable, with some strong differences favoring each sex. Factors that account for this variation have not yet been uncovered. Studies reporting only combined visual and vocal accuracy showed an average sex difference of $r = .58$ (three results).

Whether expressions were posed or spontaneous (this pertains only to visual cues) made almost no difference. The correlation between modality (coded 0 = posed, 1 = spontaneous) and the size of the sex difference (r) was − .08 (eighteen results): posed cues showed a very slightly larger sex difference than spontaneous cues.

Finally, sex of authors was examined, as in chapter 2, to test Eagly and Carli's (1981) hypothesis that authors succeed in making their own sex look good (in this case, as accurate in expression as possible). The correlation between the proportion of male authors and the size of the sex difference (r) was only .07 (twenty-eight results), indicating only a very weak tendency for studies with a higher proportion of male authors to find larger sex differences favoring females. This is contrary to the hypothesis as I have stated it. However, "looking good" would not mean the greatest expression accuracy if high expression accuracy were seen by male authors as a negative female stereotype; in that case, their own sex would look better (more masculine) if it showed less, not more, expression accuracy. Seen in this way, the result fits the hypothesis. But we should not forget that the hypothesis was rephrased with hindsight, and the relationship is extremely small anyway.

An additional question was whether specific emotions show different sex-difference patterns. This question is especially interesting in light of R. Rosenthal and DePaulo's (1979a, 1979b) accommodation hypothesis, which states that women show politeness in their nonverbal behavior. We might predict from this that women would be especially skilled in conveying pleasant feelings — love, happiness, friendliness. Unfortunately, it is hard to answer this question definitively, because most studies did not offer much detail on specific emotions. But as far as I can tell, there is no evident pattern. Females were reported to be better encoders of unfriendly and unpleasant affect, friendly affect, happiness, love, fear, anger, dominance, and surprise; and males were reported to be either absolutely or relatively better on happiness, love, disgust, sadness, pain, and pleasant and unpleasant affect.

The sex differences obtained in these empirical reviews can be compared to sex differences obtained from people's self-reports of their expression skill. Zuckerman and Larrance (1979) developed scales on which subjects rate their assessment of their own decoding and sending skills. Though in general people are poor judges of their own skills (as tested by the correlation between self-ratings and actual skills; Zuckerman and Larrance 1979; R. Rosenthal et al. 1979), the sex differences in self-report are remarkably similar to the actual sex differences described in the present chapters. For expression skill, Zuckerman and Larrance found the correlation between sex and self-rated skill to be .30 (that is, women rated themselves as more accurate in expression than men rated themselves). The analogous correlation between sex and actual accuracy, based on all thirty-five results in table 4.1 for which this statistic was known, was .25.

Another scale to measure self-rated expression, the Affective Communication Test (ACT), has been developed by Friedman et al. (1980). This scale includes nonverbal expression skill as well as charismatic traits such as emotional demonstrativeness, lack of shyness, and readiness to attract attention. Friedman and his colleagues found that women rate themselves as more expressive by this definition, but the effects were not as large as those of Zuckerman and Larrance (rs of only about .10 between sex and self-ratings). Some of the ACT's traits are not specifically nonverbal, and perhaps these traits show sex differences that are small or even reversed in direction, reducing the size of the overall sex difference.

EXPLANATIONS

Several of the hypotheses put forth in chapter 3 seem applicable. One that has received some empirical support is socialization along lines of masculinity and femininity. Zuckerman et al. (1982) investigated this hypothesis in three separate studies in which expression accuracy (measured in several different ways) was related to measures of masculinity and femininity of the sort used by Hall and Halberstadt (1981) to test the same hypothesis for decoding skill (see chapter 3). Zuckerman and his colleagues reasoned that *femininity* implies clear and willing expression of nonverbal cues; indeed, expressiveness — meant in a broad sense — is at the heart of the very concept of femininity as it is captured in most femininity scales.

Consistent with their hypothesis, Zuckerman et al. found that masculin-

ity was negatively associated with posed-expression accuracy, and femininity was positively associated. The average within-sex correlations, over all
three studies, were:

Masculinity with vocal sending, $r = -.34, p < .001$.
Masculinity with facial sending, $r = -.17, p < .05$.
Femininity with vocal sending, $r = .18, p < .05$.
Femininity with facial sending, $r = .24, p < .01$.

In addition, for the vocal channel, femininity was significantly
associated with a person's tendency to leak or inadvertently show iden-
tifiable cues of emotion when trying to suppress expression; that is, more
feminine people of either sex were likely to reveal their emotions in their
voices even against their wills.

One test of the power of this hypothesis is to see whether taking
masculinity and femininity into account can make the sex differences
decrease substantially. In fact, it does not, but in every case where the sex
difference was originally significant, taking masculinity and femininity
into account using partial correlation rendered the sex difference nonsignificant. The sex difference was, in other words, not completely eliminated
but was reduced in magnitude.

R. Rosenthal and DePaulo (1979a, 1979b) suggested that women's
superiority in expression could be an aspect of accommodation to the
wishes of others — a polite person shows others their feelings. Women's
special accuracy in facial expression would seem to be consistent with this
view, since the face, according to the authors, is the most polite, most
noticed, and least problematic channel. That Zuckerman et al. (1982)
found more feminine individuals (of both sexes) to leak vocal emotion
when trying to suppress it is also consistent with the view that the accommodating person is open about expression apparently even when they don't
want to be.

Points made in chapter 3 are pertinent here, however. Women's greater
accuracy when producing facial expressions could be due to the kinds of
cues that the face makes most salient, rather than to a trait of accommodation. The face conveys positivity *and* negativity and, as noted above,
females are often superior in expressing negative as well as positive affects.
To send a clear message of positivity or negativity may be very important
to women because of the relevance of the positivity-negativity dimension
to the quality of interpersonal relations. Men may, in contrast, be relatively more attuned to the voice and relatively better at decoding and
encoding the voice because of its relevance to establishing relations along a
dominance-submission dimension (see chapters 3 and 10 for further
elaboration of this point).

It is intriguing that a skill not summarized in the present review — skill in deceiving others, via verbal and nonverbal cues — does not show women to be superior (Zuckerman, DePaulo, and Rosenthal 1981). One could fit this with the accommodation hypothesis, arguing that polite people are not unusually good at manipulating others via deception. But one could also argue that the polite person should be superior at the altruistic, "white," lie, which eases social interaction by enabling others to avoid embarrassment or confrontation. As yet, research on deception is not well-enough focused to test these ideas.

Another possible explanation of expression-accuracy sex differences is that expression accuracy is an extension of decoding skill — that is, a person with good decoding skill develops good expression skill because both are based on the same knowledge. (This would apply chiefly to posed-expression skill.) In order for this hypothesis to be true, encoding and decoding skills would have to be positively correlated. The available evidence on the encoding-decoding relationship, reviewed by DePaulo and Rosenthal (1979), is unfortunately too mixed to inform us of the potential usefulness of this hypothesis. Some studies do show strong positive correlations between the two kinds of skill, but some show strong negative correlations. This variation has not yet been explained.

Buck (1983) has suggested the reverse hypothesis, speaking particularly about sending and receiving skill in interactional contexts. He proposed that expressiveness encourages others to be expressive in reciprocation and that, as a consequence, the expressive person lives in a nonverbal environment that is more easily decodable than that of the less-expressive person. One would have to posit further that such good decoding in specific contexts develops into general decoding skill that is measurable using standard stimuli. Thus it would be women's greater expression accuracy that leads to their greater decoding accuracy, not vice versa as suggested above.

It is possible, of course, that males and females simply learn and do what is considered appropriate for their sex, via standard social-learning processes. Consistent with this is the tendency for the expression-accuracy sex difference to increase with age. A social-learning interpretation implies that the nonverbal skill has no motivational relevance besides that of doing what oneself and others feel is suitable. In other words, the sexes' differences on other traits such as accommodation would be irrelevant to the expression-accuracy sex difference.

Expression accuracy refers to overall decodability, not to specific nonverbal behaviors. The description of specific behaviors is the concern of the remainder of this book. Since we have just been focusing mainly on facial accuracy, the next chapter will continue with a consideration of facial expression.

5 The Face

Here we are concerned with general facial expressiveness and with positive and negative facial expressions. These are aspects of sex differences about which most people have a clear intuitive idea. Kramer (1977) has documented the stereotype that women smile more than men, and Broverman et al. (1972) have shown that high emotional expressiveness (though not facial expressiveness in particular) is a key element of the female stereotype. The belief that women smile a lot is so strong that the authors of existing reviews state it as a fact with little or even no published empirical evidence to support the claim (Deaux 1976; Frieze and Ramsey 1976; Henley 1977). For social smiling, there are in fact over sixty studies of infants, children, and adults.[1] There are also studies on social laughing and on nonsocial smiling and laughing, and on general facial expressiveness and negative facial expressions, though in the last two categories there is unfortunately little research.

GENERAL FACIAL EXPRESSIVENESS

Chapter 4 showed that emotions are more easily judged from women's than from men's faces. This implies that women have more expressive, that is, more labile, faces, since accuracy of facial expression over a variety of emotions or stimuli must reflect changes from one to the next. A face that changes little when circumstances change is not an accurate source of information about a person's state. Of course, an expressive face is not necessarily an accurate one, since the expressions could be inappropriate to

---

1. Data for precollege adolescents are practically nonexistent. This is true for facial behavior as well as most other kinds of behavior examined in this book.

the prevailing feelings or situation. Buck and his colleagues have defined facial expressiveness in their research as "breakpoints," or the number of times observers see something meaningful happen on the face of an expressor who is watching emotionally arousing color slides (Buck et al. 1980). These investigators found that for female faces, both adult and preschool, the number of breakpoints was substantially correlated with facial-expression accuracy, as hypothesized above. But for males' faces in both age groups, there was no such correlation, indicating that some males who show many facial changes have accurate (that is, easily judged) faces, but some who show few such changes are also accurate.

Expressiveness can be defined in more than one way. It could refer to a person's overall level of expression, such that a person whose face is frozen into a smile is more expressive than a person whose face is characteristically relaxed. Expressiveness could also refer to the range of facial parts used, the extent of their movement, or the rate at which changes occur, whatever their magnitude. In the published literature, mainly global assessments were made, so it is not obvious which definition was employed.

Data on sex differences in expressiveness come from seven studies, one with preschool children and six with college or older subjects. The preschool study found identical overall expressiveness (breakpoints) for boys and girls, but boys showed more than girls when viewing unpleasant slides and girls showed more than boys when viewing unusual slides. Among the adult studies, five of the six found women's faces to be significantly more expressive, measured as breakpoints, ratings of facial movement, facial activity or mobility, and number of facial reactions. The average known effect size (r between sex and expressiveness) was .45 (five results), quite an impressive difference.

Women's greater facial expressiveness could yield benefits beyond those possibly gained in the social realm. Buck and his colleagues (summarized in Buck 1979), as well as earlier investigators, have demonstrated that people whose faces respond expressively have lower levels of concurrent electrodermal response than do people whose faces are relatively immobile. Electrodermal response is a measure of physiological arousal, which could signify suppressed emotion. Suppressed emotion, especially negative emotion, has long been considered a possible contributor to heart disease and other stress-related conditions (Diamond 1982). This "internalizer-externalizer" distinction (internalizing emotion versus externalizing it via the face) corresponds to the patterns of sex differences that have been documented: women tend to be externalizers (high facial response, low physiological response), while males tend to be internalizers (reverse pattern). Socialization to inhibit emotional expression in males may thus contribute to some diseases that are more prevalent in men.

POSITIVE FACIAL EXPRESSION

Smiling and laughing, like all nonverbal behavior, have somewhat ambiguous meaning without reference to the expressor's mood and intention and the social context in which the behavior takes place. Many authors have commented on, and documented, the various meanings and functions of smiling. To build on Noller's (1982) summary, smiling may reflect the following: (1) Habit acquired by observation or reinforcement. Such smiling need have no particular meaning to the expressor. (2) Warmth, friendliness, or pleasure. (3) Appeasement — an attempt to placate someone, reduce threat, obtain approval, or signal submission. (4) Social unease or nervousness. This kind of smiling is paradoxical but not at all uncommon. It may be a spontaneous expression or a deliberate attempt to mask unease.

Research on sex differences has not generally shed much light on what the observed smiles mean. There are exceptions, though. In some cases, extensive descriptive detail or experimental manipulation permits inference about the expressor's state. Stern and Bender (1974), for example, distinguished "common" from "ambivalent" smiles, which are compressed or with lip in, and also noted "apprehensive mouth behavior." Preschool boys showed more common smiling to an adult experimenter than girls did, but girls showed more of the last two behaviors, suggesting that in that situation boys' smiles meant relaxation or pleasure, while girls' smiles reflected unease. Rosenfeld (1966) conducted an experiment in which subjects were asked to role-play approval-seeking or approval-avoiding; Mehrabian and Williams (1969) observed subjects in the act of trying to persuade an experimenter about something. Because intentions are experimentally manipulated in such studies, they have the potential, at least, of providing insight into the everyday smiling intentions of men and women.

Unfortunately, though some research designs can be of some help in understanding what a smile signifies, most studies have been based either on unobtrusive observation in field settings, in which case almost nothing is known about the concurrent mood, relationship, and context, or else on observations of pairs of initially unacquainted persons interacting in a psychology laboratory. In the latter case, a person talks with an experimenter or interviewer or is asked to get acquainted with a real or supposed peer. In such situations, one can infer that the interaction is civil and probably at least superficially friendly.

The factors that are reported in many studies are approximate age of the expressors and interactant(s), sex of interactant(s), and social versus nonsocial situation (that is, expressor is with others or is alone). How smiling and laughing are measured varies. Though studies most often report on the incidence or duration of smiling or "facial pleasantness," some studies report on "smiling and laughing" as one variable, and others employ a rating scale with "frown" or "no expression" at the lowest scale value, "smile" at the middle scale value, and "laugh" at the highest scale value. Some others report on laughing only or on both smiling and laughing as separate variables. In the review that follows, studies that expressly coded smiling are summarized separately from all studies that measured laughing (either separately or together in one way or another with smiling).

Social Smiling

Because there are striking differences between young samples (infants or children) and adult samples in sex differences in social smiling, results will be presented for each group.

For infants there were eighteen results for social smiling (at experimenters, parents, or siblings). Regrettably, only five of these stated the direction of the result, of which three showed more female smiling. Only two effect sizes (r) were available, and they averaged to only $-.02$; seventeen of the results were nonsignificant, and none was significant either way. Infants, therefore, show no sex difference in social smiling on the basis of the reported data.

Table 5.1 shows the overall results for social smiling in children (aged two through twelve) and adults (college and up). Recipients of smiles included both male and female children or adults (with sex being almost universally a between-subjects factor — that is, different subjects interacted with each sex), only male or female child(ren) or adult(s), same-sex child(ren) or adult(s), or opposite-sex adult(s), but not infants.[2] Sex of recipient was unspecified in some studies.

As with previous tables of this kind, the sex differences are summarized using several indices. For children there was almost no evidence of a sex difference. The only exception is that two studies were significant in favor of girls' smiling and none was significant in favor of boys'; but considering the consistently null overall results for the other indices in the table, I would be cautious about interpreting this slight trend. Also relevant here is Cheyne's (1976) study of preschoolers in classrooms: most of the smiles observed were social, and there was no significant sex difference overall.

Among adults, by contrast, women showed remarkably consistent smiling compared with men. The correlation between age level (coded 0 = children, 1 = adults) and the magnitude of the sex difference (r) confirms this age effect: it was .45 (twenty results, p < .05).

---

2. A few results exist for parents smiling at their infants. Mothers generally smiled more than fathers, but in one study this was not so when each parent was alone with the infant (Field 1978; Parke and O'Leary 1976).

TABLE 5.1. Sex Differences in Social Smiling (by Sex of Subject, for Children and Adults)

Index	Children (20 studies)	Adults (23 studies)
Direction of effect (excluding no differ- ence or unknown)	47% (8/17) favor females (not significant)	94% (17/18) favor females ($p = .0002$)
Mean effect size (r)[a]	Between .00 (20 studies) and −.02 (5 studies)	Between .20 (23 studies) and .30 (15 studies)
Statistical significance (all studies)	10% (2/20) favor females significantly, none favors males significantly	52% (12/23) favor females significantly, none favors males significantly
Combined p	$p = .49$ (14 studies)	$p < 10^{-9}$ (19 studies)

[a] Positive values mean more female smiling.

Hence, one can conclude that females' greater tendency for social smiling develops with age, though it may exist very weakly in children, considering that the very few significant results did favor girls. One study that specifically analyzed the relationship of sex differences in smiling to age was R. M. Adams and Kirkevold's (1978) observational study of people in restaurants. They found that the sex difference (which favored females significantly over all age groups) did vary significantly with the age of the people observed.[3] The largest sex difference was for the age group eighteen through twenty-two years. This result is consistent with the above inference from the aggregate literature, since most of the "adult" studies in table 5.1 were of college students (that is, eighteen through twenty-two years old).

Though the data are scarce, it appears also that females are especially likely to smile, relative to males, when the other interactant is of the same sex. The average sex difference (r) for two adult studies for which it was available was .39 (these studies are included in table 5.1). This is consistent with one study that found women to be smiled *at* significantly more by both sexes than men were, and another in which men and women were rated as nonverbally "warmer" toward women than toward men (Weitz 1976). (Three other studies with adults found no significant effect for recipient sex.) Indeed, the same-sex situation confounds effects of subject and recipient, so it is not actually possible to determine which factor is most responsible for any results. The two tendencies — the effect for sex of

3. This study is not in table 5.1 because it did not present the results broken down by both age and the social/nonsocial distinction. The sex × age interaction effect reported here is, in fact, for pooled social and nonsocial smiling, but since presumably few people are alone in restaurants, especially under age eighteen, the result is probably mainly for social smiling.

the smiler and the effect for sex of the smile recipient (if this effect is real) — would converge to make the same-sex situation show the strongest difference for sex of smiler.[4]

Still other interesting questions can be asked, but again the data are limited. One such question concerns same-sex versus opposite-sex smiling. (Note that this is not the same comparison discussed in the preceding paragraph: there, the issue was female-female versus male-male smiling — that is, the size of the sex difference among smilers when the other person is the same sex as the smiler. Here the issue is male-male and female-female smiling versus opposite-sex smiling.) Three studies suggested that smiling is much more likely in same-sex than in opposite-sex interactions; one of these effects was highly significant and very large (Foot, Smith, and Chapman 1979). Perhaps this reflects lower levels of inhibition and more comfort in same-sex dyads, though it should be remembered that few of these dyads were well acquainted. In intimate dyads, there could actually be much more opposite-sex than same-sex smiling.

One might also ask, within opposite-sex pairs, which sex smiles the most? This question, which I shall call the asymmetry question, has special importance to those interested in the oppression theory of sex differences (see chapter 3): sex differences suggesting asymmetry in nonverbal behavior could have origins in status differences between the sexes. Though caution is in order due to scarce results, it appears that among children, boys may smile at girls more than vice versa (three results), but among adolescents and adults the reverse may be true (three results). These speculations are mainly based on the direction of the differences, not on actual significance tests or estimates of effect size, so they are indeed tentative. If adult females smile more at males than vice versa, it could mean appeasement: if the female in the interaction is trying to be more pleasant than the male, it could mean she has a weaker role and must seek to please. On the other hand, a male-female power difference could also be involved if *males* smiled more: here, the argument would be that males have the prerogative to take the initiative (a hypothesis put forth by Henley 1977 with regard to touch). Thus, a hypothesis based on status differences does not make unambiguous predictions.[5] Further, a male-female smiling

4. Among four studies of smiling by infants, male adults received more smiles than female adults: all three results of known direction favored male recipients significantly, with an average effect size (r) of $-.52$. Three studies of children's preferences for which sex to smile at yielded little usable data, but none was significant. Finally, six studies of adults, mainly mothers, smiling at infants showed them to have no clear preference to smile at either sex of infant: none was significant, and known directions were mixed. Thus the only evidence for females receiving more smiles than males is for adults smiling at other adults; unfortunately there have been few such studies.

5. I would add that from the point of view of anyone determined to invoke a status interpretation, this is fortunate, because it means that any pattern of results would do.

asymmetry does not necessarily mean that the relative status of the parties is involved at all; if females smile more at males than vice versa, it could be simply a manifestation of their tendency to smile more at *anyone* than men do.

Social Laughing and Smiling-Laughing

The picture for social laughing and smiling-laughing (that is, smiling and laughing measured as one variable) is similar to that for social smiling by itself, though more extreme with regard to the age effect. For simplicity, I shall refer to this category of behavior as *laugh* even though it includes smiling whenever smiling was not measured separately from laughing. For children, 61 percent (11/18) of the studies with known direction showed girls to laugh more than boys; but the known size of the sex difference (*r*) was − .26 (five results), which indicates more laughing by boys; and two studies favored boys significantly. One of the studies observed children in both same-sex and opposite-sex dyads, and found a slight (nonsignificant) tendency for boys to laugh more than girls in same-sex pairings but found a significant tendency for girls to laugh more than boys in opposite-sex pairings. Three other of the studies that showed more male laughing were in same-sex dyads, including one large and significant result. Thus, it seems possible that when boys do laugh more than girls, they are in a same-sex situation.

For adults, things are entirely different. All four of the available studies favored women significantly, all four were highly significant, and the average size of the difference (*r*) was .36 (four results). A propensity for more laughter in females than in males thus seems to develop with age. Adams and Kirkevold's study of people in restaurants, described earlier, found significant variation with age in the sex difference in laughing, but that relationship was curvilinear, with the largest difference (favoring females) occurring in the twelve through seventeen year-old group, a group for which other observational data are lacking.[6]

Nonsocial Smiling, Laughing, and Smiling-Laughing

Nonsocial smiling and laughing are measured when individuals are alone. Examples of such situations are a baby lying alone and a person eating alone in a restaurant, solving anagrams, or sitting in a laboratory listening to funny stories on a tape recorder. In each case, no companions,

6. That study was not summarized above because the data included both social and nonsocial laughing, a distinction I am trying to make as clearly as possible. But it is worth noting that nonsocial laughing was rare (as our intuitions might tell us); if we were to consider R. M. Adams and Kirkevold's study as one of mainly social laughing, there would be less of a boys' edge in evidence, since in this study laughing was more common in girls.

observers, or experimenters are in the immediate vicinity of the person who is observed. These studies, though comparatively few, do not suggest strong sex differences, but those that are reported seem to favor females, at least for smiling.

For infants, out of six nonsocial studies (which included situations in which the infant was alone and situations in which the infant was shown pictures of objects or faces), direction was stated in four. Three of those four found more female smiling, one of which was highly significant and one marginally so. The average sex difference (r) was .21 (two results). Both the significant and near-significant study were of infants less than four days old, and one was noteworthy in excluding all boys who had undergone circumcision (an event that is likely to reduce the frequency of smiling).

For nonsocial smiling, there were no studies of just adults. Children were observed in only three studies; none was known to be significant, and the direction ratio was 2:1 in favor of girls. Adams and Kirkevold's restaurant study did not separate children from adults, but the data are still instructive: smiling was, predictably, very infrequent for people eating alone, but even so the sex difference, though not significant, favored females. By contrast, the same comparison for people with companions showed a very significant sex difference favoring females ($p < .001$).

The nonsocial laughing and smiling-laughing categories, as defined earlier, were more plentiful. For children, the six results of known direction were evenly split between boys and girls; the average size of the sex difference (r) was only .07 (three results), but the only two results known to be significant favored girls. For adults, the four results of known direction were divided 3:1 in favor of men, with a known effect size (r) of $-.18$ (two results). None was significant. Adams and Kirkevold's restaurant study, not analyzed by age groups, showed a consistent result: though females laughed more than males whether alone or accompanied, the difference was trivial in the former circumstance and highly significant in the latter ($p = .001$). Thus, for nonsocial laughing and smiling-laughing the sex differences are minimal and possibly slightly reversed.

Comparing the nonsocial with the social data leads to the conclusion that the sex difference is a social phenomenon that develops sometime between early childhood and adulthood. The gap in the research record for adolescence up to college age is most regrettable. The closest to filling the gap is Ragan's (1982) study of high school yearbooks. In these pictures, girls did smile more than boys, a finding that is consistent with Ragan's analyses of teachers' pictures in high school yearbooks, of college students' yearbook photographs, and of university professors' media-file photographs. Though all of these groups showed more female smiling, and the overall difference was highly significant, the difference was actually small (*r* between sex and smile expansiveness = .11). Morse (1982) also found more female smiling in twelve college yearbooks (significant in eleven of the twelve). Of course, though unequivocal in demonstrating smiling norms that differentiate the sexes, these studies are ambiguous with regard to the social-nonsocial distinction. Is posing for a photographer a social situation?

Why Do Women Smile?

Almost universally, writers allude to women's role: women are expected to be, or at least to appear, pleasant. But an important distinction is whether they smile as an active strategy of appeasement or smile for more genuine or purely habitual reasons. The active strategy is most linked to the possibility that smiling serves as a display of the female role of submission. Of course, even if women smile as a habit and not to communicate anything in particular, the smile could still conceivably make them seem weak or too eager to please, a fact that would be dismaying to many women who are not this way at all.

As mentioned earlier, most studies do not provide enough contextual or other detail to answer the "why" question. One way to seek an answer is to examine studies that found large sex differences and those that found small sex differences, to see if there are striking differences in kinds of situations, interpersonal relations, or apparent motives of the persons observed. The largest social-smiling sex differences for adults were the following, all in laboratory settings unless stated otherwise: conversing with a previously unacquainted same-sex or opposite-sex peer (Bond and Shiraishi 1974; M. Davis and Weitz 1981; Frances 1979; Ickes, Schermer, and Steeno 1979; LaFrance and Carmen 1980; Pilkonis 1977b); interviewing a previously unacquainted same-sex or opposite-sex person (Sarason and Winkel 1966); tutoring a male child confederate (Chaikin, Sigler, and Derlega 1974; Chaikin and Derlega 1978; Bates 1976); and delivering persuasive or informative messages (Chaiken 1979; Mehrabian and Williams 1969). Minimal sex differences were found in the following circumstances: when smiled at by a waitress in a restaurant (Tidd and Lockard 1978); when smiled at by a passerby on the street (Jorgenson 1978); waiting with a stranger for an experiment to begin (Mehrabian 1971b); presenting arguments to another person (Mehrabian 1971a); and role-playing someone seeking or someone avoiding approval (Rosenfeld 1966).

The studies with weaker results include more fleeting, anonymous, or public encounters, where smiling might be misconstrued or be considered inappropriate. The stronger results seem to come from studies of interactions legitimated by a third party and that are defined as mutual and friendly, in which women's tendencies to behave affiliatively might be disinhibited. Both groups contain studies in which subjects had to act persuasively, so that cannot be a distinguishing factor. It is interesting, however, that Mehrabian and Williams found no significant difference between the conditions of "be persuasive" versus "be informative" in the size of the sex difference in smiling, and Rosenfeld similarly found no significant difference between the "seek approval" and "avoid approval" conditions in the size of the sex difference in smiling. These two results suggest that women's motives in smiling are not any more finely tuned to situational demands than men's are, once the relationship is recognized as having an existence, even if in a highly circumscribed way.

Some of the larger sex differences may also be attributed in part to the self-consciousness that subjects probably feel in an artificially composed, though probably nominally pleasant, conversational situation in a laboratory. Women might be more self-conscious than men, and their smiling could therefore reflect nervousness. Women do score slightly higher than men on scales of social anxiety (see chapter 11), but since these scales seem mainly to tap a person's wish to avoid social awkwardness, they in no way prove that women are in fact behaviorally more anxious in social interaction. In addition, Frances found evidence that social discomfort may be manifested in different ways by the sexes. In her study, as conversing subjects apparently became more relaxed over time, women's smiling decreased relative to men's, while men's body fidgeting decreased relative to women's. Frances also found that smiling was associated with self-rated friendliness in men but with self-rated nervousness in women. Thus, pleasantness norms in women may be compounded by a tendency to smile (and laugh) excessively when socially nervous.[7]

Further evidence supports this hypothesis. Stern and Bender (1974) found that preschool girls showed more uncomfortable smiles than boys, and boys showed more common (presumably relaxed) smiles than girls. B. Lott (1978) found that preschool girls smiled much more than cohort boys at adults but not significantly more at peers (true in both of two schools observed). Bond and Shiraishi (1974) interpreted a factor analysis of observed nonverbal behaviors as indicating that women's smiling was

---

7. In a subsequent analysis of the social-smiling studies for adults, Hall and Halberstadt (in press) employed quantitative methods to test for situational friendliness, social tension, and relative status as moderators of the sex differences. Hall and Halberstadt blind-rated on a variety of scales the situations in which subjects were observed and coded objective features of the study designs. Consistent with the arguments put forth in the present chapter, a more friendly tone, a situation inspiring more nervousness, and more face-to-face involvement were associated with larger sex differences favoring women. The relative status of the subject in the situation was not related to the sex differences.

nervous while men's was relaxed. And Pilkonis (1977b) found that though women smiled generally more than men, shy women smiled most of all.

Though probably intended and generally perceived as pleasant, a woman's smile may have the paradoxical effect of being discounted because of its very chronicity or whenever it is not entirely consistent with messages conveyed in the verbal or voice-tone channels (Bugental et al. 1970; Bugental, Love, and Gianetto 1971; Noller 1982). When discrepancies between communication channels exist, women's discrepancies tend to show greater positivity in the face, as we would expect from higher overall levels of smiling. Bugental, Love, and Gianetto found that fathers in their sample made more positive verbal statements when smiling than when not smiling, whereas mothers' verbal statements were unrelated to whether they were smiling. Such evidence, combined with the possibility that discrepant communication is harmful (for example, Bugental, Love et al. 1971; Hall and Levin 1980; Noller 1982), led Bugental to call the female face "perfidious": it sends a misleadingly pleasant message.[8]

Consistent with the idea of the female smile as having a high baseline level, when women frowned in one study it had a particularly strong negative impact relative to when men frowned (Bugental et al.). Shrout and Fiske (1981) also found that judges rating videotapes gave higher positive ratings to men when they smiled than when they did not, but did not evaluate women higher when they smiled. This suggests that the smile occurs so often in women that it loses some of its impact.

NEGATIVE FACIAL EXPRESSION

One might assume that because women smile a lot, they produce correspondingly fewer frowns, scowls, and other negative facial expressions. The last Bugental result described would imply this. But the evidence for greater *general* facial expressiveness in women, reviewed earlier, suggests

---

8. The prevailing conceptualization of communication discrepancy is that discrepancy indicates ambivalence and/or that it indicates leakage — that is, one message is intended while a concurrent message in a different channel is both unintended and presumably truer than the intended one (for example, DePaulo and Rosenthal 1979). Though this must surely be a correct presumption much of the time, it is also possible to have simultaneous *intended* messages which appear to disagree with each other but which actually reflect a superordinate communicative purpose. For example, a mother might smile while rebuking a child; though this could mean she is ambivalent about her capacity to control the child or her right to scold (and thus qualify as leakage), it could also mean that she is trying to communicate affection while making the rebuke. Discrepant communication (especially positive nonverbal paired with negative verbal, as in this example) may still have a less than optimal effect, no matter what the motive (Hall, Roter, and Rand 1981; Woolfolk 1978). But it should not be *assumed* that discrepant communication per se reflects ambivalence, insincerity, or any kind of communicative psychopathology.

the possibility that women engage in more facial behavior of all sorts than men, not just the seemingly pleasant kind.

When one looks to the literature for evidence on negative expressions, however, one is disappointed. Very few studies measure negative facial expressions.[9] This could have several explanations. First, the kind of theories under examination could have relevance for smiling but not for frowning. This seems unlikely, since nonverbal behavior is generally taken as a source of information on affect, and for this purpose negative expressions would be as relevant as positive ones. Second, some authors may feel that their measures capture both negative and positive expressions, as when the face is rated on a negative-positive continuum. But few investigators actually employ such a measure; most code or count only smiles, or laughs, or pleasant facial reactions. Third, and very likely to be a contributing factor, is the great disproportion in the frequency with which negative versus positive expressions can be observed. When investigators decide which nonverbal behaviors to code (and this can sometimes be a very large set), they are unlikely to include categories of behavior that occur with extremely low frequency. In the kinds of situations in which nonverbal behavior is often observed — public relations among friends or strangers, and laboratory-based conversations between college students — overt negative emotion is probably rarely expressed. And the fourth possible reason why negative facial expression is rarely described is the most disturbing with regard to our interest in sex differences: perhaps investigators who plan to look for sex differences focus, unconsciously, on behaviors that are the most stereotypically sex-typed. Since female smiling is probably a stronger stereotype than male frowning (its not quite logical corollary), smiling may be measured and frowning not.

If it were actually the case that women smile *and* frown more than men, then some prevailing beliefs about women's motives in expression would have to be revised. The view that women are constantly pleasant, at least in the face (while they may mask or leak their real feelings in other ways), would lose much of its appeal, as would the belief that women's smiling communicates a constant message of submission and deference (Henley 1977). Only if women's negative expressions were reflective of actual fear, which is unlikely, would the submission interpretation still make strong sense.

What do the data tell us? For infants I found six studies of negative facial expression excluding crying; these studies measured grimace, frown, or wary brow. One was significant in showing neonate boys to grimace

9. Here I do not include weeping as a facial expression. Although crying is often included among the variables observed in studies of infants and young children, it has not to my knowledge been measured in an observational study of adults.

more – importantly, before circumcision – than neonate girls. Four others were nonsignificant. In terms of direction, two showed more boy negativity, one showed the reverse. Male infants tend therefore to look more negative, if we can interpret this slim evidence.

For children there were four studies of apprehensive mouth behavior, frowning, and grimacing. None was known to be significant overall, though one subgroup of five-year-olds showed significantly more apprehensive mouth behavior by girls toward an adult experimenter; no effect size was available; and the two studies for which direction was known were split in direction (with the study favoring boys being a nonsocial situation). Young girls may, then, display more uncomfortable negativity than boys in certain situations.

For adults, there were six studies. One was significant in showing more female negative facial expression when tutoring a male child (effect size $r = .30$); four others were nonsignificant; and no other effect sizes were known. In direction, for the five studies in which it was known, the ratio was 3:2 favoring more female frowning, with one of the studies favoring males being nonsocial.

On the basis of this very slim literature, then, child and adult females in social situations tend to show at least somewhat more facial negativity, and for adult females this negativity takes the form of frowning, not expressions of fear or anxiety. The one study with a complete report of results, that on tutoring a child, found a substantial difference favoring females. Though extremely provocative, any conclusion must be held very tentatively until more data are available. One important gap is that, for adults, not a single study was of women interacting with other women; they interacted with male child confederates, with spouses, or with dating partners. Therefore it is an open question whether women frown more with any interactant, or only (possibly) with a male. Future research on negative facial expression will be most important, and may bring about revision of some theorizing about women.

AUTHOR SEX

This analysis parallels those for author sex reported in chapters 2 and 4. Only social smiling was considered, that being the largest category of independent results. Both child and adult studies were included. The correlation between the proportion of male authors on a study and the size of the sex difference (r) was .24 (nineteen results). Though nonsignificant, this result hints that the higher the proportion of male authors, the greater is the female tendency to smile relative to males.

CONCLUSIONS

As many have long believed, females do have more expressive faces and they smile and laugh more than males. But their smiling is not unqualified. Such sex differences are barely apparent for infants and children, and are robust in adults in social situations only. Women seem to be smiled at more than men, and, consistent with this, women seem especially prone to smile more than men when each is with their own sex. Same-sex interaction may be more easy for women, and this may be reflected both in the norms that govern their relations with other females and the behaviors they display with them.

No one has definitively explained why women smile more than men. Possibly it is an aspect of sex-role stereotypes to which women and men conform, mainly unconsciously, as a result of observation of people in the media and in real life; thus, people may internalize the norms which they perceive to apply to their own sex. In addition, society may actually reward and punish people for adopting and failing to adopt sex-appropriate behavior patterns, which would also enhance sex differences. A man who is too eager to smile may seem unmasculine and receive negative feedback; a woman who looks too serious for her sex may be admonished to "gimme a smile" or "cheer up." Thus, women may show more smiling not for any immediate or conscious purpose, such as to display deference, but rather because of a lifetime of subtle pressure to internalize cultural expectations. Evidence that suggests that women's smiles sometimes reflect nervousness could be a consequence of such pressure: when ill at ease, they exaggerate behavior that has been emphasized as appropriate for them during the process of socialization.

Too, women's smiling could be greatly enhanced by people's tendencies to smile *at* them. Smiling is a highly reciprocal act. The connotation of a smiling habit acquired in this way is not that of a downtrodden person who smiles to appear harmless and to please others, but rather of a person who receives and returns generally high levels of trust and warmth. An interesting study by Rosenhan and Messick (1966) is consistent with the idea that women receive and expect to see smiles around them. In an experimental task in which subjects guessed the probability that smiling versus angry faces would turn up in a deck of pictures, women were more likely than men to guess smiling faces.

Finally, an important but largely unexplored possibility is that women show more negative as well as positive facial expressions than men. Though rarely if ever entertained in theoretical discussions of nonverbal sex differences, this result, if upheld by adequate research, would strongly indicate that the different norms to which men and women subscribe are norms of expressiveness rather than norms of pleasantness. Women's facial pleasantness may be accentuated in stereotype and in research partly because the relative infrequency of negative expression makes the pleasant expressions a much more constant and characteristic difference between the sexes.

6 Gaze

Gaze is one of the most subtle and meaningful forms of nonverbal behavior. The eyes have symbolic significance in many cultures, as reflected in such superstitions as the evil eye and powers of casting spells with the eyes. Infants respond so early to schematic eyes that some writers have proposed an innate responsiveness (Hess 1975). In the animal kingdom the power of gaze is so great that morphology actually reflects it, as in eye-spots on the wings of insects and the dramatic eye markings in some monkeys that make their eyes seem larger and more staring than they actually are.

Like much nonverbal behavior, gaze has many possible meanings and functions. For example, gaze patterns help people to take turns in conversations. The most universal meaning is probably interest and attention. But beyond that, gaze can mean friendliness or an invitation to increase intimacy, on the positive side, as well as threat and anger, on the negative side. The difference between positive and negative gazes is a matter of the context of the communication, other nonverbal behavior (such as position of brows and mouth), and timing. Subordinate-dominant status has also been shown to be related to gazing behavior not only in an overall way, with more-dominant or high-ranking individuals receiving more gaze than less-dominant or lower-ranking ones (for example, Efran 1968; Exline 1972; Fugita 1974; Weitz 1976), but also in a more complex way in conversation: the more-dominant individual gazes relatively more while speaking and relatively less while listening, while the less-dominant gazes relatively more while listening and relatively less while speaking.

When discussing sex differences in gaze, which do exist and which show more gazing by and at women, writers have brought up two of the themes from the preceding chapter: warmth-affiliation and dominance-status (the latter is what I call the oppression hypothesis). Women's greater social

interest and awareness of nonverbal communication, and sex-role expectations for friendliness, all fit with women's gaze as an expression of kindly
interest and warmth. On the other hand, an emphasis on women's low
status and dependency vis-à-vis men can lead one to interpret women's
gaze both as a signal of low status and as a means of gathering vital information about others' attitudes toward them and expectations for their
behavior.

Though all writers seem to agree that women gaze at others more than
men do, detailed analyses of the literature are not available (see, for example, Argyle and Cook 1976). Perhaps, as was the case with smiling, a
strong a priori belief combined, in the case of gaze, with a few well-known
and strong research results gives the impression that the story is told. But
by compiling the large research literature, one can ask a number of different interesting questions. What one cannot do satisfactorily is to answer
the question of why the sex differences exist. One reason for this uncertainty is that very few explicit efforts in this direction have been made by
investigators.

SEX OF THE GAZER

Because there are a reasonably large number of studies in various age
groups, and because age trends are apparent, table 6.1 presents separate
summaries for infants, children, and adults. Included here are studies that
had any kind of live human target (that is, recipient of gaze) except for
studies of adults gazing at infants. This very small category is excluded
because any sex differences would be seriously confounded with traditional parenting responsibilities (that is, male and female are typically confounded with father and mother roles).[1]

Studies of infants (under age two) were based on laboratory or home
observation of infants gazing at mother, father, siblings, or male or female
experimenters, strangers, or observers. By far the most common target
made available to the infant was its own mother, either as the sole target
observed or as one of several, which could include the father and other
male or female adults. Experimenters or "strangers" who served as the
other adult targets were also mainly female. Only two of the infant studies
in table 6.1 that involved targets of reported sex used exclusively male
targets.

---

1. Though not involving live targets, Leckart, Keeling, and Bakan (1966) obtained results
that parallel those reported in this chapter. They unobtrusively observed how long subjects
gazed at magazine photos of men versus women and found that women gazed longer than
men, women's photos were gazed at longer than men's (both nonsignificant, however), and
same-sex photos were examined longer than opposite-sex ones ($r = .29$, $p < .05$).

TABLE 6.1. Sex Differences in Gaze (by Sex of Subject, for Infants, Children, and Adults)

Index	Infants (33 studies)	Children (25 studies)	Adults (61 studies)
Direction of effect (excluding no difference or unknown)	71% (10/14) favor females ($p = .18$)	82% (14/17) favor females ($p < .01$)	83% (35/42) favor females ($p < .00006$)
Mean effect size (r)[a]	Between .06 (33 studies) and .20 (8 studies)	Between .08 (25 studies) and .19 (10 studies)	Between .16 (61 studies) and .32 (30 studies)
Statistical significance (all studies)	15% (5/33) favor females significantly, none favors males significantly	16% (4/25) favor females significantly, none favors males significantly	34% (21/61) favor females significantly, 3% (2/61) favor males significantly
Combined p	$p = .07$ (31 studies)	$p = .01$ (24 studies)	$p < 10^{-9}$ (56 studies)

[a] Positive values mean more gaze by females.

Gaze was measured in various ways. The studies in table 6.1 involved frequency of looks (total or time sampled), instances of gaze aversion (a measure that was reversed in direction for the table summary), and total duration of gaze. Measures of "mutual gaze" were not included in the table but are discussed separately.

The summary indicates that girl infants gaze at others more than boy infants do, though the trends are not strong. Neither of the aggregate ps in the table for infants quite reaches significance, and the size of the sex difference (r between sex of infant and amount of gaze) is small to moderate, at best. One fascinating study of five-month-old infants (not in table 6.1 because it used pictures as stimuli rather than live targets) found that girls looked more at photographs of faces and at a drawing of a face than boys did, and less at other kinds of stimuli than boys did (Lewis, Kagan, and Kalafat 1966). This suggests that girls' gaze is preferentially given to social stimuli, starting at quite a young age.

Infants' mutual gaze, nearly always recorded with their mothers, showed no reported trends at all for infants' sex. Of five studies, none was significant and none reported the direction of the result.

Observations of children's gaze were done mainly in laboratory-based tasks or during play in school or laboratory. As with studies of adults, observation was generally unobtrusive. The range of possible targets was skewed, as for infants, toward female targets. No study used only male targets, whereas ten used mother or a female adult experimenter or confederate; only four used both male and female targets; and six used same-sex targets — that is, boys were observed with boys and girls with girls.

Measures included total duration of gaze, percentage of interaction spent in gaze, and frequency of gaze.

The results for children shown in table 6.1 are very similar to those for infants, except that both aggregate p-values are significant for children.

Studies of adults were based on laboratory interactions, such as interviews and conversations, and on naturally occurring situations, such as people passing on the sidewalk. Available targets were peers, confederates, interviewers, or experimenters. Unlike studies of infants and children, targets of both sexes were observed in the largest number of studies (twenty-five studies); almost always target sex was a between-subjects factor, meaning that a subject interacted with either a male or a female and the results were tabulated as the average over both sexes of target. Five studies had only female targets, eight had only male targets, two had targets of unreported sex, eight had only opposite-sex targets, and thirteen had only same-sex targets. Most observations were of a subject interacting with only one other person. Measures were varied, and sometimes several were reported for one study, such as total gaze, frequency of gaze, and average duration of gaze. Table 6.1 is based on total gaze or percentage of interaction spent in gaze whenever one of those was available, on the grounds that it was the most common measure; otherwise, what was entered was whatever primary measure of individual gaze was reported by the original authors, such as frequency (but never mutual gaze or mutual eye contact).[2]

The results for adults shown in table 6.1 are extremely significant, owing partly to the larger number of studies available. The size of the sex difference (r) is also larger than found for younger groups, and the proportion of significant results is greater, reflecting this larger magnitude of difference. Age trends are further discussed later in this chapter.

Adult studies are numerous enough to permit an instructive breakdown by the sexes of the targets — that is, an analysis of the sex-of-gazer effect for different groups of studies defined by which sexes of targets were available. Below are the sizes of the sex differences (r between the gazer's sex and amount of gazing) as a function of the kind of target available:

Studies with male and female targets, r = .19 (ten results).
Studies with female targets only, r = .41 (four results).
Studies with male targets only, r = .31 (four results).
Studies with same-sex targets only, r = .45 (nine results).
Studies with opposite-sex targets only, r = .22 (three results).

2. Mutual gaze or mutual eye contact, measures almost always in same-sex dyads or same-sex groups, is much more pronounced in females, as is individual gaze (which is summarized in table 6.1).

Thus, one sees that studies in which subjects are paired with others of their own sex show the largest sex differences in gazing. Studies in which females are the target show similar, slightly smaller but still substantial, differences. Studies with males as targets showed the next biggest differences, followed by studies with opposite-sex targets and studies with both sexes as targets.

What should be made of this pattern? The bigger sex difference for studies with female targets than for those with male targets implies statistical interaction, such that people gaze more at others of their own sex than at members of the opposite sex. Such an effect can also be tested by looking at same-sex versus opposite-sex gazing (that is, the statistical interaction of subject sex and target sex) *within* studies that used both sexes as targets in a fully crossed design. Such an analysis is described later in this chapter.

I would have expected the sex differences for studies with both sexes of targets to be intermediate between those found for male-target studies and female-target studies (since the former averages over male and female targets), but it was actually considerably smaller. However, inspection of the studies shows that the only two results among those with both sexes of targets showing more male than female gaze were found in circumstances quite different from the other studies considered. In one, subjects were asked to walk toward a confederate, head-on, and to stop when they felt comfortable (a method used often to measure comfortable interpersonal distance; Fromme and Beam 1974); in the other, subjects were observed unobtrusively while passing others, head-on, on the sidewalk (Cary 1978). In neither case were subjects engaged in conversation, an almost universal aspect of the other studies of gaze; the situations were therefore not definable as actual relationships, a definition which may be central in eliciting women's gazing tendencies. In these two studies an additional factor could have elicited unusually high levels of gaze by men. In each, subjects were negotiating interpersonal distance. Men may have been attempting to maintain larger distances for themselves (see chapter 7) by establishing gaze — a compensatory mechanism described in discussions of intimacy equilibrium theory (also called affiliative conflict theory; Argyle and Dean 1965). Without these two unusual studies, the average sex difference for studies with both male and female targets is $r = .32$, a figure that is indeed in between those for studies with only male targets and with only female targets.

Consideration of these two interesting reversals of the usual pattern makes it clear that more female gaze is not a universal occurrence but rather one that marks interactions defined as legitimate and friendly, as the vast majority of interactions studied in this literature were, and as

Ellsworth and Ludwig (1972) suggested years ago. Consistent with this suggestion, Exline (1963) found that circumstances of competition greatly reduced interpersonal gazing among subjects with strong affiliative needs, especially women with such needs; thus, it would appear that gazing is highest by females when they are affiliative and when the circumstances are cooperative.

Other evidence that circumstances affect sex differences in gazing comes from studies in which conversations took place at predetermined interpersonal distances, for example two feet, six feet, or ten feet (Aiello 1972, 1977a, 1977b). In these studies, the tendency for women to gaze more at the other person held at closer distances (up to about six feet), but the sex difference was consistently reversed at larger distances. Graphs of gaze time showed that men's gaze increased linearly with increases in distance but that women's dropped off abruptly. It would seem that greater distances disrupt women's ability to define an interaction as normal and friendly, which may be an important condition for their gazing and other apparently affiliative nonverbal behaviors such as smiling. This research therefore points to affiliation as an important motivator of female gazing and further supports the conclusion that the bulk of the literature taps into the kind of situations — friendly interactions at comfortable distances — in which sex differences in gazing are likely to be maximally apparent.

Returning now to the discussion of the various sizes of sex difference in gazing as a function of the target's sex, it is also instructive to note that studies with only same-sex targets showed the largest differences and studies with only opposite-sex targets showed almost the smallest. These two results, exactly consistent with two analogous trends (main effects) for smiling noted in chapter 5, suggest that women tend to gaze more at others than men do (already documented in this chapter) and that women tend to be gazed *at* more than men, a trend which does in fact exist and which will be documented shortly. The combined effects of sex of gazer and sex of target would logically make the sex difference for gazing in the same-sex situation more pronounced than it is in other situations, which in fact it is.

A final result to emerge from the analysis of sex differences in gazing concerns the difference between gaze duration (or total gaze) and gaze frequency. For ten studies where results were presented for both of these measures, the tendency for females to gaze more was stronger for duration than for frequency. For four of these, the sex differences were in fact reversed: females gazed more than males in terms of duration, but males gazed more frequently than females did. These patterns are entirely consistent with each other, however, because frequent gaze implies that one breaks gaze often, which supports the idea that men are motivated to avoid gaze or are uncomfortable with protracted gaze.

Age Trends

Table 6.1 suggests that the sex differences for adults may be stronger than those for infants and children. However, the correlation between age (coded 0 = infants, 1 = children, 2 = adults) and the magnitude of the sex difference (r) was only .22 (forty-eight results, not significant). This correlation is attenuated, however, by inconsistencies between the three age categories in the sexes of gaze recipients employed. As we just saw, this does make a difference in the size of sex differences in gazing. Age trends are more apparent when we consider only one target-sex group at a time. Below are the correlations between age, coded as above, and the size of the sex difference for three different target-sex groups. The fact that these three groups of studies are entirely nonoverlapping gives greatly added credence to the consistently positive correlations for age:

For male and female targets, r = .36 (twelve results, not significant).[3]
For female targets, r = .34 (thirteen results, not significant).
For same-sex targets, r = .85 (thirteen results, p = .004).

Thus, sex differences in the tendency to gaze do increase in a linear fashion with age, when the sex of the available targets is held constant.[4]

Sex of Authors

As in previous chapters, the proportion of male authors of each study was correlated with the size of the sex difference (r) for adult studies of gazer sex. There was no relationship: the correlation was only .06 (twenty-nine results).

SEX OF THE TARGET

A question quite independent, in principle, from which sex gazes more is which sex is gazed *at* more. Data pertaining to this question are not as plentiful, partly because a study needed, by definition, to employ targets of both sexes and partly because authors did not always report any data for target sex even when they could have. Also, with these studies there is considerable variety in the ages of gazers and targets. Nevertheless, some trends are apparent.

---

3. This correlation excludes the anomalous result of Fromme and Beam (1974), described in the text. With it, the correlation is r = .18.

4. Some individual studies also tested for age changes in gaze as a function of sex of gazer. None found a significant age effect but, consistent with the data of table 6.1, Levine and Sutton-Smith (1973) and Russo (1975) both found sex differences in gaze to increase with age.

Four studies reported whether mothers gazed more at male or female infants. Results were inconclusive, with the two results of known direction being split in direction and none being significant; the average size of the sex difference (*r*) was − .03. Three studies reported whether male or female children were gazed at more by infants, other children, or parents. In both of the studies with children or parents as gazers, girls were gazed at more; the study with infants as gazers did not state the direction of the result. No result was significant and no effect sizes were reported.

For adults the situation is clearer. Twenty-two studies reported target-sex results, with gazing by infants, children, or other adults. When gazing was by infants, all four of the studies of known direction showed more gazing at fathers than at mothers, with a substantial effect size (*r*) of − .40 (three results); two of the five available results in this category were significant in this direction.

The pattern changes, however, as the gazers become older. The one study of preschoolers found more gazing at a female than at a male adult experimenter (effect size = .32, *p* < .01). For adults gazing at other adults, as table 6.2 shows, the results clearly show women to receive more gaze than men.

In sum, it is unclear whether boy or girl infants receive more gaze by others; female children do seem to be gazed at more than male children, by peers and parents, but the data base is very small. Female adults definitely seem to be gazed at more than male adults by other adults and probably by young children, but not by infants. Males (fathers) were in fact gazed at more than females (mothers) by infants. This could reflect the infants' heightened interest in the fathers due to less-constant companionship compared to mothers; high visual fixation by infants is often interpreted as an index of stimulus novelty and low visual fixation as an index of stimulus familiarity.

SAME VERSUS OPPOSITE SEX

This analysis concerns not differences between males and females but rather whether people are more likely to gaze when with their own sex than with the opposite sex (that is, sex-of-gazer × sex-of-target interaction). Studies reporting such results are similar to those discussed earlier: observations of conversing dyads inside and outside of psychology laboratories, dyads engaging in experimental tasks, and people passing on the sidewalk. For this analysis, I used total gaze or percentage of the interaction devoted to gaze as individual gaze measures if they were available; otherwise, I used frequency, mutual gaze, or undefined gaze (each of these was rare).

There were three studies of children; two showed more opposite-sex

TABLE 6.2. Sex Differences in Gaze (by Sex of Target,
for Adult Gazers and Targets)

Index	Results (16 studies)
Direction of effect (excluding no difference or unknown)	90% (9/10) favor females (p = .02)
Mean effect size (r)[a]	Between .12 (16 studies) and .31 (6 studies)
Statistical significance (all studies)	12% (2/16) favor females significantly, none favors males significantly
Combined p	p < .02 (15 studies)

[a] Positive values mean more gaze at women.

gaze (one to peers, one to adults), but the only significant result showed more same-sex gaze (to peers, effect size = $-.74$, p < .01). For adults there were twenty studies, all but one of which involved adult dyads (one was of parents with children). Here the results were also mixed. Of seventeen results of stated direction, ten showed more same-sex gaze, a ratio that was far from significant. The size of the same-sex–opposite-sex difference (r) showed that same-sex gaze exceeded opposite-sex gaze: r was between $-.07$ (twenty results, estimating all unknown results as zero) and $-.16$ (nine known results). The combined p was not significant, though the trend was toward more same-sex gaze. These results based on within-study comparisons support the results given above for between-studies comparisons in indicating a tendency for more gaze in same-sex dyads.

It is interesting to note that of the four results showing significantly more opposite-sex gaze, three were of strangers passing on the sidewalk, a scenario that is in marked contrast to most of the studies that found more same-sex gaze, which were of naturally acquainted or newly acquainted individuals in actual interactions. This may reflect different norms and inhibitions in scenarios differing in these ways. In chapter 5, I suggested that same-sex smiling exceeds opposite-sex smiling because of lower inhibition in same-sex than opposite-sex dyads, at least in the weakly acquainted kinds of dyads mainly studied. The same interpretation would apply here. Gazing is more extended in friendly same-sex dyads because of the lower levels of inhibition and uncertainty in such dyads; it is also possible that this trend is exaggerated when the dyads are in a psychology laboratory and any signs of heterosexual flirtation might seem particularly inappropriate. But in public — passing on the sidewalk when absolutely nothing is at stake — opposite-sex interest may come to the fore. On the other hand, in very intimate dyads of the sort not commonly observed in research, opposite-sex gaze may also be heightened; this is suggested by Rubin's (1970) research that showed more gaze between members of dating couples when the couples were more in love. It would also be consistent with the not too surprising evidence presented in chapters 7 and 8 that closer distances and more touch may characterize intimate opposite-sex dyads.

An additional comparison is for asymmetry: in opposite-sex dyads, which sex gazes the most? As discussed in chapter 5, marked asymmetry could reflect the impact of dominance disparities between the sexes, but the predictions that can be made on the basis of dominance are of two very different kinds: men's prerogatives of status (the prerogatives to initiate interaction, to impose) could lead to a tendency for them to gaze more at women than vice versa. On the other hand, women's purportedly subordinate role could lead to high levels of visual attention paid to men. Further, other interpretations of any given pattern of results are also available. For example, if women gaze at men more than vice versa, it could reflect their tendencies to be open and direct (and not just with men), rather than subservient. Actually, no interpretations are necessary at this time, because the available data on direction show little asymmetry. Of the ten pairs of means for adults in opposite-sex interaction, six show more gaze by women and four show more gaze by men. Few of these comparisons were put to statistical test, so this is not a conclusive analysis. But it does not suggest asymmetry and is, in addition, exactly what we would expect given the gazer main effects and target main effects described earlier, which showed that women gaze more and are gazed at more than men are. These two main effects imply that male-male and female-female gaze differs maximally, while male-female and female-male gaze differs minimally.

A more interpretable measure of gaze-as-dominance is provided in the extensive research on patterns of gaze while speaking versus listening (Ellyson, Dovidio, and Fehr 1981; Exline, Ellyson, and Long 1975). These authors have established that relatively more gaze while speaking and relatively less while listening occur in individuals of dominant personality or of dominant social standing within the dyad. The less-dominant person shows the opposite pattern. Presumably the less-dominant person is less assertive and directive while speaking and more attentive while listening. If females as a group were to show the same gaze pattern as do less-dominant persons in such experiments, it would suggest that sex differences in dominance or social standing could also lie behind this and other sex differences in gaze. For fifteen studies, I could calculate the direction of this effect, by contrasting males' gaze while speaking and females' gaze while listening with males' gaze while listening and females' gaze while speaking (the sex of gazer × listen/speak interaction). Nine of the fifteen results (60 percent) showed females to gaze relatively more while listening (and males to gaze relatively more while speaking). Rarely, if ever, were these comparisons actually tested for statistical significance, so only a cautious conclusion can be reached. But with so small a preponderance of studies showing relatively more female gaze while listening, it would certainly seem that there is not much of a sex difference in these dominance-related gaze patterns.

CONCLUSIONS

In most studies of gaze, measurements were taken in ostensibly friendly and comfortable interactions. In such circumstances, females of all ages seem to gaze more at others than males do. Assuming that such visual directness is full-face rather than sidelong, it could explain Hammer and Kaplan's (1964) finding that young girls drew more front-view faces than boys did. Women's gazing habit could also explain Argyle, Lalljee, and Cook's (1968) finding that women were more uncomfortable than men if they could not see the person to whom they were talking. The present review also found that, controlling for sex of target, the difference between males' and females' gaze tendencies increases with age.

Females, at least adult females, are gazed at more than males are, which in combination with the sex-of-gazer main effect makes for especially high levels of gaze in female-female dyads compared to male-male dyads. More gaze also seems to occur in same-sex (male-male and female-female) dyads than in opposite-sex dyads except when, it seems, public inhibitions are few. However, since few truly intimate interactions were ever observed, because of ethical and practical constraints, this conclusion could require qualification. Opposite-sex gaze could be pronounced in public *and* in private when inhibitions are low but be minimal in public or quasi-public, high-inhibition situations, such as conversations and interviews between newly acquainted individuals in a laboratory setting.

Evidence bearing directly on explanations for sex differences in gaze is very scarce, but the documentary evidence reviewed here suggests, provisionally at least, that the warmth-affiliation motive makes more sense than does a motive based on dominance-status differences between the sexes, though it should be kept in mind that the two possibilities are not mutually exclusive. Two different analyses that could have implicated dominance-status did not show sex differences, whereas comparisons that would implicate affiliation-friendliness did, such as the comparison of female-female with male-male dyads and the reduction in female gaze as distance increases. Of course, gaze could be enhanced in female-female dyads because of possibly reduced saliency of dominance as an issue to be resolved. Male-male interaction could show lower levels of gaze partly because men are trying to avoid the confrontational implications that high gaze could have for them. Thus, dominance could still be quite relevant to sex differences in gazing, but not because women are less dominant than men; rather, it would be because women are not as concerned with dominance as men.

As mentioned earlier in this book, it is also difficult to disentangle these two basic explanations – dominance and affiliation – because of the possibility that women's lower status reduces their ability to challenge or threaten anyone, which in turn enables or requires them to act warm and nice. Dominance-status thus could have a place in a causal stream, but it would be a distant, not an immediate, cause of women's gaze habits.[5]

That people like to gaze *at* women in interaction is subject to the same two explanations: women are considered nicer and more likely to respond (warmth-affiliation), versus women are considered weak and therefore unable to prevent the violation of their privacy by others' prying eyes. Ancillary research supports the former interpretation better than the latter: people gaze more at approving than at disapproving others, and they in fact gaze *less* at low-status than at high-status others (for example, Efran 1968; Efran and Broughton 1966; Fugita 1974).

Nevertheless, the dominance-status interpretation must still be entertained, especially perhaps in indirect causal patterns such as the one described above, or in the following hypothetical sequence: women are looked at more than men because people disregard women's privacy; because looks are strongly reciprocated in reasonably friendly interaction, women therefore look at others more than men do – not because of any personal motives, needs, or traits, but only because they respond to others' gaze.[6]

The topic of the next chapter, interpersonal distance, follows naturally from the findings on gaze. Recall that Aiello showed women's and men's gaze preferences to be dramatically reversed when interpersonal distance increased. Skotko and Langmeyer (1977) also found that males engaged in more intimate self-disclosure as interpersonal distance increased, whereas exactly the reverse was true for females. One implication of these results is that men and women gaze and self-disclose the most when they are most comfortable but that they define "comfortable" differently, with women interpreting greater distances as less comfortable than men do. This is just what the research on distance suggests.

5. In a subsequent analysis of the child and adult gazing studies, described in footnote 7 of chapter 5, Hall and Halberstadt (in press) found no relationship between subjects' relative status and the size of the sex differences in gazing. Instead, more situational friendliness and more face-to-face involvement were associated with larger sex differences favoring females.

6. Bates (1976) actually found that women reciprocated the glances of a male child significantly more than men did in a teaching situation ($r = .29$). A sex difference in the tendency to reciprocate gaze could augment sex differences still further.

7 Interpersonal Distance and Orientation

The distance at which people interact has been shown to vary with many factors, including nationality, relative status, degree of friendship, nature of the situation, social class, race, age, and sex. As is generally true of the behaviors considered in this book, existing reviews of sex differences are very incomplete in their coverage or not very detailed in their analysis (for example, Evans and Howard 1973; Hayduk 1978, 1983; Harper, Wiens, and Matarazzo 1978). The author of the most recent review stated that the evidence is much too slight for a description of sex differences in personal space to be made (Hayduk 1983). I disagree with this conclusion.[1]

Discussions of possible determinants of sex differences in interpersonal distance have focused on the two themes entertained earlier, warmth-affiliation and dominance-status. An additional factor, height, has occasionally been considered but has not caught the imagination, or perhaps even the awareness, of most authors.

Three techniques of measuring interpersonal distance have been employed. Unobtrusive measurement of spontaneous behavior in the field

---

1. Though Hayduk (1983) compiled a large bibliography of studies involving personal space, analysis of them seems to have been scanty. His table 1 lists studies according to whether a sex difference was "supported," "partially or conditionally supported," or "not supported." The criterion for this rough division was most likely the $p = .05$ level of significance, a very imprecise way of summarizing results (see chapter 1). Further, studies in the table had heterogeneous methods that were poorly described; the kind of sex difference assessed was not stated (for example, subject effects versus target effects, or male-male, male-female, and female-female differences); and the direction of any sex differences obtained was never stated. It is impossible therefore to assess the basis on which Hayduk reached the conclusion that sex differences are not apparent or interpretable overall. If the conclusion was reached by noting that roughly equal numbers of studies found "support" versus "no support," such a conclusion is misguided, since under the null hypothesis of no real difference we would expect many fewer supporting than nonsupporting studies, not equal numbers.

or laboratory has been used for subjects of all ages. For children and adults, staged and projective measures have also been used. In a staged study, a subject is generally asked to approach another person, or to allow another person to approach him or her, or both. The subject is asked to speak up when an uncomfortably close distance is reached. In a projective study, a subject is asked to state preferred or comfortable distance for dolls, silhouettes of people, imaginary people, or for paper labels with such identifiers as "yourself" and "friend" written on them. The subject positions these or marks preferred distances on a board, paper, or drawing of a room. The identification of the figures, the social situations, and the angles of approach are often varied. Sometimes one of the figures is explicitly identified as "yourself," and sometimes it is not, but in either case it is usually assumed, in the nature of any projective test, that the distances chosen reflect one's own preferences or expectations.

Pairwise correlations among these three methods of assessing interpersonal distance are usually positive and sometimes as large as .60 or more (for example, Duke and Kiebach 1974; Duke and Nowicki 1972; Gottheil, Corey, and Paredes 1968; Knowles 1980; D. M. Pedersen 1973; Price and Dabbs 1974; Slane, Petruska, and Cheyfitz 1981; Tennis and Dabbs 1975). The lowest convergent validity, perhaps not surprisingly, is between unobtrusive measurement and reactive (staged and paper-and-pencil) measures (for example, Aiello and Thompson 1980; Hayduk 1983; S. E. Jones and Aiello 1979).

As with other behaviors reviewed in this book, several questions are analyzed that are theoretically distinct, such as sex of subject, sex of target (interactant), and same-sex versus opposite-sex dyads.

Some additional proxemic behaviors are reviewed here. One is actual and inferred preferences for axis or directness of body orientation during interaction. Another is seating position preferences. Fewer studies are available for these variables, but they show some consistent trends.

DISTANCE SET BY MALES AND FEMALES

Naturalistic Measures

In these studies, subjects are observed without their knowledge, or as subtly as possible, in ongoing interaction in public settings such as beaches, queues, schools, or on the street, or in quasi-structured or unstructured interaction in classrooms and psychology laboratories. In the latter type of situation, subjects might know they are in a study but not, presumably, that anyone is noting their proxemic behavior.

Unobtrusive observation is also used in so-called invasion studies, where a confederate deliberately establishes with a subject a distance that is assumed to be uncomfortably close. Subjects' reactions, such as how long they remain there, are observed. Though unobtrusive, such studies are not included in this section of the chapter because they assess preferences so indirectly and are so artificial.

In relatively controlled circumstances such as psychology laboratories, the investigator is often able to ascertain distance clearly as an individual-subject variable; for example, in many studies a confederate is already seated or standing, and the subject's freely chosen seating or standing distance from the confederate is observed. In less-controlled circumstances such as on the street, it is rarely possible to separate subject behavior from that of the interactant, because the dyad is typically already interacting at the time observation is made. This makes it unclear how much of the measured distance is a function of the subject's preference, the other's preference, or some tacitly agreed on mutual preference; it is also unclear whether the measured distance reflects the subject's behavior as a function of his or her own sex or the subject's behavior as a function of his or her awareness of the other person's sex. (Of course it can be moot in such a study as to which individual is the "subject," and sometimes the investigator does not try to decide this but instead considers the dyad as the unit of analysis. But the interpretive ambiguity remains.)

Uncertainty over whose sex determines proxemic behavior — the subject's or the other's — is additionally a problem whenever same-sex dyads are observed exclusively (that is, males with other males and females with other females), even when such observation is done in relatively controlled circumstances. This is because the sex-of-subject and sex-of-other factors are confounded. In the tables to this chapter, as in similar tables to other chapters, studies of same-sex dyads are included under "sex of subject," for lack of a better solution, though admittedly there is some ambiguity in doing so.

Table 7.1 shows sex-of-subject results for naturalistic measures. In the twenty-one studies of infants (defined as under two years old), the mother was the interactant in all but two, with or without others, who could be father, male or female adult experimenters or acquaintances, or siblings. The two studies not involving the mother used siblings or female adults. Measurement was either of actual distance, often time sampled, or of the amount of time the infant spent near the target (sometimes defined objectively, as for example in the four floor squares closest to the target person).

As the table shows, boys stayed farther from the target than girls, and the effect-size estimates (r) are moderate. (Negative coefficients mean greater distances for males.) The tendency for boys to stay farther from the target was particularly evident when the mother was available as a target, and especially when she was the only target available. The one result that showed girls to keep a greater distance, and significantly so, did

TABLE 7.1. Sex Differences for Naturalistic Measures of Interpersonal Distance (by Sex of Subject, for Infants, Children, and Adults)

Index	Infants (21 studies)	Children (28 studies)	Adults (59 studies)
Direction of effect (excluding no difference or unknown)	88% (7/8) favor males ($p = .07$)	67% (14/21) favor males ($p = .12$)	80% (32/40) favor males ($p < .0001$)
Mean effect size (r)[a]	Between $-.04$ (21 studies) and $-.23$ (4 studies)	Between $-.02$ (28 studies) and $-.11$ (4 studies)	Between $-.08$ (59 studies) and $-.27$ (17 studies)
Statistical significance (all studies)	19% (4/21) favor males significantly, 5% (1/21) favor females significantly	18% (5/28) favor males significantly, 4% (1/28) favor females significantly	27% (16/59) favor males significantly, 3% (2/59) favor females significantly
Combined p	$p < .16$ (21 studies)	$p < .04$ (22 studies)	$p = 10^{-7}$ (45 studies)

[a] Negative values mean greater distances set by males.

not involve the mother but rather other adult females, and was interpreted by the original authors to reflect greater distress by boys when the mother was absent. The data therefore show female infants to stay closer to their mothers than boys do, but it is not clear how generalizable this result is.

Studies of children two through twelve rarely employed the mother as target but rather observed subjects' behavior with adult experimenters, teachers, or peers, with the latter being the most frequent. Again, the summary data in table 7.1 show boys to set greater distances than girls, but the effect-size estimates (r) are small. One study showed a strong tendency ($r = .62$) for girls to keep *greater* distances than boys, and this study is interesting because it is somewhat different from the others, involving free play of same-sex triads of children. Possibly, such a situation invites rougher play in boys, which would naturally involve high levels of proximity and contact (see DiPietro 1981). The other studies tended to be of more structured situations, such as visiting a zoo, sitting near another child on a bench, approaching an adult in a game, or simply conversing. Without the one anomalous result, the average known effect size (r) is $-.38$, which is quite generous in size.

Seventeen of the twenty-eight studies of children involved same-sex targets. Although one would like to do a separate analysis for studies that used same-sex targets versus studies that used other kinds, the effect-size data are too limited. In terms of direction only, 62 percent (10/16) of the same-sex studies showed more distance for boys than for girls, and 80 percent (4/5) of studies using other kinds of targets showed such a result.

Turning now to adult studies in table 7.1, most or all involved adult targets, and all possible target sexes were available in the data set: male or female only, male and female (as a between-subjects variable), opposite-sex only, and same-sex only. The two most common were same-sex (26/59) and both male and female (22/59). The table shows very persuasive evidence that men set larger distances, with moderate effect sizes (r). When the effect-size data are broken down by what sex of target was employed, studies using same-sex targets and those using both male and female targets show equivalent sex differences (respectively, $r = -.32$, nine studies; $r = -.31$, four studies). The only other category with any known effect sizes was for female targets; there, the average effect size was only $r = -.10$ (three studies). One of these was an especially strong and significant reverse-direction result of $r = .45$ in a study in which subjects were observed standing in a queue next to a female confederate at an amusement park, and the result was especially strong at night. The anonymity and relative disinhibition one may assume characterize such a situation may account for men approaching the female confederate more closely than women did. Without this result, the average effect size for female-target studies is $r = -.38$ (two studies), which is in line with the other target-sex categories.

Studies reporting specifically on adolescents are very few, only three, and they are not in the table. No firm conclusions can be reached because of the small number and incomplete reporting, but the trend is consistent with other age groups: two showed greater male distance, and one showed greater female distance (no other information available).

Staged Measures

In these studies, as mentioned earlier, subjects knowingly indicated their preferred distances vis-à-vis someone. In about half of these studies, both male and female targets were employed. Most were carried out in psychology laboratories; a small number were done on the beach, where an experimenter obtained the cooperation of sunbathers. Needless to say, there are no staged studies of infants.

Table 7.2 shows that for children, the limited number of studies suggests at best a very weak tendency for males to set larger distances than females; it should be noted that no significance test, either of individual studies or of the aggregate data, achieved $p = .05$. Adult data, too, are very weak, but here at least some individual studies were significant, and all the indices of outcome point at least tentatively toward more distance preferred by men. The two available results for adolescents (not in the table) both showed greater male distances, but no other information was available.[2]

---

2. Two additional studies of adults were of subjects approaching cutouts or posters of people (Leginski and Izzett 1976; Powell and Dabbs 1976). These showed no sex differences appreciable enough to have been reported, except that one found subjects to approach a female cutout significantly more closely than a male cutout ($r = -.32$). This is consistent with sex-of-target effects reported in this chapter.

TABLE 7.2. Sex Differences for Staged Measures of Interpersonal Distance (by Sex of Subject, for Children and Adults)

Index	Children (6 studies)	Adults (19 studies)
Direction of effect (excluding no difference or unknown)	80% (4/5) favor males (not significant)	64% (9/14) favor males (not significant)
Mean effect size (r) [a]	Between $-.02$ (6 studies) and $-.08$ (1 study)	Between $-.02$ (19 studies) and $-.06$ (8 studies)
Statistical significance (all studies)	None favors either males or females significantly	16% (3/19) favor males significantly, none favors females significantly
Combined p	$p = 1.00$ (3 studies)	$p = .12$ (16 studies)

[a] Negative values mean greater distances set by males.

Projective Measures

As described earlier, all of these studies relied on subjects' indications of preferred distance as these were presumably expressed in how far apart they positioned hypothetical people. For obvious reasons, there are again no infant studies. In most of these studies, targets of both sexes were used, sometimes with additional within-study variation in the target's identity (for example, friend and stranger), setting, or angle of approach.

Table 7.3 shows no evidence whatever of a sex difference for children and only a highly marginal difference for adults, one which again suggests that men prefer bigger distances from others than women do. The three available studies on adolescents (not in the table) are inconclusive but consistent with the preceding, with two results showing greater male distance and one showing greater female distance (no other information available).

One interesting fact helping to account for the lack of overall subject-sex differences for projective measures is that, in several studies where target identity was varied, females placed the hypothetical dyads farther apart than males did for *threatening or alienating targets.* Guardo (1969) and Meisels and Guardo (1969), using eleven-year-olds and grades three through ten, respectively, found girls to use greater distances than boys for feared or disliked others but boys to use greater distances than girls for a liked other. Guardo (1976), using eleven-year-olds, found girls to use greater distances than boys for vigorous, assertive, and phlegmatic others, but boys to use greater distances than girls for tender-minded, apprehensive, and emotional others (also for a rule-breaking other, a finding that may not fit the pattern). Melson (1976), using ages three through six years, found girls to use greater distances than boys for angry dyads but boys to use greater distances than girls for friendly dyads. Finally, Knowles (1980), using college students, found women to use greater distances for a stranger

TABLE 7.3. Sex Differences for Projective Measures of Interpersonal Distance (by Sex of Subject, for Children and Adults)

Index	Children (16 studies)	Adults (26 studies)
Direction of effect (excluding no difference of unknown)	44% (7/16) favor males (not significant)	61% (14/23) favor males (not significant)
Mean effect size (r)[a]	Between .00 (16 studies) and .04 (2 studies)	Between $-.03$ (26 studies) and $-.07$ (11 studies)
Statistical significance (all studies)	6% (1/16) favor males significantly, 6% (1/16) favor females significantly	19% (5/26) favor males significantly, 12% (3/26) favor females significantly
Combined p	$p = 1.00$ (10 studies)	$p < .10$ (23 studies)

[a] Negative values mean greater distances set by males.

but men to use greater distances for a friend. Such a pattern is not universal in the literature, however, since some studies that varied the target in similar ways apparently found no such differential responding.

Nevertheless, it is worth noting that most studies of naturalistically observed distance use targets that are familiar, friendly, or at least neutral. It is therefore possible that the usual tendency for males to establish larger distances than females is limited to such affiliatively toned encounters. In threatening or unpleasant encounters, males may step forward, as it were, and females may step back, as our intuitions might tell us. This reasoning is consistent with data on touch (chapter 8), which suggest that females touch others more in actually or nominally friendly interactions, whereas males do so more when real or pretended aggression is occurring.

Age Effects

The magnitude of the sex differences (r) was correlated with the subjects' age group (coded 0 = infants, 1 = children, 2 = adults, or just the latter two when infant studies were not available) for naturalistic, staged, and projective measures. These correlations cannot be conclusive because limited effect-size data were available for some categories, as tables 7.1, 7.2, and 7.3 make clear. The correlations for age, all of which are nonsignificant, are consistent with the tables in suggesting no change in the size of the sex differences with age: for naturalistic studies, $r = -.10$ (twenty-five studies); for staged studies, $r = .03$ (nine studies); for projective studies, $r = .28$ (thirteen studies). Individual studies that included analyses of sex differences across age, for sex of subject, were almost unanimous in corroborating this lack of an age effect, though it should be added that a number of these studies did not include a very wide range of ages.

Author Sex

For sex-of-subject data, correlations to test the relationship between the proportion of authors on a study who were male and the size of the sex difference (*r*) were computed, as in previous chapters. These correlations were remarkably consistent (computed for children and adults only):

For naturalistic measures, $r = .37$, $p < .10$ (twenty-one studies).[3]
For staged measures, $r = .40$, not significant (nine studies).
For projective measures, $r = .34$, not significant (thirteen studies).

The positive signs indicate that when studies had a higher proportion of male authors, the tendency for males to set larger distances was reduced in magnitude, regardless of the method employed. To state it differently, the stereotype that females prefer smaller distances was confirmed more strongly in the work of female than male investigators.

One possible explanation for these results would be that subjects respond differently to male and female investigators, with female subjects responding warmly to female investigators and consequently using smaller interpersonal distances in whatever tasks or interactions they are put in (and, symmetrically, male subjects responding warmly to male investigators and using relatively smaller distances than they ordinarily would). This assumes that the sex ratio among authors is mirrored in the sex ratio of the personnel conducting the study. This explanation could hold even for most of the naturalistic studies because, even though subjects were supposedly unaware that their distance was being measured, nevertheless in most studies subjects were quite aware that they were in a study of some sort and therefore would have had face-to-face dealings with research personnel. If this hypothesis is correct, we would expect that when naturalistic studies are divided into those where subjects were probably not aware of being studied and those where subjects probably were, the correlation between author sex and outcome should be considerably stronger for the latter than the former. Unfortunately, this is not so: the correlation *drops* from .37 for all twenty-one naturalistic studies to .26 for the nineteen studies in which subjects were likely to have had the opportunity to interact with the investigators.

Perhaps it is observer bias, not the social psychology of the experimental situation, that produces the author-sex effect. Female investigators may start with a stronger hypothesis about sex differences in preferred distance, based on their everyday observation of the actual preferences of males and females. This would be consistent with females' greater awareness of nonverbal communication and its meanings (see chapters 2 and 3). Female investigators may inadvertently convey this hypothesis to their research

---

3. With infants included, this correlation is .34, $p < .10$ (twenty-five studies).

personnel, or may bias their own observations if they themselves serve as observers. Though intriguing and potentially important, this interpretation should not be accepted until the available literature becomes large enough so that more direct evidence for it can be found and so that the author-sex effect itself can be confirmed.

Racial and Cultural Differences

Race and culture are well known to influence interpersonal distance; their effects are reviewed by Halberstadt (in press) and by Aiello and Thompson (1980). Indeed, because of the potential importance of race and culture, the studies summarized so far and later in this chapter were entered as separate racial or cultural subgroups whenever separate reporting was made in the original research.[4] Later in this chapter, I present an analysis of the rank ordering of the distance of male-male, female-female, and opposite-sex dyads as a function of race/culture. Here I assess race/culture's relationship to sex-of-subject effects.

Unfortunately, an adequate analysis of race/culture and sex is not possible because there are so few studies for any given non-Anglo group. For neither children nor adults, for naturalistic measures, are there more than three results for any non-Anglo racial/cultural group, and by far the most common number is one. There is, however, good variety in the racial/cultural groups studied. For children these are Anglo (including studies where racial/cultural groups were mixed or unspecified), Israeli, Mexican-American, Puerto Rican, and U.S. black. For adults these are Anglo (as just defined, plus English and Australian), Indonesian, Filipino, Israeli, Costa Rican, Panamanian, Colombian, Venezuelan, Puerto Rican, Mexican-American, Italian, Chinese, French, German, Japanese, and U.S. black. Most foreign groups were observed in their own countries, but occasionally they were observed in culturally homogeneous sections of a U.S. city. Only a simple statistical test seemed reasonable, which employed the direction of the sex difference and "Anglo versus others" as classifying variables. These analyses were nonsignificant for both children and adults ($\chi^2(1) = 0.10$ and 2.11, respectively); the adult studies showed a weak tendency for non-Anglo groups to have relatively more findings of women setting larger distances than men. Overall, however, one cannot reject the null hypothesis, which says that the tendency for males to set farther distances from others than females is a universal phenomenon and not one that is limited to Anglo society.

---

4. This is a deviation from my practice elsewhere in this book, which has been to combine subgroups before entering them in the summaries, unless subgroup data were more fully reported than the total sample data or the subgroups represented the three basic age groups of infants, children, or adults.

DISTANCE TOWARD MALE AND FEMALE TARGETS

Here we are concerned with how closely people approach males versus females. As with other such discussions in this book, the sex-of-target effect is theoretically independent of the sex-of-subject effect: males and females could differ only moderately in their own distance preferences, but at the same time, people could characteristically approach females much more closely than they approach males. This is, in fact, the pattern that emerges from the data.

The studies reviewed here fall into the same three methodologies presented above — naturalistic, staged, and projective — and involve the same kinds of situations as already discussed. This is no surprise, because the analyses of target sex come often from the same studies that analyses of sex of subject come from, though they are a subset of the latter, since not all of the studies employed both male and female targets.

Naturalistic Measures

Though, as table 7.4 shows, there are fewer studies reporting specifically on sex of target, nevertheless the results are overwhelmingly consistent, persuasive, and of impressive magnitudes for all three age groups. For infants, the others involved were always mother versus father. For children, the others were either adults or peers; for adults they were apparently always other adults, either confederates, experimenters, or peers. Thus, while previous analyses found a tendency for females to place themselves closer to others than males do (a tendency that is well established among adults), the much stronger and more consistent tendency is for females to be approached more closely by others than males are. The magnitude of this effect did not change with the age group studied (correlation between age group, coded as described above, and the size of the sex difference = .05, sixteen studies).

Staged Measures

Only two studies of children presented data for target sex, both of children approaching an adult. One showed no sex difference at all, and the other showed a male to be approached closer than a female (no more information available). Adult studies, in contrast, which are summarized in table 7.5, are consistent in showing females to be approached closer than males. No analysis of target-sex differences by age group was feasible for staged studies.

Projective Measures

Projective studies of children that reported on target-sex effects were few in number, only five. They were split in direction, and the only known

TABLE 7.4. Sex Differences for Naturalistic Measures of Interpersonal Distance (by Sex of Target, for Infants, Children, and Adults)

Index	Infants (5 studies)	Children (5 studies)	Adults (20 studies)
Direction of effect (excluding no difference or unknown)	100% (5/5) favor males ($p = .06$)	100% (2/2) favor males (not significant)	92% (12/13) favor males ($p = .004$)
Mean effect size (r)[a]	− .44 (5 studies)	Between − .33 (5 studies) and − .66 (2 studies)	Between − .21 (20 studies) and − .43 (9 studies)
Statistical significance (all studies)	40% (2/5) favor males significantly, none favors females significantly	40% (2/5) favor males significantly, none favors females significantly	35% (7/20) favor males significantly, none favors females significantly
Combined p	$p = .0006$ (5 studies)	$p < .02$ (5 studies)	$p < 10^{-6}$ (20 studies)

[a] Negative values mean greater distances set for male targets.

TABLE 7.5. Sex Differences for Staged and Projective Measures of Interpersonal Distance (by Sex of Target, for Adults)

Index	Staged (6 studies)	Projective (12 studies)
Direction of effect (excluding no difference or unknown)	100% (5/5) favor males ($p = .06$)	100% (10/10) favor males ($p = .002$)
Mean effect size (r)[a]	Between − .25 (6 studies) and − .30 (5 studies)	Between − .24 (12 studies) and − .39 (7 studies)
Statistical significance (all studies)	67% (4/6) favor males significantly, none favors females significantly	50% (6/12) favor males significantly, none favors females significantly
Combined p	$p < 10^{-5}$ (6 studies)	$p < 10^{-4}$ (9 studies)

[a] Negative values mean greater distances set for male targets.

effect size (r) was .00. One result was reported to be significant, and it showed subjects to put greater distances toward hypothetical girls than toward hypothetical boys. In contrast, adult studies, shown in table 7.5, were strong in showing subjects to estimate greater distances for approaches to hypothetical males than females. No analysis of projective target-sex differences by age was feasible.[5]

5. Under ordinary circumstances, effect size (r) will be larger for a repeated-measures (within-subjects) effect than for a between-subjects effect, with correspondingly smaller p-values. One may wonder whether the stronger effects found for target sex than for subject sex may be accounted for by the possibility that the former was more likely to be

Invasion Research

The literature on "invasion" of personal space yields results that are consistent with the studies that showed that men experience larger interpersonal distances than women. Invasion is usually operationalized as a confederate sitting or approaching close to an unsuspecting subject. Latency to departure is a typical dependent measure. Both Bleda and Bleda (1978) and Krail and Leventhal (1976) found that subjects departed sooner from a male invader. This could suggest greater threat implied by the male invader, but it could also suggest that subjects become uncomfortable when a male is closer to them than expected.

In a different operationalization of invasion, Buchanan, Juhnke, and Goldman (1976) and Buchanan, Goldman, and Juhnke (1977) observed people's behavior in elevators when they could choose between two different floor-selection panels. Near one of the panels was a woman and near the other was a man (there were also other variations in their series of experiments). Subjects generally preferred to use the panel near the woman. Though these authors conceived of this situation as violation of personal space, such an interpretation should not be assumed in the absence of any direct evidence.

The validity of violation as an explanatory concept behind such behavior is actually brought into question in two field studies, which observed who displaced whom on the sidewalk when passing (Willis, Gier, and Smith 1979) and at what distance a subject stepped aside for an oncoming other (Sobel and Lillith 1975). In the first, male walkers were displaced (or displaced themselves) more often than female walkers, and in the second, subjects stepped aside farther from an oncoming woman than an oncoming man. Thus, in two studies that are much more definable as situations of violation of personal space than most, there was no evidence that women experienced a violation of their space. On the contrary, the opposite seemed to be the case.[6]

---

assessed via repeated measures, whereas the latter is almost by definition a between-subjects factor. The facts on this differ according to the measurement method and the age group employed. For naturalistic measures, infants' behavior toward male and female targets was always a repeated measure, but for children and adults all studies seemed to employ target sex as a between-subjects factor. For staged measures of children and adults, half were repeated measures and half were between-subjects, and paradoxically the between-subjects studies showed significantly larger target-sex effects than the repeated-measures studies did. For projective measures, all studies of children and adults used target sex as a repeated measure. Overall, then, whether target sex was a between-subjects or a repeated-measures factor cannot account for the difference in strength between subject-sex and target-sex differences.

6. Yet another study design consists of observing whether passersby are more likely to walk between two men in conversation than between two women. These results are mixed (Cheyne and Efran 1972; Walker and Borden 1976).

DISTANCE IN SAME-SEX VERSUS OPPOSITE-SEX DYADS

Here we are concerned with the statistical interaction of sex of subject with sex of target, which is synonymous with same-sex versus opposite-sex distance.

Naturalistic Measures

For five studies of children in which the direction was reported, four showed greater distances for same-sex dyads and one showed greater distances for opposite-sex dyads. But the one study for which full data were available showed more opposite-sex distance, with an appreciable effect size (r) of .34 and a p of .001. Thus the children's data are ambiguous.

For nineteen studies of adults in which direction was known, seven showed more same-sex distance and twelve more opposite-sex distance. Only two effect sizes (r) were available, whose average was $-.20$; the negative sign indicates that the average distance was actually greater for same-sex dyads, though the two results that were significant both showed more opposite-sex distance.

One study casts light on a possible factor behind the inconsistencies in same-sex versus opposite-sex distance. Heshka and Nelson (1972) photographed natural dyads on the street in London and found that in acquainted dyads same-sex distance exceeded opposite-sex distance, but that the reverse was the case for stranger dyads. This stands to reason, since we would expect unacquainted men and women to be more reserved toward each other than acquainted men and women.

Using the twenty adult studies for which direction was known (counting Heshka and Nelson's stranger and acquaintance subsamples separately), a rough further test of this hypothesis is possible if one classifies all observation in public as representing acquaintances and all laboratory-based interactions as representing strangers. This is a conservative test, because in public observations the dyads may not all have been acquainted and in laboratory studies subjects were probably newly acquainted rather than literally strangers. Nevertheless the correlation between the two dichotomous variables (same-sex more/opposite-sex more and acquaintance/stranger) is consistent with the hypothesis ($r = .25$): stranger dyads tend to show more opposite-sex than same-sex distance, and acquainted dyads tend to show the reverse.

Staged Measures

For four studies of children, three showed more opposite-sex distance and one showed more same-sex distance. The average effect size (r) was .24

(two studies), showing more opposite-sex distance (these were the only two significant results). For three adult studies for which direction was reported, one showed more same-sex distance and two more opposite-sex distance, though the average effect size (*r*), known for only two studies, was − .10 (more same-sex distance). Two results were significant, one in each direction.

Projective Measures

For ten studies of children, three showed more same-sex distance and seven more opposite-sex distance. The average effect size (*r*), available for only two results, was .61, showing more opposite-sex distance, and three of the opposite-sex results were significant, all at *p* ‹ .001. Adults, by contrast, showed the reverse pattern, with all six studies of known direction showing more same-sex distance, with a known effect size (*r*) of − .31 (three studies), and two being significant (both showing more same-sex distance).

Naturalistic and projective measures show an interesting discrepancy between adults' observed behavior and their stated preferences. In the former, opposite-sex distance tended, weakly, to be greater, but in the latter, same-sex distance was clearly greater. This parallels a similar discrepancy to be discussed in chapter 8 for same-sex versus opposite-sex touch. These patterns of results may indicate that in naturalistic settings people are actually more at ease with same-sex others, but when they perform projective and self-rating tasks their responses reflect the greater social desirability of expressing heterosexual interest. Indeed, respondents may fear that any indication of liking same-sex more than opposite-sex others is a confession of homosexuality.

Other Comparisons

Sometimes in discussions of sex differences in distance, authors focus on the relative distances shown by male-male, female-female, and opposite-sex dyads (compare Hayduk 1983). I examined the data in this way, too, using naturalistic studies of adults. For twenty studies for which the three distances or their ordering were supplied, in eleven the ordering, from most to least distance, was male-male, opposite-sex, and female-female. The remaining nine were varied with regard to the order, but seven of them showed opposite-sex dyads to have the greatest distances. The modal pattern of intermediate distances for opposite-sex dyads is consistent with the results of earlier analyses in this chapter: main effects for both sex of subject and sex of target, and a small interaction (that is, same-sex versus opposite-sex) effect. The secondary pattern of greatest opposite-sex distances were all, interestingly, of neither non-U.S. or non-Anglo cultural or ethnic groups: U.S. black, Chinese, Puerto Rican, British (acquainted), Filipino, Israeli, and Costa Rican. Only five of the eleven studies with the modal pattern described above were of such groups: U.S. black, British (strangers), Colombian, Panamanian, and Mexican-American. This difference is significant when tested by chi-square ($\chi^2(1) = 5.71$, $r = .56$, $p < .02$). Possibly, social norms among U.S. Anglos permit relatively more public familiarity between the sexes than is allowed in more traditional, non-U.S., or non-Anglo cultural groups, or alternatively, prohibitions on male-male familiarity may be particularly strong in U.S. Anglo culture.

An issue related to opposite-sex behavior is asymmetry, discussed in earlier chapters as the comparison, for opposite-sex dyads only, of men's behavior toward women as opposed to women's behavior toward men. This question has theoretical significance because of the possibility that male-female status differences may dictate each sex's behavior toward the other (compare Henley 1977). In the case of distance, the comparison is not conclusive because not many studies reported the relevant data. However, the results are consistent. For naturalistic studies of adults, six studies found men to approach women closer than women approached men, one found a tie, and none found the reverse. No significance tests or effect sizes were available. In interpreting this, one could indeed hypothesize that males' higher status earns them larger interaction distances, though there are some problems with such an interpretation, which will be discussed later in this chapter. However, the asymmetry comparison is, of course, confounded with the overall target-sex effect, so it may be indicating simply a generally strong tendency for women to be approached more closely than men are.

EXPLANATIONS FOR DISTANCE RESULTS

The two most obvious interpretations of the trends reviewed here are familiar from earlier chapters. The first is that women are more affiliative than men and therefore prefer the positive-affect connotations of closer distances; and, relatedly, that their real or perceived affiliativeness also encourages others to approach them more closely. The second is that women have lower social status than men and therefore cannot command as large a personal space. When writing in the latter vein, as I have noted, authors are likely to refer to "violations" of women's personal space.

Research supports the association of positive affect with closer distances (reviewed in Hayduk 1983). For example, Gifford (1982) found that subjects who described themselves as cold preferred larger interpersonal distances on a paper-and-pencil task, and those who described themselves as warm preferred smaller distances. Wittig and Skolnick (1978), who manipulated the warmth versus coldness of a confederate and observed how closely subjects approached him or her, found that subjects approached a warm confederate much closer than a cold one, with most of this effect being due to unusually large distances set by both male and female subjects toward a cold male confederate. Thus, greater real or perceived warmth in females could account for their own distance preferences and others' distance preferences toward them. Perhaps women's greater real or perceived warmth is what made subjects in one study behave less nonverbally "anxious" toward them than toward men in a laboratory-based conversation (Weitz 1976).

The status hypothesis is somewhat more problematic. First, as described earlier in this chapter, some studies whose design had the potential to imply space violations more than do the designs of most observational studies did not find any evidence that women's spaces were in fact violated.

Second, status does not seem to have a simple relationship to distance. The smallest distances are not generally set for people of lower status than oneself and the greatest for people of higher status. Instead, the smallest distances seem to be set when the participants have equal status, and larger distances are set when the other is either higher *or* lower (Gifford 1982; Latta 1978 [two studies]; D. F. Lott and Sommer 1967). Jorgenson (1975) also found that equal-status pairs faced each other significantly more directly than unequal-status pairs, and that equal-status pairs interacted at closer distances, though this trend was not significant. Further, Mehrabian (1968) found no status effect when *only* others of higher and lower status, relative to the subjects, were used in a role-play study, which is consistent with all the preceding findings. Not all studies show this pattern, however: two studies that used an equal-status versus higher-status other found no difference (M. J. White 1975; Wittig and Skolnick 1978); one study found that naval men approached others of equal and subordinate rank equally close but stayed significantly farther away from others of higher rank (Dean, Willis, and Hewitt 1975); and one found that two kinds of equal-status pairs showed different distances (high-status pairs more than low-status pairs; Jorgenson 1975). To find the smallest distances (and more direct orientation) for equal-status individuals, as the most consistent group of studies does, is consistent with the warmth effect noted earlier, since one would presumably have the most affiliative feelings toward someone of the greatest perceived similarity to oneself.

In light of the apparent curvilinear effect of status on distance, one is led to question whether it is justified to view people's tendency to approach females more closely than males as evidence of females' low status, since the closest interaction is actually with equal, not low, status others. At the same time, the curvilinear status effect may indeed be related to the same-sex versus opposite-sex effect noted earlier, which showed that same-sex dyads tend to interact more closely on the average than opposite-sex dyads do, at least among adults; same-sex dyads can be seen as equal in status and opposite-sex dyads as unequal. But *among* unequal status (that is, opposite-sex) dyads, the curvilinear status effect would predict little difference between the distance to which men approach women and to which women approach men. This was not so, however, in the asymmetry data reported earlier: there, men approached women closer than vice versa.

Third, if women's low status is a kind of social stigma, then the literature on stigma and interpersonal distance should concur in showing stigmatized persons to be accorded smaller distances. But this literature shows the opposite: stigmatized individuals are given more, not less, space than unstigmatized ones (for example, Barrios et al. 1976; Langer et al. 1976; S. E. Taylor and Langer 1977).

And fourth, the tendency for females to approach others closer than males do can be seen as inconsistent with the status hypothesis, because such behavior would have to imply that females characteristically violate their own personal space by setting smaller distances than they need to. Of course, one could argue that society forces females to use small distances and to persuade themselves that they like doing so, even though this perpetuates their oppression. I find such an argument to be strained.

To the warmth-affiliation and status interpretations can be added a third, which has only rarely been mentioned, perhaps because it is less arresting theoretically. Women are smaller than men, and smaller individuals *within* a sex seem to experience closer interpersonal distances than larger individuals. This has been shown experimentally for height, using both a staged task with adults (Hartnett, Bailey, and Hartley 1974) and unobtrusive observation of adults (Caplan and Goldman 1981). An additional study that used six-foot five-inch confederates in a staged task (Frankel and Barrett 1971) obtained larger than usual approach distances. Bailey, Caffrey, and Hartnett (1976), however, experimentally varied confederate height and failed to get a significant effect.

Further, among children using paper-and-pencil tasks, researchers have found that obese-looking others are given larger distances (Lerner 1973; Lerner, Iwawaki, and Chihara 1976; Lerner, Karabenick, and Meisels 1975; Lerner, Venning, and Knapp 1975). Though this is easily conceptualized as a stigma effect, it can also be thought of in terms of sheer size. Consistent with such results, research has found that personal space increases with age (reviewed by Hayduk 1983). Height obviously increases with age as well. Further, in two studies, which both used same-sex pairs in a staged task in grades one, three, nine, and twelve, the male-male versus female-female difference in interpersonal distance grew steadily larger as age advanced, starting from virtually none in grade one (Price and Dabbs

1974; Tennis and Dabbs 1975). This increase in the sex difference for distance parallels increasing height differences between the sexes over this age span.

If height is implicated in sex differences in interpersonal distance, it might help to explain why the target-sex effect is stronger than the subject-sex effect. In interpersonal interaction, the height of the other person is likely to be a more salient fact than is one's own height. One's own relative height is probably hard to gauge in ordinary interaction; it is my impression that when a mirror shows us along with others we are often surprised to see how tall or short we actually are in relation to others. Thus, the fact that men are taller than women on the average should contribute to the larger distances accorded to men, and the reduced awareness of one's own height should contribute to a smaller subject-sex effect.

The data presented here suggest that females' greater approachability is a function of their real or perceived warmth-affiliativeness or size, rather than their low status. But there is obviously room for further research on this matter. It is also important to add that these various hypotheses are not necessarily independent. For example, small size may connote weakness, or smaller people may feel more affiliative with others because their physical threat potential is relatively low.

DIRECTNESS OF ORIENTATION

Closely associated with the study of interpersonal distance — indeed, usually measured in conjunction with it — is people's angle of orientation while interacting. The most direct is face-to-face, and other angles are less direct. On this question there are not a great many studies. The available data for naturalistic measures are summarized in table 7.6. As usual, people were observed with a variety of possible others: both male and female, female only, opposite-sex only, or same-sex only. Most were same sex.

Table 7.6 shows that in general, for children and adults, females interact more directly with others than males do, though the size of the sex difference (r) is small. The paucity of effect-size data makes it impossible to ascertain whether the magnitude varies with the sex of the other person in the dyad.

Other methods for assessing orientation have occasionally been used. One study using a staged measure with preschool children found girls to be significantly more direct when approaching an adult than boys ($r = .21$). One study using a projective measure with adults found no significant difference (effect size and direction unknown).

The only other comparison for which data from several studies are available is for same-sex versus opposite-sex dyads. For naturalistic

TABLE 7.6. Sex Differences for Naturalistic Measures of Directness of Orientation (by Sex of Subject, for Children and Adults)

Index	Children (5 studies)	Adults (18 studies)
Direction of effect (excluding no difference or unknown)	75% (3/4) favor females (not significant)	92% (11/12) favor females ($p = .006$)
Mean effect size (r)[a]	Between .07 (5 studies) and .12 (3 studies)	Between .02 (18 studies) and .15 (3 studies)
Statistical significance (all studies)	60% (3/5) favor females significantly, none favors males significantly	11% (2/18) favor females significantly, 6% (1/18) favor males significantly
Combined p	$p = .0003$ (5 studies)	$p < .12$ (14 studies)

[a] Positive values mean more direct orientation by females.

measures, in seven samples of adults in which the direction of the result is apparent, three showed more directness for same-sex dyads and four for opposite-sex dyads; virtually no other data are available for these studies. In two studies of preschool children where staged measurement was employed, same-sex dyads were more direct, and in one study this was a significant effect ($r = .22$).

Finally, four studies examined age changes in these sex differences for orientation. No study found a significant effect, but one found a tendency for female-female dyads to interact more directly with increasing age, compared with male-male dyads, over grades one through eleven.

On the basis of a very limited literature, then, it appears that females interact somewhat more directly with others than males do, at least in the same-sex dyads where most observation was made. This would fit with the warmth/affiliativeness theme entertained in previous discussions.

Another way that investigators have studied orientation behaviorally is to observe naturalistic seating patterns and, relatedly, to infer orientation preferences from people's behavior when approached by uninvited confederates. The orientations noted most often in such studies are "adjacent" and "across from," usually seated.

Studies of this sort show a very suggestive pattern whereby sex differences in preference for "adjacent" versus "across from" depends on whether the other person is a friend or a stranger (often an invader, as described earlier). A large proportion of such studies showed statistically significant results. In two of three studies of friends or acquaintances in natural interaction, females sat more often in adjacent positions and males more often in across positions (across a table, for example). In an additional study where a confederate agreed with or was depicted as similar to the subjects, females preferred the adjacent position and males preferred the across position. In contrast, five out of five studies of strangers or invaders found a mirror-image pattern: females reacted more negatively to the adjacent position and males to the across position, as measured by latency to departure, attempts to block or intervene with their arms or possessions, or mood. An additional study had mixed results: females leaned away from an adjacent invader, while males leaned away from one who was across (which is consistent with the preceding five studies), but females also did more blocking of an invader who was across and males did slightly more blocking of an adjacent one.

It seems clear that a female and a male have different affective responses to having others in these two positions and that each has an aversion to another being in a preferred position on an uninvited basis. As Fisher and Byrne (1975) speculated, the two positions may have different threat values for the sexes. Face-to-face encounters may arouse a challenging type of threat for males, whereas an approach from the side may present the threat of molestation for females. Of course, relatively benign places like a college library do not inspire one to fear either fistfights or muggings. One must assume that whatever responses people have in such places are generalized responses which would in fact be much stronger in less-safe or less-inhibited circumstances. If this interpretation is true, then it follows that for men and women to *prefer* the across and adjacent positions, respectively, with friendly others is an indication of trust and acceptance.

CONCLUSIONS

The literature indicates that males and females of all ages have different preferences for interpersonal distance: males set larger distances toward others than females do. Unlike the common finding in psychology that results are stronger for self-report than for behavioral measures, this result was stronger for naturalistic observation than for staged and projective methodologies. Several results from the projective literature suggest that this sex difference may be reversed when the other person has alienating qualities, an attribute rarely if ever present in the other interactant in the naturalistic studies. This may therefore help to account for the larger sex differences for naturalistic observation than for self-report. Additional, more limited, analyses showed that there is a weak tendency for females to face others more directly during interaction than males do in naturalistic interaction.

Considerably stronger than the subject-sex differences for distance were the target-sex effects for naturalistic observation, for all age groups: females are approached more closely than males are. Though this was also evident for adults in staged and projective studies, the staged and projective studies on children did not show it, though they were also few in number.

Though the comparison of same-sex with opposite-sex dyads was somewhat ambiguous for both children and adults, there was a tendency among adults under naturalistic observation to interact more closely with same-sex others, and there was also evidence that the nature of this effect varies with whether the dyad is acquainted or not. With projective measures, in contrast, adults show a consistent tendency to put larger distances between same-sex individuals.

As with other sex differences discussed in this book, not much research has been done specifically to examine the sources of these differences. At present I find the status explanation to be unconvincing. Clearly, much more research is needed.

8 Touch

The possibility of sex differences in touch has aroused more theoretical interest than any other nonverbal sex difference. This is because the oppression hypothesis, which has been entertained in some form in every chapter of this book, has been most fully developed, or at least most publicized, for touching behavior. The most articulate spokesperson for this point of view has been Henley (1973, 1977), and following her, other authors have given it prominence in their discussions of sex differences in touch and, by extension, other nonverbal sex differences as well.

Part of Henley's impact was her timely introduction of feminist ideas into social psychological theorizing, and part of the impact was her influential 1973 research on touch in public places, which has remained by far the most cited research in the area to this day. Until very recently, other pertinent research was largely nonexistent, unknown, or ignored. Only in 1981 did a substantial review of sex differences in touch appear (Major 1981), and even that review had relatively limited coverage of the literature. Even as of this writing, observational research on sex differences in touch is of smaller quantity and more problematic nature than is the case with the topics considered in previous chapters.

The relative scarcity of research can be attributed to several factors. First, investigators have been hampered by the fact that interpersonal touch is a statistically rare event, at least in the public places where most observational research is done (Jourard 1966; Perdue and Connor 1978; S. J. Williams and Willis 1978; Willis, Reeves, and Buchanan 1976). And, as Major (1981) has noted, because observation has been mainly unobtrusive and anonymous, investigators have obtained very limited knowledge about the age, status, and relationship of the individuals and about the meanings of the observed touches, either as intended by the toucher or as perceived by the recipient. The interpretation of touch seems particularly ambiguous and context-dependent, even more so than other nonverbal behaviors, making information on intentions and perceptions especially important. Because of the difficulty of obtaining observational data, investigators have relied more on self-report and stereotype data than has been the case in other areas of nonverbal research.

A second reason for the relatively small literature on touch is more speculative. The fact that Henley's early research (1973) showed striking results, especially on one major question — whether men touch women more than vice versa — paired with her strong statement of the oppression explanation, may have served to reduce investigators' motivations to pursue the topic. The answer and the explanation both seemed to have been provided: the answer was that men do touch women more than vice versa, and the reason was men's prerogatives of status. In addition, other research, when it was done, was often overlooked, with the result that one can easily gain the impression from reading various authors' discussions of the matter that Henley's research is both unique and definitive.

My colleague, Deborah S. Stier, and I in reviewing the literature on sex differences in touch discovered that neither of these assumptions is necessarily true: the literature is actually much larger than most writers seem to be aware of, and the appropriate interpretation of sex differences is hardly settled in our view (Stier and Hall 1984). However, we found it to be a very difficult literature to review. Methodological consistency among observational studies is low, and methodological problems result in many ambiguities in understanding and summarizing studies' findings. These problems and ambiguities are discussed in the course of this chapter, as well as in Stier and Hall, where more detail on the empirical literature is also presented.

SEX OF SUBJECT

Henley (1977) suggested that men, by virtue of their status in society, are freer than women to touch others and therefore do so. The results bearing on this question appear in table 8.1. Measurement techniques of the studies reviewed took several different forms, including percentage of individuals seen to touch, number of touches per individual, rate of touch, duration of touch, and total frequency. Total frequency is difficult to interpret because it does not take into account the number of males versus females observed. Thus, if the total frequency of female-initiated touches is higher than the total frequency of male-initiated touches, it could reflect the presence of more females in the population observed rather than different *proportions* of females versus males seen to touch. All sexes of potential targets are included in the table, except for opposite-sex only,

TABLE 8.1. Sex Differences in Touch (by Sex of Subject,
for Infants, Children, and Adults)

Index	Infants (25 studies)	Children (20 studies)	Adults (18 studies)
Direction of effect (excluding no difference or unknown)	86% (6/7) favor females ($p = .12$)	70% (12/17) favor females ($p < .09$)	67% (10/15) favor females (not significant)
Statistical significance (all studies)	12% (3/25) favor females significantly, none favors males significantly	5% (1/20) favor females significantly, 10% (2/20) favor males significantly	22% (4/18) favor females significantly, none favors males significantly
Combined p	$p < .21$ (25 studies)	$p = .50$ (favors males) (12 studies)	$p = .006$ (12 studies)

that is, which sex initiates touch more in opposite-sex dyads. This theoretically highly important comparison is dealt with later.

Another deviation from earlier analogous tables is that effect sizes for the sex differences are not included. This is done for two reasons: (1) effect sizes were rarely available, and (2) studies used a mixture of parametric and nonparametric statistics (that is, statistics based on means versus frequencies), with the consequence that derived effect sizes are not directly comparable. Where an attempt to summarize effect sizes was done, they proved to be extremely small on the average, not only for the sex-of-subject comparison but for other comparisons taken up in this chapter as well (Stier and Hall).

Infant studies were, as in most nonverbal research, done under fairly controlled situations, with the mother as the sole possible target or as one possible target along with father, siblings, or adult strangers. Children and adult studies had both sexes of targets as well as same-sex targets.

The table shows different patterns of results for different age groups. For infants, girls seem to touch others more than boys, but since the available target was so often their mother, generality of this is unknown. For children, the data show inconsistent patterns depending on the index of outcome, with direction favoring girls, but p-values favoring boys. The safest tentative conclusion is one of "no difference." For adults, a clear trend emerges favoring females in touch initiation. All the studies using the questionable total-frequency variable described earlier found male touches to equal or exceed female touches; without these results the pattern suggested in table 8.1 is even stronger.

Additional data, not in the table, are for adolescents and for many age groups combined. The three adolescent studies show evenly split directional trends and one marginally significant result favoring males in touch initiation. The study of many ages, observed in six areas of the world, found females to initiate touch more than males at $p < .001$ (Berkowitz 1971). When directional trends are examined in Berkowitz's twenty-four groups (four age groups × six areas of world), female touch was more prevalent in twenty-three of them, the only reversal being for U.S. children, and that reversal was small.

The excess of female over male touch initiation suggested for adults presents some problems of interpretation, however. First, studies in field settings (such as the Berkowitz study just described) must be interpreted cautiously, because naturally occurring groups show a marked tendency for the sexes to segregate themselves (Batchelor and Goethals 1972; Sommer 1967; Willis and Hofmann 1975; Willis and Reeves 1976; Willis, Reeves, and Buchanan 1976; Willis, Rinck, and Dean 1978). Because observation may actually have been mainly of same-sex dyads, it is therefore sometimes impossible to distinguish between an apparent tendency for females to touch others more in general and a tendency for female-female touch to exceed male-male touch.

The second problem with interpreting the apparent excess of touch by females is that even in studies where gender segregation was not a problem, as in experiments where dyads were paired by the experimenter, the reports sometimes did not present enough data for us to tell whether the effect may actually have been due to high levels of female-female touch rather than to high levels of females touching both males and females. The data for asymmetry in opposite-sex dyads, discussed shortly, suggest that this could be the case, since the incidence of females touching males is not strikingly high. It is therefore possible that the bulk of the touch-initiation main effect is actually due to female-female touch.

Yet another consideration is that the vast majority of the touches reported in the table are nonaggressive. Sometimes authors explicitly excluded aggressive touch from consideration, and in many other studies it is safe to assume that obviously aggressive touch was rare or nonexistent, based on the description of the observation context. Evidence on physical aggression in adults certainly favors males, not females, as initiators, and research on children has found higher levels of assault, either playful or aggressive, in boys than in girls (for example, DiPietro 1981; B. B. Whiting and Whiting 1975). Thus the touch-initiation sex difference would seem dependent on the nature of the ongoing interpersonal interaction.

A study not included in table 8.1 because it is not strictly observational is by Willis and Rinck (1983), who asked college students to keep a log of touches they received. Because subjects were asked to record touches immediately after they occurred, it has more empirical value, on the face of it at least, than studies based on general self-report and belief. Analysis of the toucher's sex showed that females initiated significantly more touch than did males.

Another study not included in table 8.1, this time because of artificiality, is by Riggio, Friedman, and DiMatteo (1981). Males did touch significantly more than females during role-played greetings, as defined by hugging, touching on arm or shoulder, or shaking hands. However, the authors noted that this result was due mainly to the difference in shaking hands, with men both initiating this behavior more and engaging in it more with other males than with females. This is consistent with results from three observational studies in which male-male handshaking was more frequent than female-female (Greenbaum and Rosenfeld 1980; Heslin and Boss 1980; Kendon and Ferber 1973).

SEX OF TARGET

Henley (1977) argued that women are touched more than men are, implying that women are more approachable and more vulnerable to personal violation by virtue of their lower status. The number of studies addressing this question is small, and, as with studies reporting on subject-sex effects, there are serious ambiguities. Foremost is the fact that several of these results for adults were based on the measure of total touch frequency, which was discussed earlier as problematic because one does not know whether the observed frequencies are out of proportion with the number of individuals of each sex observed.

In five studies of infants where direction was reported, three showed more touch receipt for boys and two showed more for girls. Almost all of this was initiated by the mother. Two of these results were significant, one favoring each sex.

In five studies of children where direction was reported, four showed more touch receipt for girls and one for boys; none was known to be significant. For three studies of teenagers where direction was reported, two showed more touch receipt for boys (neither significant), and one showed no difference.

In eleven studies of adults where direction was reported, seven showed more touch receipt for women and four for men. But three of the results showing more female receipt, including the only significant result, were based on the total-frequency measure which was earlier shown to be very difficult to interpret.

Willis and Rinck's (1983) study based on students' personal logs of touches received, described earlier, also has data on touch receipt. The authors found no difference in receipt of personal touch by male versus female college students.

On the basis of the available data, therefore, it seems justified to conclude that convincing sex differences in receipt of touch are hard to find.

SAME SEX VERSUS OPPOSITE SEX

The same-sex versus opposite-sex comparison for touch data presents several interpretational problems. Some studies counted total frequency of touches, as described earlier, so that frequency differences could reflect the proportions of same-sex and opposite-sex dyads available for observation rather than the individuals' touch preferences. Sex segregation is a possible problem in some studies as well, as S. J. Williams and Willis (1978) have suggested. For example, when observers noted the activities of a given subject over a specified length of time (as in a schoolroom), if that subject interacted mainly with his or her own sex, then the rate of opposite-sex touch would inevitably be low. Another interpretational problem arises if, in field studies, opposite-sex dyads were better acquainted than same-sex ones, as could be the case if the former tended to be married couples; then a touch difference could be an artifact of degree of intimacy, not the sex composition of the dyad per se. In studies in which dyads were the units of analysis rather than individuals, sex segregation is no problem but acquaintanceship may be; in experiments where subjects were paired arbitrarily, neither is a problem.

The data for the studies reporting this comparison reveal a steady trend for same-sex touch to decrease as subjects grow older. The percentages of studies showing more same-sex than opposite-sex touch for three age groups of touchers are: children, 88 percent (7/8, $p = .07$; two of the eight had significantly higher same-sex touch); adolescents, 67 percent (2/3, not significant; two of the three had significantly higher same-sex touch); adults, 53 percent (10/19, not significant; two of the nineteen had significantly higher same-sex touch, three of the nineteen had significantly higher opposite-sex touch).

Unfortunately, among the adult studies, eight of the nine studies showing more opposite-sex touch employed the total-frequency measure that does not control for possible differences in the numbers of same-sex and opposite-sex dyads observed, whereas only one of the ten showing more same-sex touch did. Further, several that showed more opposite-sex touch were conducted in field settings where differential intimacy could also be involved, as in mixed-league bowling, where in fact all three significant opposite-sex-more results occurred. Studies showing more same-sex touch tended to involve, by contrast, nonintimate or stranger dyads and dyads in public places where opposite-sex touch might be avoided (on the subway, in church or synagogue, in school, in cafeteria lines). Thus, any statements about same-sex versus opposite-sex touch frequency must be qualified by the age of the touchers, by contextual factors, and by methodological considerations. But the pattern revealed does fit with intuitive expectations:

that children would engage in more same-sex touch, and that adults would engage in relatively more opposite-sex touch.

MALE-FEMALE ASYMMETRY

The issue that has drawn the most attention when sex differences in touch are discussed is asymmetry: do men touch women more than vice versa? Henley (1973) proposed that men initiate touch with women more often than do women with men and that such asymmetry is due to a status difference between men and women. This status difference gives men a touching privilege which, in turn, contributes to their domination of women.

The best-known study addressing the asymmetry question is Henley's (1973) observational study of intentional touches with the hand, in which young adult men were seen to touch young adult women significantly more than vice versa. Besides this result, the literature on children, adolescents, and adults yields a number of other pertinent results. These were reported in terms of rate of touch, frequency, which sex initiated a touch, or duration.

In terms of direction, all five results for rate consistently indicated that females touched males more than vice versa; but all of these results involved preschool children as touchers or recipients, so generality is unknown. Statistical significance was hardly ever reported for this group of studies.

For the results stated in terms of opposite-sex dyads showing male versus female touch-initiation (the other main category of dependent variable), it is easy to do significance tests whenever it is reasonable to assume that each dyad was counted only once; expected values are set at 50 percent of sample size, since the null hypothesis says that male-to-female touch and female-to-male touch are equally frequent. Three of the ten such results were significant but inconsistent in direction (all three involving adolescents or adults). The remaining seven were generally far from significance, and were almost evenly split on which sex was seen to touch the other more. The combined probability of these ten results was .22, favoring male-to-female initiation.

For all studies addressing asymmetry, excluding ties, a slight preponderance (63 percent, or 12/19) showed more female initiation. Excluding both ties and studies involving children as touchers, the proportion is more even: 57 percent (8/14) showed more female initiation.

Though they stand alone in showing significant asymmetry favoring males, the results of Henley (1973) and Major and Williams (1980, reported in Major 1981) are important. Unfortunately, Henley did not say what kind of touch was involved (other than that it was intentional, with the hand), what relationship the people had to each other, what they were doing, or their exact ages. In the available report of the Major and Williams study, such information is also lacking. The age group of Henley's significant result is roughly similar to that of Willis, Rinck, and Dean (1978), who found a significant result in the opposite direction.

In Henley's sample, male-to-female asymmetry occurred only outdoors. Henley speculated that men use manual control over women outdoors and some other method of control indoors. Willis, Rinck, and Dean found significantly more female-to-male touching in an indoor setting, and Major and Williams found no difference between indoors and outdoors. So this issue is unresolved.[1]

Henley's and Major and Williams' studies are also unique in that they coded only touches that were considered intentional by the observers. It is certainly possible that male-to-female asymmetry can be observed only for intentional touches, and that this asymmetry may be swamped when the data include accidental touches. This is an important point, because Henley's theory would seem to assume intentionality. Unfortunately, little is known about the ratio of intentional to unintentional touches in the other studies, with the exception that Willis, Reeves, and Buchanan (1976) commented that touch in their samples was often inadvertent (these samples showed little asymmetry). Clearly, the intentionality issue merits further research. In the meanwhile, it seems safe to say that the male-to-female asymmetry proposed by Henley has not been demonstrated to be a very general phenomenon.[2]

OTHER OBSERVATIONAL DATA

Obviously, overall counts of touches by men and women, to men and women, tell only a limited amount about touch. The most important differences may lie in a more differentiated discussion of the nature, context, and participants' perceptions of touch. Unfortunately, the literature is very scanty on these important issues (see Stier and Hall 1984). The few robust

---

1. Henley (1973) also found that significantly more male-to-female touches went unreciprocated than did female-to-male touches. Henley interpreted this to mean that women tacitly acknowledged the legitimacy of men's touch. It seems equally likely, however, that to ignore someone's touch is a sign of indifference or even of rebuke. It may actually be premature to debate this issue, since Major and Williams found a trend opposite to Henley's.

2. The analysis of author sex, which has appeared in all other chapters, has not been done for the touch data. Too few effect sizes are apparent. An analysis based only on first-author sex and the direction of the result for "asymmetry" studies revealed no difference at all for male versus female authors.

qualitative differences that have been documented include men's greater proclivity to shake hands, at least in the United States, and men's greater readiness to engage in physical aggression. Heslin and Boss (1980) also found female-female dyads to hug more solidly and to touch more intimately in airports than male-male dyads did. What we would like to know is how the touches initiated by males and females may be qualitatively different: might males and females express the same things with different types of touch, or perhaps different things with the same type of touch? In order really to understand such qualitative differences in touch, the manner and location of touch, context, and perceptions of the participants must all be established, which would be a major effort to accomplish.

Another, very different, kind of observational research involves people's responses to being touched in experiments where touch by a confederate was an independent variable. As noted by Major (1981) and Stier and Hall (1984), studies generally find positive overall effects of these brief, presumably friendly or at least neutral, touches, as measured by such variables as subjects' ratings of slides on their aesthetic qualities, compliance to a request, or evaluation of a counselor. Though not all studies of this kind find sex differences, a substantial proportion do, and in every case it is females who respond more favorably — and usually regardless of the toucher's sex. These studies involve brief, prosocial touches by library clerks, peer-confederates, experimenters, or nurses (Fisher, Rytting, and Heslin 1976; Silverthorne et al. 1976; Sussman and Rosenfeld 1978; Whitcher and Fisher 1979). The suggestion that women's positive response to being touched is due to their greater experience of being touched (Fisher, Rytting, and Heslin) is not strongly supported by the available data on touch frequency and, in fact, seems to be undermined by the finding of Alagna et al. (1979) of no relationship between subjects' self-reports of body accessibility and their evaluative responses to being touched.

SELF-REPORT AND BELIEFS ABOUT
THE FREQUENCY OF TOUCH

Self-report and stereotype data figure more highly in the touch literature than is the case with other kinds of nonverbal behavior, presumably because the observational literature is smaller. Most nonobservational studies involve questionnaires given to college students. Since this literature is discussed in detail in Stier and Hall, I shall only summarize it here.

First, the only strong and consistent result is that subjects believe that opposite-sex touch is more frequent than same-sex touch. This discrepancy with the overall results for observational studies (described above) could be due to subjects' tendencies, when responding in the paper-and-pencil mode, to think of more intimate encounters than those routinely observed, or to their reluctance to acknowledge same-sex touch because of its possible homosexual implications. Also, same-sex touch is likely in fact to be more casual than opposite-sex touch and therefore more likely to be forgotten.

Sex-of-subject and sex-of-target differences — that is, who touches more and who receives more touch — are generally weak in nonobservational studies. People do believe, however, that men touch women more than vice versa. This belief is consistent in the small group of studies where it has been ascertained (for example, Radecki and Jennings [Walstedt] 1980), but it is not necessarily very strong, at least as far as can be determined from the published accounts.

THEORETICAL ISSUES

Although the most theoretically charged sex difference — touch asymmetry between the sexes — received only equivocal overall support empirically, it is still important to discuss theoretical issues, since future observational research could easily be more conclusive. The main theoretical point to be considered here is whether high status implies the prerogative to touch, a point that is obviously central to Henley's arguments about sex differences. Many authors have asserted that this prerogative exists, but the quantity of empirical support cited for such a claim is surprisingly small. Often the main basis is to cite Henley's (1973) well-known male-to-female asymmetry result and to conclude that, because men did touch women more, it had to be because of their greater power and dominance vis-à-vis women. Because of the importance of this issue and the lack of detailed reviews by other authors, I shall describe the available literature in some detail. However, even more detail is available in the Stier and Hall article.

The most compelling source of data should be observational research. Unfortunately, the observational research does not present a clear picture. Both Henley (1973) and Major and Williams (1980) inferred the socioeconomic statuses of people touching in public. Socioeconomic status was only vaguely defined, with the only example (supplied by Henley) being "waitress-customer," which is a questionable example, at best. In any case, both studies found that the person higher in socioeconomic status touched the lower person more frequently than vice versa (significantly only in Henley's study).

A study that defined status differently, however, found a different pattern. Goldstein and Jeffords (1981) recorded intentional touch, excluding handshake, between male legislators in a state house of representatives. Status was determined using information on committee membership, committee standing, and past government service. Here, the lower in status initiated touch with the higher *more* often than vice versa, a difference that almost reached significance ($p = .07$).

Yet other research on status yielded mixed results. Juni and Brannon (1981) performed two experiments in which status was manipulated by dress or by title. In the first, the potential recipient of touch posed as a blind person seeking directions. Naive subjects touched the low-status "blind" person relatively more frequently than they did the high-status "blind" person ($p = .07$). In the second experiment, subjects had to guide a blindfolded person across a floor maze. There was no status main effect for the proportion of time subjects spent touching the blindfolded person, but there was a tendency for the high-status male to be touched *more* than the low-status male.[3]

Age has served as another operationalization of status. The relevant studies are Henley; Major and Williams; Goldstein and Jeffords (all described above); and Heslin and Boss (1980), who observed touches during airport greetings and departures. The age comparison generally yielded striking tendencies for older to touch younger more than vice versa; the combined p for the five available studies (Heslin and Boss supplying two) is $p < .00006$. It has not always been a foregone conclusion, however, that age is equivalent to status: Heslin and Boss suggested that younger people may avoid touching their elders out of distaste rather than deference.

Data also exist in the form of casual observation, self-report, and belief. The idea that power implies the prerogative to touch was proposed by Goffman (1967), who described the "touch system" in a research hospital. There, doctors could initiate touch with lower ranks, but lower ranks did not initiate such interaction. Questionnaire studies confirm the belief that higher-rank individuals have more freedom to touch than lower (Brown and Ford 1961; Henley 1977; Radecki and Jennings [Walstedt] 1980).

In several other studies, subjects rated the dominance of individuals portrayed in photographs, slides, or videotapes (Forden 1981; Major and

---

3. A study by Rago and Cleland (1978) found a moderate ($r = -.25$) but nonsignificant tendency for less-dominant institutionalized retarded men to touch others in a nonaggressive manner more than did more-dominant men. Though the authors viewed this as contradicting Henley's hypothesis by showing that less-dominant individuals initiated more rather than less touch, their methodology makes this interpretation doubtful. Since dominance was defined as amount of aggressive behavior, most of which involved touch, the result seems to mean simply that those who used more aggressive touch used less nonaggressive touch and vice versa.

Heslin 1982; Summerhayes and Suchner 1978). These studies concur in showing that subjects perceived the relative dominance of touchers (either female, or both male and female) to go up after initiating touch with someone else.

The pattern that emerges from this literature dealing with power implications of touch is largely but not entirely consistent. People's beliefs, anecdote, self-report, observational studies of socioeconomic status and age, and one true experiment favor either the power-privilege idea or the idea that relative dominance increases as a consequence of touch initiation. However, one study that employed unusually careful measurement of status hinted at a reversal of the power-privilege hypothesis. It is worth noting that most of the evidence supporting the power-privilege hypothesis is ambiguous in one way or another; either the operationalizations of the status/power concept are debatable, or the results are based on belief and self-report.

CONCLUSIONS

Though touch is often talked about as though it shows marked sex differences, the observational literature shows less consistent and persuasive sex differences than we have yet seen in this book. Perhaps if the literature were more voluminous and more standard methodologically, the trends would be more evident. More touch initiation by adult women is the chief positive conclusion that can be reached, but even this is somewhat ambiguous because it may rest mainly on women touching other women.

To the extent that power or status is a factor in opposite-sex touch, one might be surprised that opposite-sex touch asymmetry is not a more consistent finding, since few would argue with the proposition that men are accorded more status than women in our society. But the research suggests that a countervailing factor could be at work that masks the expression of male dominance in heterosexual touch. This possible countervailing factor was documented in studies where the perceived relative dominance of a person was increased when that person touched someone else. The closing of the status gap thus accomplished is a plausible motivational basis for Goldstein and Jeffords' finding that the lower-status individual in a dyad of legislators tended to touch the higher-status individual more than vice versa. The higher-status individual may not always need to express status or to control the other overtly, but the lower-status individual may have a strong desire to redress the status imbalance or to establish a bond of familiarity and solidarity that could come in useful at a later date. Thus, though men may be granted more status than women, it may be the women who, at times at least, seek opportunities to touch.

When male-to-female touch asymmetry is found, there is a great need to try to document when, where, and in what relationships it occurs, and whether it is limited to certain kinds of touches. And when male-to-female asymmetry is demonstrated, it is also unwarranted to *assume* that it is due to status discrepancy between the sexes, as some authors seem to do (for touch as well as for other nonverbal sex differences; for example, Borden and Homleid 1978; Silverthorne et al. 1976; D. E. Smith, Willis, and Gier 1980). One possibility, supported by the touch-response literature discussed earlier, is that women enjoy being touched and that men, in touching them, are merely recognizing this fact. Indeed, men may respond to some subtle eliciting cue. Women's greater appreciation of touch could, of course, have a connection to their lower status, but, if so, status has only an indirect effect on touch asymmetry.

Sex differences in touch seem to be more complex and less well understood than is often assumed. Sufficient empirical data are not available to shed much light on qualitative differences in male and female touch. We do not know, for example, the proportions of power-connoting versus affiliative touches exchanged between men and women, nor even what constitutes a power-connoting versus an affiliative touch. Research is complicated by the fact that a given touch may be quite affiliative in both its intention and perception but its very occurrence could reflect the actual or aspired status or dominance of the toucher. Research is also made difficult because touch itself is infrequent, and touches that have anything to do with power or status may be more infrequent still.

9 Body Movement and Position

Sex differences in body movement have not received abundant empirical attention. The quantity of research is in inverse proportion, it would seem, to the abundance of everyday observation and popular stereotype that one can find in some books on nonverbal behavior. Even a young child can put on an impression of how each sex walks and moves. Mass-market books on nonverbal communication are filled with claims about male and female "body language" (for comments on such books, see Koivumaki 1975). When scholars try to summarize sex differences in movement, they either find little to summarize and therefore say little (for example, Harper, Wiens, and Matarazzo 1978; LaFrance and Mayo 1978; M. Davis and Weitz 1981), or they fill the void with impressions or unpublished data (for example, Henley 1977).

The major theoretical theme that emerges in available writings focuses on sex-role prescriptions. Women are said to move in ladylike ways, betraying lack of social power (Henley) via such habits as taking up as little physical space as possible (LaFrance and Mayo). Women are said to avoid being crude, sloppy, or overbearing in their physical movement, while men are said to avoid delicate, small movements and even to eschew certain gestures altogether, lest their masculinity be in doubt (as, in the United States, sitting with one's legs crossed at the knees rather than with one ankle resting on the other knee).

Traditionally, and to a lesser extent even today, women's freedom of movement has been hampered by their clothes: awkward or inherently uncomfortable shoes; long skirts or, at the other extreme, skirts so short that constant effort is required to prevent displaying their underwear; tight clothes; clothes made out of fragile fabrics. Every generation seems to produce new discomforts in women's clothes. The tightness of women's clothes in other centuries has even been known to kill (Stone 1979). Even in

119

the 1980s, when many women wear relatively practical and unconfining clothes, shoes with high, spiked heels are still popular. Most women would probably agree that wearing "unisex" (which really means masculine) clothes such as trousers and flat shoes confers much greater physical freedom and lack of self-consciousness about how they walk, sit, stand, and lean over. Feminist writers have advocated, as a form of masculine consciousness-raising, that men try walking and sitting in the ways required by women's skirts and blouses (Henley 1977). It is therefore hard to distinguish between sex differences in movement and position that might be mandated by dress styles and those that stem from sex-role socialization.

The behaviors covered in this chapter are varied, not only in their form but in their probable meanings. Included are movements of the head, body, arms, hands, legs, and feet, as well as posture, lean, position of arms and legs, and ways of carrying books. It is often difficult to identify the meanings of these behaviors. In research studies, bodily behaviors are sometimes described carefully, but the investigators must sometimes guess at what they signify. Even the same act, touching the hair for example, could indicate states as different as sexual invitation, acute social discomfort, or the need to adjust a stray lock. Of course, most nonverbal behaviors are ambiguous without reference to the social context and other verbal and nonverbal behaviors; but the plethora of variables included under the heading of body movement makes the job of understanding unusually difficult, as does the small number of studies that have reported on each movement variable.

To summarize the literature requires a somewhat different approach from that taken in previous chapters. Though, as usual, the available evidence is more ample than generally recognized, it is still too small and varied for a strictly quantitative approach to be used. In addition, some kind of thematic organization is called for, which must of course be provisional at best because of the interpretational ambiguity of many of the nonverbal behaviors measured.

Tables 9.1 and 9.2 show observational (not role-played) results for adults. There are two differences between these and previous tables. First, individual results are shown (table 9.1). This is done because the general categories of behavior listed are based on my interpretations of the specific behaviors measured; it is necessary to identify the specific variables and their results in case a reader disagrees with my inferential categories. (A few behaviors that did not fit these categories are not in the tables but are described later.) Second, there is a large amount of nonindependence in the entries, resulting from the common practice of coding a batch of behaviors for a given sample of subjects. Because of this, no significance tests of the aggregate data were performed. The studies in the table were based on all possible sexes of interactants (that is, targets — males and females, males or females only, opposite sex, and same sex). Only studies involving social interaction (which occurred mainly in newly acquainted dyads in laboratory situations) were included; body movements in non-social situations are discussed later.

The tables invite several interpretations. Men are clearly more relaxed; the effect sizes for this category were substantial. This is consistent with the stereotype documented by Kramer (1977): subjects in her study believed that men lounge and lean back more than women do. Men are also much more expansive. Both results are consistent with clothing differences (legs wide, for example), but also with the effect of behavioral norms not related to dress (arms wide, for example). But men are also consistently more restless, and again the effect sizes are substantial. Note that "restlessness" includes mainly gross and lower body movements, whereas "self-consciousness" is based mainly on self-touching (self-adaptors; Ekman and Friesen 1969a). On the latter, women exceed men.

The male pattern of restlessness may signify awkwardness and nervousness but not, possibly, the more acute self-consciousness that seems more implied in women's movements. On the other hand, male "restlessness" and female "self-consciousness" may actually be manifestations of exactly the same kind of social discomfort channeled in different ways. Men's clothing permits more lower body movement, at least without embarrassment, while women's clothes, makeup, and hair arrangements invite constant tending and therefore more self-touching hand movements. Thus the outlet found for nervous energy may be determined by clothing and hair styles, and it is even possible that some of women's movements do not signify anxiety or discomfort at all but simply the habits built up by many years of having to attend to their physical appearance.

Consistent with the view that men and women do not differ much in their underlying levels of social discomfort, Frances (1979) found that men's apparent restlessness decreased over time in interactions, whereas women's smiling and laughing decreased. This suggested that initial nervousness or self-consciousness may be expressed in gross body movement by men and in exaggerated pleasantness by women. Further evidence that women do not have a monopoly on social discomfort lies in research on speech errors, usually taken to be signs of anxiety in the voice, where men exceed women (chapter 10).

The tables contain the apparently contradictory findings that men are both more restless *and* more relaxed than women. One possibility is that men are more uninhibited physically and more likely than women to use their bodies — at least their trunks, feet, and legs — in *any way*. It is also

TABLE 9.1. Sex Differences in Movement and Position
in Dyadic Interaction (by Sex of Subject, for Adults)

Behavior	Direction	r
Restlessness		
Fidgeting	M	− .50 *
Manipulating objects	M	− .50 *
Foot gestures	M	− .31 *
Shifts of body position	M	− .26 *
Leg shifts	M	− .24 *
Foot and leg movements	M	− .23 *
Body activity	M	− *
Trunk swivel	M	−
Foot and leg movements	M	−
Torso shifts	−	−
Posture shifts	−	−
Foot and leg movements	−	−
Foot and leg movements	−	−
Foot and leg movements	−	−
Relaxation		
Trunk tilt to side	M	− .41 *
Backward lean	M	− .33 *
Relaxation in arms and body lean	M	− .32 *
Feet on table	M	− .25 *
Symmetrical reclining	M	−
Relaxation	−	−
Expansiveness		
Wide knees	M	− .68 *
Legs open	M	− .55 *
Body open	M	− .46 *
Arms wide	M	− .45 *
Elbows not held to side	M	− .38 *
Arms open	M	− .21 *
Involvement		
Nods	F	.50 *
Forward lean	F	.36 *
Nods	F	.31 *
Head tilt to side	F	.31 *
Nods	M = F	.00
Nods	M = F	.00
Forward lean	M	− .38 *
Forward lean	M	−
Forward lean	M	−
Forward lean	−	−
Forward lean	−	−
Forward lean	−	−
Forward lean	−	−
Nods	−	−
Nods	−	−
Nods	−	−
Nods	−	−
Nods	−	−
Expressiveness		
Gesticulating	F	.50 *
Articulation of fingers, wrist, and hand	F	.49 *
Head, body, and hand emblems	F	.44 *
Expressive gestures	F	.39 *

TABLE 9.1 — *Continued*

Behavior	Direction	r
Head movement	F	.29
Expressive gestures	F	.26*
Expressive gestures	M	−.39*
Gesticulation	F	—
Hand gestures	F	—
Hand gestures	M	—
Gesticulation rate	M	—
Expressive gestures	—	—
Gestures	—	—
Gesticulation rate	—	—
Gestures	—	—
Self-consciousness		
Self-manipulation of feet	F	.50*
Hands near face	F	.50*
Self-touch	F	.25*
Hands to chin	F	.17*
Self-touch	M	−.31*
Self-manipulation	M	—
Nervous gestures	—	—
Self-manipulation	—	—
Self-adaptors	—	—
Stroking hair	—	—
Preening clothes	—	—

Note: Entries are not all based on independent samples. M and F indicate which sex showed more of the named behavior.

*p < .05.

TABLE 9.2. Summary of Movement and Body Position Results from Table 9.1

Category of behavior	Results
Restlessness (14 results)	100% (9/9) favor men; r between −.14 (14 results) and −.34 (6 results); 100% (6/6) favor men significantly, none favors women significantly.
Relaxation (6 results)	100% (5/5) favor men; r between −.22 (6 results) and −.33 (4 results); 67% (4/6) favor men significantly, none favors women significantly.
Expansiveness (6 results)	100% (6/6) favor men; r = −.46 (6 results); 100% (6/6) favor men significantly, none favors women significantly.
Involvement (18 results)	57% (4/7) favor women; r between .06 (18 results) and .16 (7 results); 22% (4/18) favor women significantly, 6% (1/18) favor men significantly.
Expressiveness (15 results)	73% (8/11) favor women; r between .13 (15 results) and .28 (7 results); 33% (5/15) favor females significantly, 7% (1/15) favor men significantly.
Self-consciousness (11 results)	67% (4/6) favor women; r between .10 (11 results) and .22 (5 results); 36% (4/11) favor women significantly, 9% (1/11) favor men significantly.

Note: Indices of results are calculated as in table 2.2 and other similar tables.

possible that men's restlessness and relaxation indicate "leakage," in that they deliberately try to look relaxed via torso and arm positions, but their restless legs and feet give them away. While this is possible, it is not demonstrable in these studies, because generally the restlessness and relaxation results come from different studies; thus there is no indication in this research that the same man appeared simultaneously relaxed and restless in different parts of the body. Incidentally, the studies from which these results emerged are similar in superficial aspects of context and interpersonal relations, so no explanation based on social psychological differences between research settings is suggested.

Women emerge from the tables as appearing slightly more interpersonally involved and as more expressive and self-conscious, though the effect sizes are not as large as the male excesses are for restlessness, relaxation, and expansiveness.

A small group of results not in the tables involves nonsocial movement; for adults the tasks involved solving problems or taking tests. To summarize just the results of $p < .10$, men engaged in more foot and leg movements and more touching or picking of the face, and women engaged in more fidgeting with clothes or objects, "manicuring" their fingers, touching hair, biting nails, and touching parts of the body besides head and hands. Though not completely consistent with the social data shown in the tables, these results give considerable support to the conclusion that men are more apt to move the lower body and women to engage in self-adaptive behavior.

Another group of results for adults, not in the tables, involves behaviors which are hard to visualize or interpret. I shall mention only results of $p < .10$. In this group fall the following behaviors: symmetrical leg positions, upper limbs moving as a unit, arm between legs, folded hands, resting fist, fingers interlaced, and nose wiping (all done more by men); palm in lap and crossed wrists (both done more by women).

Some other behaviors whose psychological significance is also not at all clear may reflect anatomical sex differences or different tasks assigned to the sexes, and as such may have come to be expected as an aspect of sex-appropriate behavior but have no psychological or communicative meaning per se. For example, women have been found to cross their arms over their chest and avert their body when passing someone on the street (Collett and Marsh 1974). This could reflect the perceived need to protect the breasts or to be less physically vulnerable in general. Women's and men's gaits are also distinctive. Cutting, Proffitt, and Kozlowski (1978) showed that viewers could identify men from women in total darkness when the only cues were small lights attached to prominent joints. The authors suggested that men and women have different "centers of movement" that permit such detection. Birdwhistell (1974), relying on anthropological observation and local informants, described men as moving the arms more independently of the trunk and tilting the pelvis back more than women, both of which, if true, could relate to muscular and skeletal differences. Hewes (1957), also using an anthropological approach, noted sex differences in sitting and standing positions across cultures. In general, women's positions are less expansive than men's, which could reflect the nature of female clothing as well as differences in men's and women's activities.

A final result that may stem from anatomical differences is the easily documented tendency for males and females to carry things differently, mainly books in the observations made to date. Males prefer to carry them at their side, whereas females prefer to carry them in front of their chest. This difference appears after kindergarten. Scheman, Lockard, and Mehler (1978) suggested hip-protrusion differences as a physiological basis for the sex difference. This could well be, but widespread observation of the difference in pre-pubescent children indicates modeling and generalization as well, so that the practice preferred by each sex must be seen as normative rather than as simply more comfortable physically.

Research on people younger than adults is even less voluminous than research on adults. Infant studies are not useful because body movements are not well differentiated in infancy. Studies on preschool-age children in social interaction find the following significant sex differences: rough and tumble play, masturbation, and hand in back of body are all done more by boys; touching hair and scalp, playing with fingers, hand to mouth, face, or head, and hand in front of body are all done more by girls. Studies of school-age children in nonsocial activity (that is, some kind of solitary play) have shown the following significant differences: self-grooming, hand clasping, palm to head, limp wrist, hand flutters, and flexed elbow are all done more by girls (last three significant in two studies each).

By and large, then, the studies of children, both social and nonsocial, depict girls as apparently more self-conscious, as reflected in their use of self-adaptors. The research also points to early sex stereotypy in movement even in a noninteractive situation. Behaviors such as fluttering the hands and holding the wrist limp are so stereotypical that they are primary ingredients in caricatures of "feminine" movement. The early appearance of such behaviors is especially interesting, because they seem to have no basis in emotion or anatomy but seem only to be imitatively learned emblems of one's sex.

For adolescents (as usual, studied rarely) two studies in nonsocial situations found that only the palm-to-head gesture differentiated the sexes even marginally significantly (girls more), though to a nonsignificant degree girls showed more limp wrist, hand flutters, hands on hips, flexed elbow, hands near mouth, face, or hair, and movement of feet, while boys showed more overall restlessness, clenching fingers, and touching ears.

Social situations would seem a more fruitful place to look for sex differences in body movement, and it is unfortunate that only for book-carrying have the observational settings for adolescents been at least partly social.

For movements determined by the sex of the recipient, that is, sex-of-target effects, only a very small amount of research is available, and it is inconclusive. The only significant results show adult females to receive more demonstrative and intense gestures than adult males (by both sexes) and for a concealed female child to receive more head nods during a teaching session than a concealed male child (in a study that had only female subjects). Women may inspire more animation and approval than males. A handful of studies reporting on forward lean found no describable sex-of-target effects.

Another small group of studies reported on same-sex versus opposite-sex movements. The four significant results showed adults in opposite-sex dyads to use more hand gestures, to manipulate objects more, to lean forward more, and to engage in more full extensions of the arms or legs than those in same-sex dyads. All of these are consistent with one's intuitive expectations for heightened animation or arousal between members of the opposite sex. Such opposite-sex arousal is what Scheflen (1973) has called "quasi-courtship": heightened involvement, self-consciousness, and self-preening in heterosexual encounters.

These results showing more intense body movement in opposite-sex than in same-sex interaction appear to be inconsistent with data on smiling and gazing presented earlier. Opposite-sex dyads were shown to do less smiling and gazing than same-sex dyads, though the results were not strong. One possible resolution of this inconsistency lies in the differential controllability of the face versus the body (see chapter 3). Newly acquainted people in opposite-sex interaction may be able to monitor their facial and gazing patterns and control them so as to avoid the appearance of flirtation or arousal. But they may be much less successful at monitoring and controlling their body movements, with the result that their physiological or psychological arousal would be detectable in their body movements.

To summarize, females' movements and positions, as documented in this limited literature, are almost always smaller or less open than males', which is consistent with Birdwhistell's (1974) anthropologically based observation. This could, as many writers have suggested, reflect inequities in sex-role norms: men have space and freedom, women must be demure and physically unimposing (for example, LaFrance and Mayo 1978). On the other hand, females' smaller movements may be geared more to communicative goals. Such movements would include head movements and hand gestures in conversation, as well as facial expressiveness and skill in facial communication documented in previous chapters. Men's larger movements, in contrast, may express more gross states and messages, whether intentionally (for example, wanting to appear at ease), unintentionally (for example, revealing social awkwardness), or incidentally (for example, discharging physical energy). This interpretation would certainly fit with the evidence, so abundant throughout this book, that women are more attuned than men to other people and to the immediate social situation.

10 Voice

Research on the voice bears a resemblance to that on movement in that both areas of research are fragmented. Many different vocal characteristics are studied, and within each the quantity of research is limited. For this reason, the summary of the research must be organized into more categories and cannot rely as fully on quantitative summary as other chapters have done.

There are other difficulties in discussing vocal sex differences. One is that the dividing line between what is nonverbal and what is verbal is not entirely clear. Some writers simply refer to "speech," thereby avoiding the nonverbal-verbal distinction, and others make a variety of other distinctions that do not map exactly onto the nonverbal-verbal dichotomy (see Harper, Wiens, and Matarazzo 1978, for a discussion of various taxonomic systems for speech-related variables). Voice quality, such as harshness or pleasantness as determined from content-free speech tapes, is clearly nonverbal, and syntax is clearly verbal. But speech rate, total quantity of speech, tendencies to interrupt, and speech errors seem to fall in between. In this chapter, I include a review of sex differences for these and several other ambiguously "nonverbal" behaviors.

Of course, behavior that is unambiguously verbal, such as vocabulary choice, can convey messages or be expressive because of a quality created by the words chosen. Similarly, sentences that are constructed in different ways can convey different impressions about the speaker, impressions that can be much like those created by purely nonverbal behavior. For example, language that is filled with vague or qualifying phrases could appear weak and unconvincing; language that is grammatical or polite, as opposed to clumsy or rude, similarly conveys a distinct impression about the speaker's background, personality, or mood. Much theoretical and empirical attention is being paid to sex differences in sentence structure, pronunciation, and vocabulary, an enterprise that began with the provocative arguments of Lakoff (1973) about the poor impression that women's speech style makes. The proposed "female register" is said to include tag questions (for example, it's a nice day, isn't it?), hedges and qualifiers (for example, I guess), and "empty" adjectives and adverbs (for example, the movie was so good) (Crosby, Jose, and Wong-McCarthy 1981).

One could well argue that linguistic sex differences like these deserve coverage in this book. I have not included them, however. It seemed too large a deviation from the nonverbal theme of the book. Suffice it to say that two recent reviews have concluded that more features are believed to differentiate the verbal behavior of the sexes than actually seem to (Kramer, Thorne, and Henley 1978; P. M. Smith 1979).[1]

Another difficulty in delineating what vocal behaviors should be discussed here is that with the voice one quickly confronts physiological differences, a topic clearly beyond the coverage of this book. Sex is easily identified from voice samples, even very brief ones. Differences in the size of men's and women's vocal tracts undoubtedly contribute to differences in fundamental frequency and in the distribution of frequencies in higher bands (R. O. Coleman 1971, 1976). But sex differences in fundamental frequency are said to be greater than one would predict on the basis of physiology alone (Mattingly 1966), leading to the obvious possibility that sex-typed vocal styles augment endowed differences. For that reason, voice frequency is included in this chapter.

Finally, there are unique methodological issues in studying vocal nonverbal behavior. The voice is harder to describe in words than are behaviors that we can see with our eyes, but easier to describe using mechanical devices or computer. Parameters measurable by machine are frequency, amplitude, frequency variation, amplitude variation, and length of pauses. Also, human judges are used as a surrogate for mechanical readings to rate pitch and loudness.

Because vocal behavior is hard for listeners to describe in terms of discrete cues, judges' impressions of affect are often used. These are registered on such rating scales as dominance, anxiety, and warmth. Probably because the molecular variables scored mechanically are sometimes inconvenient to produce and are not easily interpreted, the use of such inferential ratings is more common in voice research than for other modalities of nonverbal behavior. Ratings, despite their global nature, do at least capture emotional qualities of the voice very well (see, for example,

---

1. Investigators have also examined males' versus females' written, as opposed to spoken, language (for example, Hiatt 1977). Hall, Aist, and Pike (1983) examined the occurrence and vividness of references to nonverbal behavior in novels by male and female authors. In general, there are few striking documented sex differences in written language.

Hall, Roter, and Rand 1981). Unfortunately, ratings can be problematic when one is studying sex differences, for reasons mentioned both in chapter 1 and below.

Four categories of vocal behavior will be considered: disturbances, voice characteristics, speech quantity, and dialogic behavior. Within each category, several individual variables are considered. Most of the data pertain to the speaker's sex, though some results are for the target's sex and the same-sex versus opposite-sex comparison. Infant behaviors — babbling, crying, "vocalizing" — are not discussed.

SEX OF SPEAKER

Disturbances

Analyses of speech disturbances are usually based on the definitions provided by Mahl (1956). Some investigators follow Mahl's coding system exactly; others apply some, or variations, of the original concepts. Speech disturbances are of two basic kinds. One is errors, defined as repetitions, omissions, slips of the tongue, sentence corrections, sentence incompletions, stutters, and intruding incoherent sounds. The other kind is the "ah" or filled pause, which is a disturbance in that it delays and disrupts the flow of speech, but which is not an error per se. Most writers consider the filled pause to indicate cognitive uncertainty and the desire to keep the floor while deciding what to say, rather than emotional uncertainty or anxiety, which is the chief interpretation of the seven behaviors defined as errors (Kasl and Mahl 1965; Lallgee and Cook 1969; summary by Harper, Wiens, and Matarazzo 1978). In the summary below, speech errors and filled pauses are considered separately.

I located fourteen studies reporting on sex differences in speech *errors.* Twelve of these were of adolescents or older (mainly college students); two were on children, preschool and fifth grade, respectively. Nearly all involved dyadic conversation, though one used dramatic readings and at least one involved talking alone, on instructions from an experimenter. The results are very clear, and in line with the stereotype documented by Kramer (1977), which said that men's speech is less smooth than women's. All eight results of stated direction showed more errors in the speech of males (a proportion that was significant at $p = .008$). The effect sizes (r) fall between $-.17$ (based on all fourteen results, including unknown effect sizes as zero) and $-.32$ (based on the seven known effect sizes). Four, or 28 percent, of the results were statistically significant, and the combined p was .003. The effect size of $r = -.24$ for the study of two-year-olds, included in the summary just described, fell squarely in the total range of effect sizes, suggesting little in the way of developmental trends (though of course it is too small a data base to warrant certainty on this point).

That very young boys have less fluent speech than their female peers is consistent with Garai and Scheinfeld's (1968) conclusion, in a large literature review, that boys have less fluent speech and more actual speech and reading disorders, such as stuttering and dyslexia, than girls. Verbal skill in women, as measured by standard paper-and-pencil tests, does exceed that of men (see chapter 11). Though speech errors are commonly considered to reflect anxiety, the sex differences suggest the possibility that they are part of generally depressed verbal skill in males rather than a manifestation of emotional state.

If males' more numerous speech errors do instead stem from anxiety, that anxiety could still be related to their depressed verbal skill. Males' depressed verbal skill may lead to anxiety about speech production, which in turn could cause speech errors to occur more often in males. (Such anxiety could also make them speak faster, as shown later, and to make more errors as a consequence.) This hypothesis does not fit well, however, with the evidence presented later that shows males to talk more than females. One would not expect a person who lacks confidence in verbal skill to be eager to expose that deficiency to an audience.

Another possibility is that males are not anxious about talking in particular but are anxious when in interpersonal interaction. They may feel they lack certain communication skills, a fear that is not entirely unfounded. They may also be particularly uncomfortable when talking about themselves, as the evidence on self-disclosure suggests (see chapter 11). It must be noted, however, that not all of the conversations analyzed in the present literature were personal in nature. One of the largest sex differences did not even come from a dyadic situation, but rather from dramatic readings. Though men display more bodily signs of restlessness than women do, which supports the idea of male social anxiety, women seem less relaxed in the body, seem to do more nervous smiling, engage in more self-touching that probably reflects self-consciousness, and report slightly higher levels of social and overall anxiety than men do (see chapter 11). It is therefore debatable whether a male excess of social anxiety can be justified as an explanation for males making more errors while speaking.

Yet another possibility, suggested by these patterns of male speech errors and restlessness and female nervous smiling and self-touching, is that the sexes differ in how they reveal anxiety, not in how much anxiety they experience. If so, the nature of that expression would suggest that the sexes differ in the intensity of their interpersonal orientation and perhaps even in the adaptiveness of their social behavior. Women's smiling and laughing, even if nervous, probably serve to smooth awkwardness and heighten openness. Even women's self-conscious self-touching reflects a concern with the other's perceptions. Men's bodily restlessness and vocal disturbances seem, in contrast, to serve no communicative function but rather to be simply an outlet. They indicate less of a focus on the interpersonal relationship and less interpersonal awareness than women's actions do.

The *filled pause*, "ah" or its equivalent (such as "uh"), is best thought of as a cognitive holding pattern. Though debatably a disturbance in the sense of reflecting emotional discomfort, it nevertheless signals hesitancy and does intrude, sometimes irritatingly to a listener, into the flow of speech. Research reporting on filled pauses shows, for adolescents and older subjects, extraordinarily large and consistent sex differences. All six of the studies (all dyadic) showed more filled pauses by men, with an average effect size (r) of $-.51$ (known for all six). In addition, all six results were statistically significant, five of them being significant at $p = .01$ or better. (It seemed unnecessary to calculate a combined probability for these studies.) Interestingly, the one study on children (fifth grade) showed no significant difference and no other reported results, hinting that the sex difference was very small. This fits with the distinction drawn above between the psychological meaning of speech errors versus filled pauses: if filled pauses were equivalent to speech errors in reflecting a disturbed psychological state, they should show similar sex differences across age groups. Instead, the filled pause seems more likely to be a device employed by more mature males to give themselves time to consider their next words, either as a way to help avoid making speech errors or as a way to avoid yielding the floor prematurely, or both. Interestingly, Frances (1979) found that a high filled-pause rate in males was associated with low self-rated dominance. Though seemingly paradoxical, such behavior may be a compensatory response to perceiving oneself as low in social power. Frances found no corresponding result for females.

Voice Characteristics

Women's voices are higher in *pitch* than men's. Though studies have not always reported statistical tests, the differences are obviously large, sometimes nonoverlapping. The most common method of measurement is the fundamental frequency, which is the rate of vibration of the laryngeal folds and which is highly correlated with subjectively perceived pitch. For this variable, the only effect size (r) I found for adults is .93, a huge difference indeed. Interestingly, a study of judges' ratings of pitch found an even larger difference ($r = .98$), which suggests that a sex stereotype of higher pitch in women contributes to judges' estimates of pitch level.[2] Such a stereotype was documented by Kramer (1977).

Cross-sectional evidence suggests that sex differences in voice frequency appear around puberty. Though females' fundamental frequency shows a steady lowering between age eight and adulthood, males' takes a sudden drop about age fourteen (Duffy 1970). Studies of infants and young children rarely find sex differences. As mentioned earlier, it has also been argued that females' voices are higher than mandated by the physiology of their vocal tract. Additional, indirect, evidence for this comes from a study on children five through twelve years old who, in talking to a baby rabbit, did show a significant sex difference in fundamental frequency, girls' voices being higher overall ($r = .39$), as well as higher at every age tested except ages five and six. Though it is conceivable that girls' natural speaking voices are actually higher than those of their male peers, contrary to other evidence, it is also possible that the situation of talking to a baby rabbit elicited sex-role behavior in the children, which led the girls to raise the pitch of their voices in an exaggeratedly motherly or affectionate way.[3]

Though stereotype (Kramer 1977) and casual observation indicate that women's voices are more variable in pitch — that is, musical, or expressive — than men's, there is not much empirical research on this question. In the study where children talked to rabbits, variability in fundamental frequency was indeed significantly greater for girls overall ($r = .50$), and was consistently higher at every age level between five and twelve years old. (As above, judges' ratings of "exaggerated intonation" for the same sample showed a much larger sex difference, $r = .80$, again suggesting the contribution of sex stereotypes to such ratings.)

Related to pitch is *intonation contour*. Naive stereotype says women are more likely to employ a rising contour, such that the end of a sentence rises

---

2. P. M. Smith (1979) cites additional evidence, which I did not locate, for women's higher vocal pitch, as well as for two other behaviors discussed later in this chapter, pitch variability (women more) and total speech (men more).

3. Additional evidence that there are differences between the voices of young boys and girls comes from research in which the sex of children three through five years old was easily guessed by listeners (Meditch 1975; Weinberg and Bennett 1971). Meditch argued that if differences in pitch contributed to this discrimination, such differences would have to be due to sex-role behavior in children rather than to physical differences since (citing several studies) preadolescent boys and girls do not differ in vocal-tract physiology when they are *matched* on height and weight (Eakins and Eakins 1978 repeated this argument). The latter part of this argument is flawed, because preadolescent boys and girls are not in fact equal in height and weight, and therefore there is still the obvious possibility that vocal-tract differences could create differences in voice frequency. Differences in vocal-tract dimensions could also lead to sex differences on other variables besides fundamental frequency, as Weinberg and Bennett have suggested and as R. O. Coleman (1971, 1976) has shown for formant frequencies and vocal-tract resonance, respectively. Females, in other words, produce a different distribution of frequencies than males do.

relative to the beginning, with the effect that a declarative sentence has a questioning tone. Such a stereotype was documented by Edelsky (1979). Scholars have made such claims, too, but such claims are not always based demonstrably on data (for example, Brend 1975). Empirical evidence on this question appears limited. Pellowe and Jones (1978) found such sex differences in British speakers, but Edelsky, in a large sample from a U.S. college population, did not.

Another voice characteristic, *loudness,* has received little empirical attention as far as I can tell, perhaps because everyone assumes men speak louder than women, as stereotype indeed says that they do (Kramer 1977). Of the three studies I located, two found college men to speak significantly louder than college women, as measured by mechanical instruments, with an average known effect size (r) of $-.29$.

A final group of voice characteristics, defined in terms of *global affective quality,* has been studied using judges' ratings of voices. Such data are problematic for two reasons. First, though some investigators used electronically filtered voice tapes (described in chapter 2) to eliminate verbal information, a number either have gathered ratings from full (unfiltered) voice tapes only or have gathered ratings in several speech conditions such as filtered voice, unfiltered voice, and typed transcripts, but have not reported results separately by condition. Thus, it is sometimes hard to know what contributions have been made by the purely nonverbal components of the voice.

Second, the ease with which a listener can identify a speaker's sex and the global nature of the ratings promote bias by sex stereotypes, just as I argued in the cases of pitch and pitch variation, above. Telling evidence for such bias comes from Edelsky's (1979) voice-rating study, in which women were judged from their voices to be significantly more "easily influenced" than men. This seems to me to be a trait inference that cannot possibly be made from voice quality alone. Most likely, judges in that study (as probably in others described below) were registering their views of women versus men, instead of, or in addition to, their judgments of female versus male voice quality per se.

Not surprisingly, considering the likelihood of such bias, the literature (all for adult speakers unless noted) shows that females' voices are judged to be more positive, more pleasant, more honest, less confident, less dominant (though not less assertive, interestingly), more meek (children), more personal, more admiring, more respectful, more anxious (though also less tense, in a study of children), less awkward (children), more delicate (children), and more enthusiastic than males'. (As always, not every study shows such differences, but the majority do.) These results are quite consistent with naive stereotypes documented by Kramer (1977): men are believed to speak demandingly, bluntly, dominantly, forcefully, and militantly, while women are believed to speak in a gentle, polite, enthusiastic, and friendly way. This is not to say that none of these ostensible differences is real; it is merely to say that judgments by raters are not the ideal way to assess them.

Speech Quantity

For *speech rate,* stereotype says women talk faster than men (Kramer 1977). But among ten studies I located (almost all on adults), none showed females to talk significantly faster, whereas three found males to talk significantly faster, either to another person or in monologue. Considering the direction alone, of the studies of known direction, four favored males and two favored females. The average effect size (r), known for only four studies, was only $-.03$, due to one study which though nonsignificant did show a large difference favoring women instead of men ($r = .43$). The one study on children (fifth grade) showed the largest sex difference favoring males ($r = -.28$). The combined probability for the ten studies was $p = .06$, favoring males. Males thus speak faster than females, but it is not a striking difference.

For *total speech production,* stereotype would seem to take two forms. On the one hand, women are seen as talkative — indeed, the gabbing woman is a common caricature. It seems indeed possible that females, when they are together with other females, may devote more of their time to talking (especially about personal topics; see chapter 11) than males do when they are together. On the other hand, men are seen in stereotype as insensitive and dominant, traits that would go along with commanding a large share of talking time for themselves when in a group with women.

Actual studies I located, numbering twenty-two, and again mainly on adults, were based on dyadic, group, and monologue situations. Unfortunately, there are not enough studies to permit a definitive breakdown according to age, group size, and sex composition. Speech production was also defined heterogeneously, further making summary a problem. Speech production was defined as total number of words or sentences spoken, total number of speech acts, total duration of speech, number of time blocks in which the subject was speaking, or length of speaking turns. Of the seventeen studies with stated direction, fourteen favored males on speech production and three favored females ($p = .01$). Six results favored males significantly and two favored males at $p = .10$, while only two favored females significantly (one of which was a study on children whose author attributed the result to girls' linguistic superiority). The overall combined p was less than .01, favoring males.

But in spite of this clear and robust pattern, the average known effect size (r) was only $-.02$ (ten results). Corroborating this small effect size is Carli's (1982) quantitative review of such studies. which came to my attention after the present review was undertaken. Carli found an average sex difference (r) of only $-.09$ favoring men, based on the four studies not included here.

Thus the consistency of the picture showing males to talk more is blurred only by the average effect size of $-.02$, an anomaly due perhaps in part to effect size being available for relatively few studies. In addition, the largest sex difference of all showed women to talk more than men in same-sex dyads ($r = .54$) — that is, when women were with other women compared with men talking with other men. Most of the significant differences favoring men in speech production were in mixed-sex groups, while the very limited data on opposite-sex dyads did not show pronounced effects. These patterns, if verified when more studies become available, would suggest two important hypotheses. First, the stereotypes described above may have some basis in fact, with women devoting more of their time to talking when with their own sex than men do, but talking less when men are around. Second, stronger sex effects in mixed-sex groups than in opposite-sex dyads would suggest that the tendency for men to outtalk women may be due more to intrasex competition than to a desire to dominate women; in other words, the key element in male speech production could be the presence of other men in a mixed-sex group, not the presence of women.

It is interesting that two strong effects favoring men came from studies that used monologues — describing pictures, either to a tape recorder or to a passive experimenter. This certainly does not suggest male dominance or competition. Instead, it could be due to men's less-developed verbal skill, which might require them to use more words to say what they mean; or, it may be because men exercise less self-restraint than women do in a situation in which no one is wanting to have the floor. Thus the view that men's greater speech production under some circumstances is due to their dominance may be somewhat overstated.

Speech production as a reflection of dominance is suggested in Frances's (1979) finding that self-rated aggression was related positively to speech production in both sexes, and in Hershey and Werner's (1975) study, where women who were active in the women's movement talked proportionately more when in conversation with their husbands than did women who were not (though other interpretations are possible). Sheer verbal production, when around men at least, is certainly an important element in the assertiveness advocated by many feminists.[4]

---

4. Though I have dealt only with total speech production, there is a related literature that deals with sex differences in the distribution of talk according to various categories of verbal content. The most common approach examines aspects of the task-versus-socioemotional dichotomy (for example, Heiss 1962; Kenkel 1957; Piliavin and Martin 1978). This literature is not discussed here because it seems to represent too much of a digression from nonverbal matters, though it is included in the review of other sex differences presented in chapter 11.

Dialogic Behavior

Here I refer to behaviors that are closely related to turn taking in conversation: interrupting, breaking silence (that is, taking the initiative when there is a pause), and using back-channel responses, which are short responses, mainly "uh-huh," uttered while the other is speaking. They are not attempts to interrupt but rather to reassure the speaker that one is listening to, and comprehending, what is being said.

As is often stated in discussions of sex differences, men *interrupt* more than women do. Among nine studies, the direction of known results was five favoring men and one favoring women. Four were significant in favor of men, and one was significant in favor of women (combined $p = .01$, nine studies). The average effect size (r) was $-.48$ (available for only two studies).

Interruption can mean more than one thing. LaFrance and Carmen (1980), though finding men to exceed women nonsignificantly on interruptive statements, found women to exceed men significantly on interruptive *questions*. Conceivably, the study mentioned above that found significantly more female interruptions included many interruptive questions. It would seem that the female style of interrupting is more prosocial than that of men, since a question clearly leads the other person to elaborate on what they are already talking about. As such, it is hardly an effort to usurp the floor.

Being the first to *break a silence* is related to interruptions, in that it indicates a claim to the speaking floor. One study examined this and found men to do so significantly more than women. Interestingly, this was the very same study that found women to interrupt more, overall. Perhaps compensatory processes were at work, such that women claimed the floor by interrupting and men by breaking silence. Or, as suggested, perhaps women's interruptions were of a questioning rather than declarative nature.

Back channeling, also called listener responses, was coded in four studies but was nonsignificant, with no other information available, in three of the four. In the remaining study, girls and women showed significantly more back channeling than boys and men ($r = .61$).

SEX OF TARGET

The literature on vocal nonverbal behavior does not offer much on target-sex effects. Some trends are apparent, however. Recall that for several previously discussed behaviors, women both gave out and received in excess of men — for example, women gaze more, and are gazed at more, than men. A similar pattern is provisionally apparent for several vocal behaviors, though this time it is men who give out and receive more than women.

For quantity of talk, in terms of direction only, men received more than women in all three studies where it was reported on; this was marginally significant ($p < .10$) in one of the studies (effect size $r = -.10$). Men were talked to louder than women in two studies of dyadic interaction; this was significant in one of the two studies ($r = -.33$). People's utterances to men on television programs in transcript, original (unfiltered) speech, and filtered speech were rated as significantly more dominant than utterances to women (rated blind as to sex of target), a difference that was also very large ($r = -.89$). In the same study, people also spoke in a manner that was rated as significantly more businesslike, condescending, and unpleasant to men than women (rs $= -.88$, $-.85$, and $-.63$, respectively).

All of these behaviors or speech styles were shown in the preceding pages to be also *produced* more by men than by women (for total quantity of talk, this was generally true except for female-female versus male-male dyads). The existence of two such main effects means that male-male dyads' voices are maximally loud, dominant, and so on, while female-female dyad's voices are minimally so. In discussing the television-ratings study, I earlier suggested (Hall and Braunwald 1981) that a process of dominance-matching may occur when two men interact: in order not to lose in the balance of power, each responds to the other's actual or perceived dominance by becoming more dominant himself. Thus, escalation occurs. I also suggested that the correspondingly low levels of rated dominance in female-female vocal communication could reflect norms that bar the expression of dominance, competition, or ego-oriented motives in female-female interaction. Such norms would, at the same time, encourage the expression of trusting, prosocial, or other-oriented attitudes in female-female communication, attitudes that are very likely also manifested in the kinds of behaviors documented previously: gazing, smiling, close distances, and touching. While some psychologists may view the female behavior pattern as reflecting mainly social submission, these patterns can also be seen as reflecting female attitudes that favor social involvement and encouragement of further positive interaction.

In contrast to the positive target-sex effects just discussed, some vocal variables seem to show no target-sex differences. In particular, six studies found apparently negligible effects (at least, all nonsignificant) for speech disturbances; in no case was the direction evident. Though only limited interpretation should be made of so small a literature, one can raise the interesting possibility that the positive target-sex effects for dominance, loudness, and total talk are created by people's general recognition that those behaviors are central to the male stereotype. Expectations may thus shape the behavior of people toward men and toward women: men are believed to be loud (for example) and therefore people speak loudly to them. (The likely self-fulfilling nature of such an expectation is, of course, obvious.) In contrast, it is probable that people have weak expectations about men's greater tendencies to commit speech errors and to fill their pauses with "ah" or its equivalent. Lacking an expectation, people would then be less likely to produce more of these behaviors when speaking to men.

SAME SEX VERSUS OPPOSITE SEX

Only rarely has the sex-of-speaker × sex-of-target interaction been examined (this interaction tests the difference between same-sex and opposite-sex vocal behaviors). Three studies have found no significant interaction for speech disturbances. But some interactions have emerged. Two studies examined this interaction for loudness, and in one it was significant in showing that opposite-sex speech was louder than same-sex speech. The study in which voices on television were rated, mentioned earlier, showed opposite-sex communications to be rated as significantly more dominant than same-sex communications, as well as more business-like, condescending, and unpleasant. Another ratings study, this one involving transcript, original speech, and filtered speech of college students delivering a teaching monologue over the telephone, also found opposite-sex communications to be more unpleasant than same-sex ($p < .06$), as well as significantly more anxious.

In these studies showing interaction effects, female-female loudness, dominance, unpleasantness, businesslike tone, and anxiety were notably less than in dyads of other sex compositions. Again, norms encouraging females to be nice with each other are suggested. In Hall and Braunwald, I discussed these patterns at length, with considerable attention given to the fact that the low female-female rated dominance was contrary to the stereotypes actually held by raters, who believed that if a woman sounded dominant she was probably addressing another woman — in other words, that women would defer to men in dominance. Instead, women seemed to defer to each other in dominance and to increase their dominance with men, though not to the levels demonstrated by men speaking to men.

CONCLUSIONS

Though no individual vocal variable has received as extensive investigation as have communication skill, gazing, smiling, or distance, sex differences nevertheless emerge. Some of these are notably large, such as the use of filled pauses. Research indicates that females' voices are more fluent, softer, slower, higher pitched, and perhaps more variable in pitch; women also talk less in mixed groups and interrupt less, overall, than men do. In terms of global ratings, which are prone to bias in the direction of sex stereotypes, women's voices are also, to summarize a number of different findings and different rating dimensions, more pleasant and more unassuming. It also seems to be the case that for the more sex-typed variables — such as loudness and rated dominance — men also receive more of the same kind of behavior that they themselves engage in.

An interesting line of future investigation could explore the possible connection between the kinds of sex differences documented for visual channels versus vocal channels and the kinds of information communicated in those modalities. Women are particularly good, compared to men, at judging and expressing in the face and body channels (especially face), and they attend more to the face; their faces are more active, and they smile more; they use body movements in a way that expresses interpersonal involvement, as in using hand gestures. Men are relatively, though not absolutely, better at judging and sending cues via the voice, and their vocal style can be construed as conveying strength and interpersonal control. Even men's more numerous speech errors, while probably not conveying strength or control, do indicate that the voice is more of an outlet for emotion in men than in women. Women and men seem thus to be modality specialists: women specialize in visual communication and behavior, men in vocal. What is intriguing is the research, mentioned in chapter 3, that suggests that the visual modality (really, the face) conveys degrees of positivity-negativity well, while the voice conveys degrees of dominance-submission particularly well.

Putting these results together yields the hypothesis that the sexes specialize in the modalities that are most relevant to them. If women are attuned to degrees of interpersonal harmony and men to degrees of social dominance, then they could each profit from attention, skill, and a behavioral repertoire centered on the modalities most suited to their respective motives. This implies more than that women show their pleasantness by the best available means, the face, and that men show their dominance by the best available means, the voice. Though this certainly may be true, the evidence also implies that it is *degrees* of positivity and dominance, not any particular level of positivity and dominance, that the sexes preferentially deal in. Thus, we have the facts that women are better judges of negative affect cues than men (chapter 2) and may also use more frowns than men (chapter 5). The point, then, is that the sexes may consciously or unconsciously put their efforts into different modalities of expression, as well as having generally preferred messages to convey.

11 Summary, Comparisons, and Conclusions

We all know that men and women are different in many more ways than the purely biological. But those differences often seem elusive, indefinable. Children, when asked to describe the difference between men and women, point to obvious features of figure, dress, or hair style. But these are not the aspects of maleness and femaleness that matter in social relations. The aspects that matter include all the nonverbal behaviors and skills that guide our actions toward others and that reflect and maintain our sexual identities. These nonverbal sex differences are subtle and difficult to measure but are not totally elusive, as the research described in this book demonstrates.

Although this book describes many sex differences in nonverbal skills and behaviors, its very thoroughness reveals where our knowledge falls short. There are gaps in the documentary evidence, and the literature shows an extraordinary lack of direct evidence bearing on explanations for the sex differences. But despite these problems, the amount of empirical evidence available for evaluating nonverbal sex differences is as extensive as for any psychological sex differences yet reviewed systematically.

Because so many results have been presented, it is important to try to summarize the main ones. Such a summary is, of course, a simplified picture of nonverbal sex differences; many moderating factors were discussed in the preceding chapters. But such a summary is important for making comparisons with other psychological sex differences to be discussed shortly. Table 11.1 presents the results of all the major analyses of subject sex and target sex, whenever there were five or more studies for which effect sizes (correlation between sex and the behavior) were available. For most categories of results, the table breaks the results down by age. Unlike previous tables, the average effect sizes are presented for only those studies where they were reported or could be calculated using the procedures described in chapter 1. These effect sizes may be somewhat larger

TABLE 11.1. Average Sex Differences (*r*) for Nonverbal Skills and Behaviors

Variable	Age group	r[a]	Number of studies
Decoding skill	All ages	.21	64
Face recognition skill	Children and adolescents	.15	5
	Adults	.17	12
Expression skill [b]	All ages	.25	35
Facial expressiveness	Adults	.45	5
Social smiling	Children	− .02	5
	Adults	.30	15
Gaze	Infants	.20	8
	Children	.19	10
	Adults	.32	30
Receipt of gaze	Adults	.31	6
Distance of approach to others			
Naturalistic	Adults	− .27	17
Staged	Adults	− .06	8
Projective	Adults	− .07	11
Distance approached by others			
Naturalistic	Infants	− .44	5
	Adults	− .43	9
Staged	Adults	− .30	5
Projective	Adults	− .39	7
Body movement and position [b]			
Restlessness	Adults	− .34	6
Expansiveness	Adults	− .46	6
Involvement	Adults	.16	7
Expressiveness	Adults	.28	7
Self-consciousness	Adults	.22	5
Vocal behavior			
Speech errors	Adolescents and adults	− .33	6
Filled pauses	Adolescents and adults	− .51	6
Total speech [c]	Adults	− .05	12

[a] Positive correlations mean higher values on the named behavior by females.
[b] Studies within these categories are not independent.
[c] Pooled results of present review and that of Carli (1982).

than actual nonverbal sex differences are because smaller effect sizes may often have failed to reach statistical significance and not been reported. Though the results in table 11.1 may thus be slightly inflated, for comparative purposes any such bias is not a problem since the other average effect sizes to be discussed later were calculated on exactly the same basis.

Elsewhere in this book I have assessed the credibility of various nonverbal sex differences using tests of statistical significance. In many cases these *p*-values were extremely small and therefore highly convincing. Occasionally the evidence based on effect sizes and statistical significance were not consistent, usually due to sampling problems. For example, a clear preponderance of studies found men to talk more than women in dyads or groups, but the effect size of − .05 does not reflect this difference. Most of the time, however, a clear and consistent picture was obtained across indices of study outcome. Nevertheless, it should go without saying that the summary of effect sizes in table 11.1 is only one way of describing nonverbal sex differences, one that is emphasized here only because it is so well suited for comparisons with results from other areas of research.

Further, many other results that readers may find important are not presented in this table. This includes behaviors for which few effect sizes were available, often the case in infant studies. Other exclusions are same-sex versus opposite-sex behavior, omitted because this comparison is not frequently enough available for behaviors outside the nonverbal domain, and sex differences in touch, omitted for lack of comparable effect sizes.

As in previous tables, the effect size is the point biserial correlation (r) between sex, coded 0 for males and 1 for females, and each nonverbal behavior or skill. This index is standard in that it falls between − 1.00 and + 1.00, and its square represents the amount of variation accounted for in the dependent variable (nonverbal behavior or skill) by the independent variable, which is in this case sex. This index is subject to influence by several features of research design. One such feature is the reliability of the research instruments (tests, scales, or observations); less-reliable instruments produce smaller correlations. Another feature is the precision of data analysis. Efforts to reduce extraneous variation will usually produce larger correlations; this is often done by using homogenous groups of males and females or by controlling statistically for other measured traits in the groups. But to the extent that such efforts are employed to roughly the same degree across research topics, then the average effect sizes will still be comparable.

Table 11.1 shows that females are better at decoding nonverbal cues, at recognizing faces, and at expressing emotions via nonverbal communication than are males. Females also have more expressive faces, smile more (except, apparently, children), gaze more, receive more gaze (at least, adults), employ smaller approach distances to others when observed unobtrusively, and are approached closer by others. Women use body movements and positions that appear to be less restless, less expansive, more involved, more expressive, and more self-conscious than men do. Finally, they emit fewer speech errors and filled pauses. These relationships range in magnitude from "small" (r about .10) to "large" (r about .50; J. Cohen 1969).

The size of most of these nonverbal sex differences is moderate. For the largest difference, for filled pauses, sex accounts for a full 26 percent of the measured variation in that nonverbal behavior — an impressive amount considering that many other factors are also contributing. Most of the

TABLE 11.2. Average Sex Differences (*r*) from Existing Quantitative Summaries

Source	Variable	Age group	r[a]	Number of studies
Warr 1971	Attributes positive traits to stimulus people	Adults	.21[b]	6
Hattie 1979	Self-actualization	Adults	.08	6
R. Rosenthal & DePaulo 1979b	Self-monitoring	Adults	.11	10
Eagly & Carli 1981	Persuasability	Adolescents and adults	.08	33
	Conformity under group pressure	Adolescents and adults	.16	46
	Conformity in other situations	Adolescents and adults	.14	11
Hyde 1981	Verbal ability	11 years and up	.18	11
	Quantitative ability	11 years and up	−.23	7
	Visuospatial ability	11 years and up	−.21	8
	Field independence	14 years and up	−.24	14
Carli 1982	Socioemotional contribution in small groups	Adults	.28	9
	Task-oriented contribution in small groups	Adults	−.28	10
	Divides rewards equally	Adults	.05	17
	Divides rewards equitably	Adults	−.10	10
	Takes smaller rewards for self	Adults	.14	11
	Behaves cooperatively with same sex in prisoner's dilemma game (mixed-motive situation)	Adults	−.02	41
	Same as above but with opposite sex	Adults	−.14	6
Frieze et al. 1982	Attributes successful performance to:	Adolescents and adults		
	Ability		−.10	13
	Effort		.06	9
	Task		−.001	9
	Luck		.14	12
	Attributes unsuccessful performance to:	Adolescents and adults		
	Ability		−.11	12
	Effort		−.11	9
	Task		−.01	8
	Luck		.18	12
N. Eisenberg & Lennon 1983	Cries at sound of infants crying	Infants	.18	5
	Self-report of empathic response to pictures or stories	Preschool through 10 years	.08	12
Hyde (in press)	Self-report of empathy on questionnaires	Grade 1 through adult	.44	17
	Aggression	Children and young adolescents	−.27	50
		College and older	−.24	21

[a] Positive correlations mean higher values on the named behavior by females.
[b] Correlation calculated from data provided in Warr 1971.

144

relationships are smaller than that, however. But the more important question for present purposes is how they compare with sex differences for other psychological variables. Luckily, other quantitative summaries of sex differences have been performed.

The results of quantitative summaries that have included average effect sizes are given in table 11.2. For each of the topics shown in the table, the summarizing authors actually performed more detailed analyses, but only the overall sex differences are shown here, to simplify comparison. As with the nonverbal sex differences summarized in table 11.1, only studies with known effect sizes are included, and sex is coded so that positive correlations mean that females were higher on the variable in question, and negative correlations mean that males were higher.

Most results are in the direction one might expect, on the basis of everyday observation and stereotype. Women are more likely to see the good in hypothetical others and less likely to try to monitor their own social behavior according to a self-monitoring scale. They tend to be more conforming than men in experimental situations. They are more verbally skilled and less skilled quantitatively, visuospatially, and in ability to detach themselves cognitively from their surroundings or to disembed hidden figures (less field independent). Women make more socioemotional contributions in small groups and fewer task-related contributions; women tend to take smaller rewards for themselves in experiments; but women also tend to behave *less* cooperatively than men in certain structured game situations. Women are less likely than men to explain their own performance in terms of ability and more likely to explain it in terms of luck (though, interestingly, these tendencies do not apparently depend on whether the performance was successful or not). Females are more empathic as infants (defined by reflexive crying), and more empathic as adults on self-report scales. Finally, girls and women are less aggressive than men, based on such measures as self-report scales and direct observation.

How strong are sex differences for these behaviors compared to sex differences for nonverbal skills and behaviors? The answer is clear: sex differences are larger for the nonverbal variables. Many of the nonverbal sex differences in table 11.1 are of comparable magnitudes to the very largest of the sex differences shown in table 11.2. One can argue, of course, that only a few behaviors are represented in table 11.2 and that there are many other psychological variables that may show larger differences. But one should take note of the fact that the behaviors in table 11.2 were not randomly sampled by their reviewers. Rather, they are behaviors for which the reviewers must have had strong a priori expectations for *large* sex differences. It is therefore all the more interesting that the effects are smaller on the average than are nonverbal sex differences.

However, to address the selectivity of the variables shown in table 11.2, I performed my own search for sex differences in four journals beginning in 1975: *Journal of Personality and Social Psychology, Journal of Personality, Journal of Personality Assessment,* and *Sex Roles.* I chose these journals because of their high likelihood of reporting sex differences, and within each I examined every article over the designated time span. Though this search is clearly not exhaustive either temporally or in terms of publication sources, it is probably unbiased and provides at least a starting point for further comparisons.

Table 11.3 presents overall sex differences for all behaviors, either self-rated or observed, which met the following criteria: (1) the number of studies within a category was at least five; (2) age was high school or older; (3) the samples were clinically normal; and (4) effect size (r) was presented or could be calculated or estimated.

Table 11.3 indicates that women are, compared with men, less masculine and more feminine (as measured on independent masculinity and femininity scales), more liberal in their sex-role attitudes, more anxious and neurotic, less psychotic, more external in locus of control (they see external forces as more in control of their lives), emotionally closer to others, and more self-disclosing in conversation. Again, these sex differences fit with stereotypes as well as with prevailing opinion among psychologists. Yet, again, they are generally smaller than nonverbal sex differences. Even for self-rated masculinity and femininity, traits for which sex stereotypes held by the subjects themselves must surely contribute to the size of the differences, the differences are still smaller than for some nonverbal variables.

The differences between nonverbal and other sex differences are especially impressive in light of the fact that with only two exceptions (staged and projective measures of distance), all nonverbal measures were either unobtrusive or objective (as in a decoding test). In contrast, many of the behaviors in tables 11.2 and 11.3 were measured totally or partially by self-report, a methodology that should, other things being equal, increase sex differences due to better reliability and the inflating contribution of sex stereotypes.

On the other hand, nonverbal studies and studies of other psychological variables differ in another way that could produce an opposite bias, one that would artifactually inflate some of the nonverbal sex differences. This is observer bias, resulting from the fact that observers are inevitably aware of the sexes of the people whose behavior they are describing. For decoding and encoding skill and face-recognition skill there is almost no possibility of such bias, since accuracy is calculated by scoring right and wrong answers or with reference to the ease with which others could judge a person's expressions. A person's scores on these skills, in other words, do

TABLE 11.3. Average Sex Differences (r) from Four Journals since 1975

Variable	r [a]	Number of studies [b]
Grade point average	.02	5
Self-esteem	−.06	10
Masculinity	−.25	12
Femininity	.37	12
Liberal sex-role attitudes	.25	6
Fear of success	.03	11
Achievement motivation and values	−.05	13
Social poise, dominance, and assertiveness	−.06	14
Anxiety, including social anxiety	.16	14
Loneliness	−.08	6
Depression	.08	5
Neuroticism	.16	14
Psychoticism	−.14	8
External locus of control	.12	16
Extraversion	.02	17
Liking and emotional closeness to others	.22	10
Self-disclosure	.18	10

[a] Positive correlations mean higher values on the named behavior by women.
[b] All results are for adolescents and older.

not rest upon the scorer's judgments. For most other behaviors, however, a person's score depends directly on observers' descriptions of their behavior. Judgments of the frequency and duration of various behaviors, the interpersonal distance established between two people, and the like, could possibly be distorted by sex stereotypes. Judges' ratings of emotional qualities in the voice have already been mentioned as being particularly vulnerable to stereotype bias, due to the difficulty of describing the voice and the global nature of the ratings used. The possibility of bias is probably less when observers make less-inferential judgments such as seconds, inches, or the number of times a behavior occurs. Coders making such measurements are generally trained to achieve good reliability and are undoubtedly conscientious in their tasks. Nevertheless bias could influence their coding.

No definitive assessment of the possible impact of such bias can be made at present. But it is worth noting that those sex differences that are free of possible bias due to methodology are not consistently smaller than those that are vulnerable; I refer to decoding and encoding skill, face-recognition skill, and some of the target-sex results for voice quality, described in chapter 10, where raters judging the voices did not know the sex of the person being addressed.

In comparing the nonverbal sex differences with others, then, we must speculate about two possible biases, first that the nonverbal differences are exaggerated due to the infusion of stereotype into observers' descriptions, and second that some of the other differences are exaggerated due to subjects' infusion of stereotype into their own self-ratings. In addition there is the possibility that observers or subjects themselves could respond to stereotype knowledge by bending over backwards *not* to be biased, in which case results would show sex differences that are artifactually small. Important future research could focus on these issues. Unfortunately, it ranges from difficult to impossible to blind observers and subjects to the factor of sex. An alternate strategy, though not an ideal one, would be to experimentally manipulate the stereotypic expectations of observers and subjects and measure the effect upon sex-difference results.

The behaviors included in tables 11.2 and 11.3 do not exhaust the universe of variables that might show sex differences. Other psychological variables for which sex differences are probably large include sex-typed activities and interests: toy and game preferences in children, activity preferences and skills in adolescent and older groups, and occupational choices. And there are domains, such as cognitive psychology, that are poorly represented in the list of behaviors considered here. In summary, then, it can be said that although nonverbal sex differences are not large in absolute magnitude, they are as large or larger than those found for most of the psychological variables that have been summarized so far.

Interestingly, most of the larger sex differences in tables 11.2 and 11.3 involve or imply face-to-face behaviors, such as aggression, empathy, socioemotional contributions in groups, "femininity" (which, for the scales used, mainly means positive orientation toward others), and emotional closeness to others. Thus, behaviors that are social but not explicitly nonverbal show enhanced sex differences which, like the nonverbal behaviors reviewed here, portray women as having a positive and involved psychological orientation toward others.

The question of why nonverbal sex differences take the form that they do is not easily answered. Throughout, I have emphasized that the research does not warrant firm conclusions about the motives, intentions, or other factors that underly these differences. Though many explanations have been discussed, the oppression hypothesis has received particular attention. This hypothesis has proved intriguing to many writers and students of nonverbal sex differences, no doubt because of its obvious social and political significance. But it has also been subject to little critical scrutiny.

The main distinction I have imposed in analyzing the oppression hypothesis is between a direct and an indirect impact of differences in social power and status between women and men on their nonverbal behaviors and skills, and, analogously, on how men and women are treated nonverbally. If the connection is direct, then the degree of oppression experienced by a woman would determine the extent to which she engaged in certain nonverbal behaviors or developed certain nonverbal skills. She would be coping with her oppression by adjusting her nonverbal repertoire to minimize oppression's ill effects. To give an extreme example, she would smile appeasingly to avert physical abuse.

A direct role for oppression would be amenable to empirical assessment, though the task would by no means be easy. Basically, some operational definition of oppression would have to be measured in a group of individuals and statistical analyses performed to see if controlling for that variable can make a given nonverbal sex difference substantially smaller. If it did, oppression would be implicated as a cause, and further research could help rule out rival causal factors. And if the sex difference were unaffected after repeated efforts of this sort, one would be in a reasonably strong position to argue that oppression as thus defined is not an explanatory factor, since differences among individuals in that factor are unrelated to the sex difference one seeks to explain.

An indirect role for oppression is much harder to test. If women's historical oppression led to certain role expectations — smiling, for example — those expectations could perpetuate such a nonverbal sex difference via same-sex modeling and reinforcement, even if oppression played no role in the lives of individual women, indeed even if inequities between the sexes were to vanish from society. In this situation, oppression would be a causal factor but such a remote one that it would be hard to envision any empirical method that could be marshalled to demonstrate it. If the connection is remote, and other factors have a more immediate impact on nonverbal sex differences than does social inequality, then one might choose to emphasize the positive side of women's social behavior as it currently exists rather than the negative conditions under which it might have originated. In sum, how alarmed we are at contemplating a role of women's oppression in the development of their nonverbal traits and the nonverbal treatment they receive must depend on how directly oppression is affecting nonverbal behavior and how negative are the actual consequences of women's nonverbal traits.

Efforts to evaluate the oppression hypothesis, in any form, are frustrated by the limited quantity of theoretically relevant research. In addition, available empirical methods may be inadequate, not only to detect a very indirect causal path, as just mentioned, but also to detect a direct relationship that actually exists. For example, women's own experience may lead them to believe that when men touch women it is a reflection of status differences. This could, of course, be a wrong inference if the frequency of status-motivated or status-reflecting touch is distorted in their recollections, or if they interpret touch in a way that it was never intended. But a woman's conviction that power is a major factor in touch patterns *could* be correct even though the best efforts of social science cannot validate it. Touch is, after all, extremely difficult to study. It is rare in public, and its purposes may be opaque to observers using accepted, standard procedures but quite clear to the participants themselves. "Objective" research methods may therefore be too insensitive at the present to provide appropriate support for the oppression hypothesis of sex differences.

Nevertheless, because of the apparently strong a priori credibility of the hypothesis, it is worthwhile to repeat some of the problems with it that have emerged in previous chapters. How serious these problems are considered will undoubtedly depend on how committed to the hypothesis a reader already is.

A small number of tests of a more or less direct role for oppression in skill in decoding nonverbal cues have been done in which oppression was defined as a woman's endorsing traditional values regarding women's role in society. This research, though far from conclusive, gave no overall support to the idea that women's decoding advantage is due to their disadvantaged social position. Related evidence regarding racial differences in decoding skills is also negative. Women have been compared to blacks in some discussions of group differences in nonverbal sensitivity, on the grounds that both groups are oppressed and should therefore show superior decoding ability. However, the most recent comprehensive review does not find blacks to be better nonverbal decoders than whites (Halberstadt, in press).

In another important case, evidence that would support the oppression argument is not forthcoming: this is the assumed linear relationship between status and interpersonal distance. Again, there is not much research. But it would seem that instead of a linear relationship whereby the largest distances of approach are to high-status others and the closest to low-status others, there seems to be a curvilinear relationship, such that people approach equals more closely than they approach either higher or lower status others. Thus one is on weak grounds to argue that women are approached closely because of their lower status. Research on stigma also predicts negatively: stigmatized individuals are given more, not less, interpersonal space.

Actual sex differences have not consistently shown patterns that suggest a role for oppression. Asymmetry in touch between men and women has not been definitively demonstrated. Women's preference to approach others more closely than men do can even be interpreted as *assertive* behavior; an oppressed or intimidated person might linger on the fringes of socially appropriate distance rather than approaching closely. And men and women's relative amounts of looking while speaking and looking while listening fit only weakly what would be expected on the basis of research relating status to these gaze patterns.

On two dialogic variables, quantity of speech and interruptions, men exceed women, and this is indeed easily attributable to status differences between the sexes. (The effect-size data for quantity of speech, shown in table 11.1 does not suggest this, but the overall trends discussed in chapter 10 do.) But these nonverbal differences could also stem from differences in social skill. Again, one could argue that only the oppressed need social skills, but this has not been demonstrated.

A final interesting pattern of results is also pertinent to our understanding of nonverbal sex differences. This pattern emerged repeatedly in separate analyses of the sex of subject and of the sex of the target, or recipient, of nonverbal behavior. It is the double main-effects pattern, whereby members of one sex receive more of the same kinds of nonverbal communications that they engage in. As examples, women gaze more and are gazed at more; women approach others closer and are approached closer. This pattern translates into maximal differences between male-male and female-female dyads and minimal differences between males' behavior toward females and females' behavior toward males. If one visualizes a 2 × 2 matrix in which the rows are male versus female recipient and the columns are male versus female subject, one pair of diagonal values will be very different (male-male and female-female) while the other pair is not very different at all (the two opposite-sex cells). Nonverbal sex differences are, therefore, most pronounced when one is with one's own sex. One way to interpret this is that, with the opposite sex, people moderate their behavior so that it approaches the other sex's norms. Thus, on the average, men gaze (for example) more at women than at other men, while women gaze less at men than at other women.

Such an interpretation leads us to examine the norms that may be controlling nonverbal behavior in same-sex and opposite-sex interaction. The nonverbal flexibility of mixed-sex dyads and the more extreme sex-typed behavior of same-sex dyads suggest that norms and expectations are stricter in same-sex dyads. In other words, deviation from stereotypically sex-appropriate behavior may be most noticeable and most unacceptable when it is with one's own sex.

This could mean, contrary to the assumptions inherent in many discussions of sex roles, that prototypically "feminine" behavior in women is displayed more with other women than with men. Though women still play their socioemotional role as a general rule, it is not at all clear that they exaggerate it around men, as the role complementarity concepts of Parsons and Bales (1955), for example, would suggest. Consistent with the present argument, women have in fact been found to be more socioemotional with other women than with men (Piliavin and Martin 1978), and to be less cooperative in opposite-sex than in same-sex dyads, compared to men (Carli 1982).

Some of my own previous research further supports the relative strength of same-sex norms. In one study, women's vocal communications to other women on television shows were rated as less dominant, condescending, and businesslike than were their vocal communications to men (Hall and Braunwald 1981). And men's vocal communications were most dominant to other men, not to women. In another study, women with traditional (nonfeminist) sex-role attitudes were more vocally dominant when teaching health facts to men than when teaching them to women (Hall, Braunwald, and Mroz 1982). Traditional women also made the poorest impression as teachers when interacting with other women. In interpreting these findings, we suggested that social norms require women to behave affiliatively and nonassertively with one another, and that in traditional women these norms are so compelling that they actually conflict with the role of an effective teacher.

It should perhaps come as no surprise if same-sex norms are powerful governors of behavior. Segregation by sex, whether by choice, law, or tradition, is common throughout our lives. Among nonhuman primates, same-sex clusters are more prevalent than opposite-sex ones (for example, Rosenblum, Coe, and Bromley 1975). Human children prefer same-sex dyads and groups in a variety of cultures (for example, B. B. Whiting and Whiting 1975). Observational studies among U.S. children and adults repeatedly show the same thing (see chapter 8). Segregation and sex-typing in games, hobbies, sports, interests, and occupations inevitably mean that one will have more in common with, and spend more time with, one's own sex. Small wonder if rules for social intercourse within one's sexual group are well established. Why those rules should be so different for the sexes is still a question. It is possible that the common, albeit simplistic, distinction between men's activities of engaging in economic activity, fighting, exploring, and competing for social and political rank versus women's activities of child rearing and domestic responsibility may have shaped the particular form that these same-sex norms take. But even if true, such a statement of course just pushes back one step the question of where those sex differences come from, and that is a question that far exceeds the scope of this book.

If same-sex norms are indeed strong forces behind social behaviors, then the oppression hypothesis, which would seem to stress asymmetries in the behaviors permitted each sex in interaction with the other and the ways in which such norms become general sex differences, is further challenged, at least insofar as oppression plays a direct role in face-to-face relations. If women and men actually experience more behavioral latitude when together than when separate, then two presumable tenets of the oppression hypothesis — men's purported desire to dominate women and women's purported needs to show they are harmless — become less plausible as explanatory factors.

Though I have argued that more evidence is needed before any explanation of nonverbal sex differences is fully satisfactory, there are important realities to confront even in the absence of theoretical certainty. Chief among these is the possibility that female nonverbal communication feeds negative stereotypes. Women's nonverbal communication could occasionally give the impression that they are too pliable, too eager to please, and not sufficiently serious, all of which I unhesitatingly assert are false. How do we deal with such destructive impressions?

One response, often present or implied in writings on nonverbal sex differences, is to say that women should change their nonverbal style so as to appear more affectively distant and insensitive. This advice has questionable merits. Though there may be short-term benefits of a woman's trying to be more like a prototypical man in terms of nonverbal behavior, what would be sacrificed is the deeper value to self and society of a behavioral style that is adaptive, socially wise, and likely to facilitate positive interaction, understanding, and trust. And by adaptive, I do not mean it in the sense of a woman's making the best out of her degraded social situation. Research shows that nonverbal skills are related to skills in teaching and clinical psychology, to popularity, to adjustment, and even to how intelligent one seems to others (R. Rosenthal et al. 1979; Halberstadt and Hall 1980). Women's experience of greater emotional closeness to others, documented earlier, surely stems partly from their nonverbal behaviors and skills. Women's nonverbal repertoire should therefore not be glibly attacked as an impediment to their personal adjustment and their social standing.

More deserving of attack are the flawed reasoning and questionable values that lie behind negative attributions of women's nonverbal behavior. The problem with negative interpretations is not just their inaccuracy, but also the fact that in a sexist society a woman's behavior is vulnerable to negative interpretation no matter what it is. I would rather see us work to change overall attitudes toward women and develop a better understanding of healthy interpersonal behavior than exhort women to change their expressive style in response to sexist judgments. That such advice is well meaning and often comes from profeminist quarters makes it no less wrong. I would argue that to call women "victims of years of conditioning" in their face-to-face behavior (Eakins and Eakins 1978) is an affront, not an encouragement, to women.

Writers on nonverbal behavior and many other topics often condemn the perpetuation of myths about women. Yet whenever it is assumed that women's nonverbal behavior is undesirable, yet another myth is perpetuated: that male behavior is "normal" and that it is women's behavior that is deviant and in need of explanation. But one can as easily view women's traits as normal and men's traits as needing remediation. In this sense, it is men who are victims of years of conditioning, and they who have the most to gain from a thorough understanding of nonverbal sex differences and of the meanings and functions of nonverbal communication.

Appendix:
Empirical Studies Reviewed

    Listed are the sources that contributed to the quantitative summaries of documentary sex differences described throughout this book. Whenever a reader finds descriptions or summaries of studies that are not referenced by author and year, the relevant references appear in the list below under the appropriate topic heading. Sources for theoretical and methodological discussions and sources of additional data not included in the quantitative summaries are identified by author and year in the text and therefore are not included in the list below, unless they also contributed to the quantitative summaries.

DECODING OF NONVERBAL CUES

Earlier Group of Studies Reviewed

    Allport 1924; Beldoch 1964; Buck 1976; Buck, Miller, & Caul 1974; Buzby 1924; Carmichael, Roberts, & Wessell 1937; J. C. Coleman 1949; Dickey & Knower 1941; Dimitrovsky 1964; Dusenbury & Knower 1938, 1939; Ekman & Friesen 1971; Fay & Middleton 1940a; Fernberger 1927; Fields 1953; Frijda 1953; Gates 1923; Gitter, Black, & Mostofsky 1972a, 1972b; Gitter, Kozel, & Mostofsky 1972; Gitter, Mostofsky, & Quincy 1971; Guilford 1929; Hunt 1928; Izard 1971; Jenness 1932; Kanner 1931; Kellogg & Eagleson 1931; N. Levy & Schlosberg 1960; P. K. Levy 1964; F. A. Moss 1929; Pfaff 1954; R. Rosenthal et al. 1979; Staffieri & Bassett 1970; Sweeney & Cottle 1976; Vinacke 1949; Vinacke & Fong 1955; Weisgerber 1956; Zaidel & Mehrabian 1969; Zuckerman et al. 1976; Zuckerman et al. 1975; Zuckerman & Przewuzman 1979.

Later Group of Studies Reviewed

    Abramovitch 1977; Abramovitch & Daly 1978, 1979; D. Archer & Akert 1977; Bassili 1979; Britton & Britton 1969; Buck et al. 1980; Camras 1980; Carlson & Levy 1973; Cunningham 1977; P. Eisenberg & Reichline 1939; Fay & Middleton 1939, 1940b, 1940c, 1941a; M. Feldman & Thayer 1980; Foley 1935; Fujita, Harper, & Wiens 1980; Gallagher & Shuntich 1981; Gitter, Mostofsky, & Guichard 1972; Gladding 1978; Isenhart 1980; H. G. Johnson, Ekman, & Friesen 1975; Kirouac &

Doré 1983; Kratochwill & Goldman 1973; Leathers & Emigh 1980; Lyons & Goldman 1966; Michael & Willis 1968, 1969; Noller 1980a, 1981; Post & Hethering-ton 1974; Rosenfeld, Shea, & Greenbaum 1979; Sabatelli, Dreyer, & Buck 1979; Samuels 1939; Scott 1974; Sweeney, Cottle, & Kobayashi 1980; Van Rooijen 1973; Wasz-Höckert et al. 1964; Weisgerber 1957; Westbrook 1974; Zuckerman, Larrance et al. 1979.

FACE RECOGNITION

Blaney & Winograd 1978; Brigham & Barkowitz 1978; Carey, Diamond, & Woods 1980; Chance, Goldstein, & McBride 1975; Chance, Turner, & Goldstein 1982; Cornell 1974; J. F. Cross, Cross, & Daly 1971; Ellis, Shepherd, & Bruce 1973; Fagan 1972, 1973, 1974, 1976, 1977; Feinman & Entwisle 1976; Flin 1980; Going & Read 1974; Goldstein & Chance 1964, 1970; Howells 1938; Laughery, Alexander, & Lane 1971; McKelvie 1978, 1981; Nowicki, Winograd, & Millard 1979; Shepherd, Deregowski, & Ellis 1974; Shepherd & Ellis 1973; Yarmey 1974, 1979; Yin 1969; A. W. Young & Ellis 1976; Young-Browne, Rosenfeld, & Horowitz 1977.

EXPRESSION ACCURACY

Earlier Group of Studies Reviewed

Buck 1975, 1977; Buck, Miller, & Caul 1974; J. C. Coleman 1949; Dickey & Knower 1941; Dimitrovsky 1964; Drag & Shaw 1967; Dusenbury & Knower 1938, 1939; Fay & Middleton 1941b; Gitter, Black, & Mostofsky 1972a, 1972b; Hall et al. 1977 (unpublished); Levitt 1964; P. K. Levy 1964; Michael & Willis 1968; R. Rosen-thal et al. 1979; D. F. Thompson & Meltzer 1964; Zaidel & Mehrabian 1969; Zuckerman et al. 1976; Zuckerman et al. 1975; Zuckerman & Przewuzman 1979.

Later Group of Studies Reviewed

Abramovitch & Daly 1979; Buck et al. 1980; Cunningham 1977; Friedman, DiMatteo, & Taranta 1980; Fujita, Harper, & Wiens 1980; Gallagher & Shuntich 1981; Hamilton 1973; Knower 1941; Michael & Willis 1969; Noller 1980a; Sabatelli, Dreyer, & Buck 1979; Zuckerman et al. 1982; Zuckerman, Larrance et al. 1979.

GENERAL FACIAL EXPRESSIVENESS

Bem, Martyna, & Watson 1976; Buck, Baron, & Barrette 1982; Buck et al. 1980; Buck, Miller, & Caul 1974; Cherulnik 1979; M. Davis & Weitz 1981; Mehrabian & Williams 1969.

POSITIVE FACIAL EXPRESSION

Ames 1949; J. Archer & Westeman 1981; Bates 1976; Beckwith et al. 1976; Beier & Sternberg 1977; Blehar, Lieberman, & Ainsworth 1977; Bond & Shiraishi 1974; Brackett 1933; Bretherton, Stolberg, & Kreye 1981; Brodzinsky 1977; Brodzinsky, Barnet, & Aiello 1981; J. Brooks & Lewis 1976; Brooks-Gunn & Lewis 1981; Campos et al. 1975; Chaiken 1979; Chaikin & Derlega 1978; Chaikin, Sigler, &

Derlega 1974; Challman 1932; Chapman 1973a, 1973b, 1974, 1975; Chapman & Chapman 1974; Crawley et al. 1978; Cupchik & Leventhal 1974; M. Davis & Weitz 1981; Ding & Jersild 1932; Eckerman & Rheingold 1974; Fein 1975; J. F. Feldman, Brody, & Miller 1980; Foot, Chapman, & Smith 1977; Foot, Smith, & Chapman 1979; Frances 1979; Fuller & Sheehy-Skeffington 1974; Gerber & Routh 1975; Goodenough 1930; Gottfried & Seay 1974; Graves 1937; Haas 1981; Harter 1974; Harter, Shultz, & Blum 1971.

Ickes & Barnes 1978; Ickes, Schermer, & Steeno 1979; Jorgenson 1978; Justin 1932; Kagan et al. 1966; Korner 1969; LaFrance & Carmen 1980; Lamb 1976, 1977a, 1978a, 1978b; Langlois, Gottfried, & Seay 1973; Lester et al. 1974; H. Leventhal & Cupchik 1975; H. Leventhal & Mace 1970; Lewis 1969, 1972; Lewis & Kreitzberg 1979; Lochman & Allen 1981; B. Lott 1978; Mackey 1976; McClintock & Hunt 1975; McGhee 1974, 1976; Mehrabian 1971a, 1971b; Mehrabian & Williams 1969; Moskowitz, Schwarz, & Corsini 1977; H. A. Moss 1967; F. A. Pedersen & Bell 1970; Pien & Rothbart 1976; Pilkonis 1977b; Rosenfeld 1966; R. Rosenthal 1976; Sarason & Winkel 1966; Shultz & Horibe 1974; Skarin 1977; Stern & Bender 1974; Tauber 1979; M. C. Taylor 1979; Tidd & Lockard 1978; Weinraub & Putney 1978; Zelazo 1971; Zigler, Levine, & Gould 1966.

NEGATIVE FACIAL EXPRESSION

Bates 1976; Campos et al. 1975; Chaikin & Derlega 1978; J. F. Feldman, Brody, & Miller 1980; Ickes & Barnes 1978; Langlois, Gottfried, & Seay 1973; Lochman & Allen 1981; Noller 1982; S. Phillips, King, & Dubois 1978; Seham & Boardman 1934; Skarin 1977; Stern & Bender 1974; Tauber 1979; Weinraub & Putney 1978; D. G. Williams 1973.

GAZE

Achenbach & Weisz 1975; Aiello 1972, 1977a, 1977b; Anderson & Willis 1976; Argyle & Dean 1965; Argyle & Ingham 1972; Argyle et al. 1973; Ashear & Snortum 1971; Ban & Lewis 1974; Bates 1976; Baum & Greenberg 1975; Beach & Sokoloff 1974; Beckwith et al. 1976; Beier & Sternberg 1977; Bretherton 1978; Bretherton, Stolberg, & Kreye 1981; J. Brooks & Lewis 1974, 1976; Campos et al. 1975; Cary 1978, 1979; Chaiken 1979; Chaikin & Derlega 1978; Chapman 1974, 1975; Chapman & Chapman 1974; Cherulnik 1979; Cherulnik et al. 1978; Coates, Anderson, & Hartup 1972; L. J. Cohen & Campos 1974; Coutts & Schneider 1975; Crawley et al. 1978; Dabbs et al. 1980; Ellyson, Dovidio, & Fehr 1981; Exline 1963; Exline, Ellyson, & Long 1975; Exline, Gray, & Schuette 1965; Exline & Winters 1965.

S. S. Feldman & Ingham 1975; Field 1977; Finley & Layne 1971; Foddy 1978; Foot, Chapman, & Smith 1977; Foot, Smith, & Chapman 1979; Frances 1979; Fromme & Beam 1974; Galassi, Galassi, & Litz 1974; Goldberg & Lewis 1969; Goldman et al. 1977; Griffitt, May, & Veitch 1974; Gunnar & Donahue 1980; Hammen & Peplau 1978; Harris 1968; Hittelman & Dickes 1979; Ickes & Barnes 1977, 1978; Ickes, Schermer, & Steeno 1979; Kendon 1967; Kendon & Cook 1969; Kendrick & Dunn 1980; Kleinke, Desautels, & Knapp 1977; LaFrance & Carmen 1980; LaFrance & Mayo 1976; Lamb 1976, 1977a, 1978a, 1978b; Lasky & Klein 1979; Lester et al. 1974; Leung & Rheingold 1981; Levine & Sutton-Smith 1973;

Lewis 1972; Lewis & Kreitzberg 1979; Lewis & Weinraub 1974; Libby 1970; Libby & Yaklevich 1973; Ling & Ling 1974.

Maccoby & Feldman 1972; Maccoby & Jacklin 1973; McCall 1974; McCauley, Coleman, & DeFusco 1978; McClintock & Hunt 1975; McDowell 1972; Mehrabian 1971a, 1971b; Messer & Lewis 1972; Moskowitz, Schwarz, & Corsini 1977; H. A. Moss 1967; Muirhead & Goldman 1979; Nevill 1974; Noller 1980b; M. L. Patterson 1973, 1977; F. A. Pedersen & Bell 1970; Pilkonis 1977b; Robson et al. 1969; R. Rosenthal 1976; H. S. Ross & Goldman 1977; M. Ross et al. 1973; Rubin 1970; Ruble 1975; Ruble & Nakamura 1972, 1973; Russo 1975; Rutter, Morley, & Graham 1972; Sarason & Winkel 1966; Scheman & Lockard 1979; F. W. Schneider, Coutts, & Garrett 1977; Schwarz 1972; Skarin 1977; Slane et al. 1980; Spelke et al. 1973; Strongman & Champness 1968; Tauber 1979; Weinraub & Frankel 1977; Weinraub & Putney 1978; Wittig & Skolnick 1978.

DISTANCE

Naturalistic

Adler & Iverson 1974; Aiello & Aiello 1974; Aiello & Jones 1971; Allgeier & Byrne 1973; Ban & Lewis 1974; Barrios et al. 1976; Barrios & Giesen 1977; Batchelor & Goethals 1972; Baxter 1970; Beach & Sokoloff 1974; Brady & Walker 1978; Bretherton, Stolberg, & Kreye 1981; J. Brooks & Lewis 1974; Coates, Anderson, & Hartup 1972; L. J. Cohen & Campos 1974; Dabbs & Stokes 1975; DeJulio & Duffy 1977; Eberts & Lepper 1975; Fein 1975; S. S. Feldman & Ingham 1975; Finley & Layne 1971; Giesen & McClaren 1976; Gifford & Price 1979; Goldberg & Lewis 1969; Hammen & Peplau 1978; Hendrick, Giesen, & Coy 1974; Heshka & Nelson 1972; Ickes & Barnes 1977, 1978; Ickes, Schermer, & Steeno 1979; S. E. Jones 1971; S. E. Jones & Aiello 1973; Knowles 1980; Lamb 1976, 1977a, 1978a, 1978b; Langer et al. 1976; Langlois, Gottfried, & Seay 1973; Latta 1978; Lester et al. 1974; Lewis & Weinraub 1974; Lomranz et al. 1975.

Maccoby & Feldman 1972; Maccoby & Jacklin 1973; Mehrabian 1971a, 1971b; Mehrabian & Diamond 1971; Melson 1977; Moskowitz, Schwarz, & Corsini 1977; Nesbitt & Steven 1974; Noesjirwan 1977; Norum, Russo, & Sommer 1967; Pagán & Aiello 1982; A. H. Patterson & Boles 1974; M. L. Patterson 1973, 1977; Pellegrini & Empey 1970; Powell & Dabbs 1976; Sarafino & Helmuth 1981; Schwarzwald et al. 1977; Sechrest, Flores, & Arellano 1968; Serbin et al. 1973; Severy, Forsyth, & Wagner 1979; Shuter 1976, 1979; Slane et al. 1980; Smetana, Bridgeman, & Bridgeman 1978; H. W. Smith 1981; Spelke et al. 1973; Sussman & Rosenfeld 1982; D. R. Thomas 1973; Tolor & LeBlanc 1974; Tracy, Lamb, & Ainsworth 1976; Van Lieshout 1975; Weinraub & Frankel 1977; M. J. White 1975; Willis 1966; Willis, Carlson, & Reeves 1979; Wittig & Skolnick 1978; Yando, Zigler, & Gates 1971.

Staged

Ashton & Shaw 1980; Bailey, Hartnett, & Gibson 1972; Bailey, Hartnett, & Glover 1973; Bauer 1973; Carducci & Webber 1979; Cozby 1973; Dosey & Meisels 1969; Edney & Jordan-Edney 1974; Edney, Walker, & Jordan 1976; Fromme & Beam 1974; Hartnett, Bailey, & Gibson 1970; Hartnett, Bailey, & Hartley 1974; Hendricks & Bootzin 1976; G. Leventhal, Matturro, & Schanerman 1978;

G. Leventhal, Schanerman, & Matturro 1978; C. Loo & Kennelly 1979; Meisels & Dosey 1971; D. M. Pedersen & Heaston 1972; Price & Dabbs 1974; Severy, Forsyth, & Wagner 1979; H. W. Smith 1981; Stern & Bender 1974; Stratton, Tekippe, & Flick 1973; Tennis & Dabbs 1975; Tolor & LeBlanc 1974; Wasserman & Stern 1978.

Projective

Adler & Iverson 1975; Ashton & Shaw 1980; Bass & Weinstein 1971; Cooley & Seeman 1979; Dies & Greenberg 1976; Dosey & Meisels 1969; Duke & Nowicki 1972; Edwards 1977, 1980; Engebretson & Fullmer 1970; Gifford 1982; Gifford & Price 1979; Guardo 1969, 1976; M. J. Horowitz, Duff, & Stratton 1964; Ihara 1978; Knowles 1980; Leginski & Izzett 1976; Lerner 1973; Lerner, Iwawaki, & Chihara 1976; Lerner, Karabenick, & Meisels 1975; Lerner, Venning, & Knapp 1975; G. Leventhal, Matturro, & Schanerman 1978; Little 1968; Melson 1976, 1977; Naus & Eckenrode 1974; Nowicki & Duke 1972; D. M. Pedersen 1973, 1977; D. M. Pedersen & Heaston 1972; Petri et al. 1974; J. R. Phillips 1979; Sanders 1976; Severy, Forsyth, & Wagner 1979; Tennis & Dabbs 1975; Tolor 1975; Tolor & Orange 1969; Veitch, Getsinger, & Arkkelin 1976.

DIRECTNESS OF ORIENTATION

Angle of Orientation

Aiello & Aiello 1974; Aiello & Jones 1971; Beach & Sokoloff 1974; Ickes & Barnes 1977, 1978; Ickes, Schermer, & Steeno 1979; S. E. Jones 1971; S. E. Jones & Aiello 1973; Mehrabian 1971a; Pagán & Aiello 1982; M. L. Patterson 1973, 1977; Pellegrini & Empey 1970; Shuter 1976, 1979; Stern & Bender 1974; Wasserman & Stern 1978.

Adjacent Versus Across

Byrne, Baskett, & Hodges 1971; Fisher & Byrne 1975; Krail & Leventhal 1976; G. Leventhal, Lipshultz, & Chiodo 1978; Mahoney 1974; Norum, Russo, & Sommer 1967; M. L. Patterson, Mullens, & Romano 1971; Polit & LaFrance 1977; Tyler, Waag, & George 1972.

TOUCH

Ban & Lewis 1974; Beier & Sternberg 1977; Berkowitz 1971; Bretherton, Stolberg, & Kreye 1981; Coates, Anderson, & Hartup 1972; L. J. Cohen & Campos 1974; Eckerman, Whatley, & Kutz 1975; Fein 1975; Finley & Layne 1971; Foot, Chapman, & Smith 1977; Ford & Graves 1977; Goldberg & Lewis 1969; Goldman et al. 1977; Gottfried & Seay 1974; Greenbaum & Rosenfeld 1980; Henley 1973; Heslin & Boss 1980; Juni & Brannon 1981; Lamb 1977a, 1977b, 1978a, 1978b; Langlois, Gottfried, & Seay 1973; Lewis & Kreitzberg 1979; Lewis & Weinraub 1974; Lochman & Allen 1981; B. Lott 1978; Maccoby & Jacklin 1973; Maines 1977; Major & Williams 1980; McCall 1974; Messer & Lewis 1972; Noller 1980b; Perdue & Connor 1978; Rheingold & Samuels 1969; Rinck, Willis, & Dean 1980; Savitsky & Watson 1975; Shuter 1976, 1979; D. E. Smith, Willis, & Gier 1980; Spelke et al.

1973; Tracy, Lamb, & Ainsworth 1976; Weinraub & Frankel 1977; B. B. Whiting & Whiting 1975; S. J. Williams & Willis 1978; Willis & Hofmann 1975; Willis, Reeves, & Buchanan 1976; Willis, Rinck, & Dean 1978.

MOVEMENT AND POSITION

Bates 1976; Beier & Sternberg 1977; Bem, Martyna, & Watson 1976; Bond & Shiraishi 1974; Chaikin & Derlega 1978; Chaikin, Sigler, & Derlega 1974; M. Davis & Weitz 1981; DiPietro 1981; Frances 1979; Hanaway & Burghardt 1976; Ickes, Schermer, & Steeno 1979; D. A. Jenni & Jenni 1976; M. A. Jenni 1976; Kendon & Ferber 1973; Koch 1935; Krout 1954; Lochman & Allen 1981; McClintock & Hunt 1975; Mehrabian 1971a; Mehrabian & Williams 1969; M. L. Patterson 1977; Poling 1978; Rekers, Amaro-Plotkin, & Low 1977; Rekers & Mead 1979; Rekers & Rudy 1978; Rekers, Sanders, & Strauss 1981; Rosenfeld 1966; R. Rosenthal 1976; Sarason & Winkel 1966; Scheman, Lockard, & Mehler 1978; S. M. Schneider & Kintz 1977; Seham & Boardman 1934; Spottswood & Burghardt 1976; Stern & Bender 1974; Tauber 1979; M. C. Taylor 1979; D. G. Williams 1973; F. M. Young 1947.

VOICE

Speech Disturbances

Brady & Walker 1978; Brotherton & Penman 1977; Chaiken 1979; S. Feldstein, Brenner, & Jaffe 1963; Frances 1979; L. M. Horowitz et al. 1977; LaFrance & Carmen 1980; Lalljee & Cook 1973; Levin & Silverman 1965; Mehrabian 1971a; Rosenfeld 1966; Rutter & Stephenson 1977; Sarason & Winkel 1966; M. C. Taylor 1979; Yairi 1981.

Frequency and Loudness

R. O. Coleman 1976; Duffy 1970; Ford, Cramer, & Owens 1977; Lass et al. 1976; Levin & Hunter 1982; Loveday 1981; Markel, Prebor, & Brandt 1972; Mehrabian 1971b; Murry, Amundson, & Hollien 1977; Weinberg & Bennett 1971; Zuckerman, DeFrank, et al. 1979.

Global Ratings

Bates 1976; Bugental, Henker, & Whalen 1976; Chaiken 1979; Edelsky 1979; Hall & Braunwald 1981; Hall, Braunwald, & Mroz 1982; Mehrabian 1971b; Sachs 1975; Zuckerman, DeFrank, et al. 1979.

Speech Quality

Argyle, Lalljee, & Cook 1968; Aries 1976; Beier & Sternberg 1977; Brotherton & Penman 1977; Brownell & Smith 1973; Chaiken 1979; Cherulnik 1979; Cherulnik et al. 1978; Edelsky 1981; S. Feldstein, Brenner, & Jaffe 1963; Frances 1979; Gall, Hobby, & Craik 1969; Haas 1981; Hershey & Werner 1975; Ickes & Barnes 1977; Lalljee & Cook 1973; Levin & Silverman 1965; McMillan et al. 1977; Mehrabian 1971a, 1971b; Natale, Entin, & Jaffe 1979; Nemeth, Endicott, & Wachtler 1976; Strodtbeck, James, & Hawkins 1957; Strodtbeck & Mann 1956; Swacker 1975; Wood 1966.

Dialogic Behavior

Dittmann 1972; Frances 1979; LaFrance & Carmen 1980; McMillan et al. 1977; Natale, Entin, & Jaffe 1979; Nemeth, Endicott, & Wachtler 1976; Shaw & Sadler 1965; Zimmerman & West 1975.

OTHER SEX DIFFERENCES

Grade Point Average

Olds & Shaver 1980; Prociuk & Breen 1975; Sparacino & Hansell 1979.

Self-esteem

Fleming & Watts 1980; Lerner, Sorell, & Brackney 1981; Olds & Shaver 1980; O'Malley & Bachman 1979; Rios-Garcia & Cook 1975; Schaie & Parham 1976; Spence, Helmreich, & Stapp 1975; Stericker & Johnson 1977; Underwood, Froming, & Moore 1980; G. L. White 1981.

Masculinity and Femininity

Bernard 1981; Brewer & Blum 1979; Flaherty & Dusek 1980; Helmreich et al. 1980; Helmreich, Spence, & Holahan 1979; S. J. Johnson & Black 1981; Krasnoff 1981; Orlofsky 1981b; Orlofsky, Ramsden, & Cohen 1982; Spence, Helmreich, & Holahan 1979; Spence, Helmreich, & Stapp 1975; Storms 1979.

Liberal Sex-role Attitudes

K. A. Adams & Landers 1978; Helmreich, Spence, & Holahan 1979; Holahan & Stephen 1981; Orlofsky 1981b; Spence, Helmreich, & Stapp 1975; G. L. White 1981.

Fear of Success

Bremer & Wittig 1980; Jackaway & Teevan 1976; Janda, O'Grady, & Capps 1978; Macdonald & Hyde 1980; Olds & Shaver 1980; Orlofsky 1981a; Zuckerman & Allison 1976; Zuckerman et al. 1980.

Achievement Motivation and Values

Conley 1978; D. T. Cross, Barclay, & Burger 1978; Falbo 1981; Griffore & Lewis 1978; Helmreich et al. 1980; Hoffman 1975; Macdonald & Hyde 1980; Mehrabian 1977; Olds & Shaver 1980; Schaible 1975; Stericker & Johnson 1977; Zuckerman et al. 1980.

Social Poise, Dominance, and Assertiveness

K. A. Adams 1980; K. A. Adams & Landers 1978; D. T. Cross, Barclay, & Burger 1978; E. E. Jones 1978; Mehrabian 1977; Orlofsky & Windle 1978; Scarr et al. 1981.

Anxiety

Conley 1978; DeGregorio & Carver 1980; Krasnoff 1981; Macdonald & Hyde 1980; Mehrabian 1977; Rios-Garcia & Cook 1975; Scarr et al. 1981; Spielberger & Jacobs 1982; Vleeming & Engelse 1981.

Loneliness

Falbo 1981; Loucks 1980; Russell, Peplau, & Cutrona 1980; Russell, Peplau, & Ferguson 1978.

Depression

Padesky & Hammen 1981; Radloff 1975.

Neuroticism

Farley et al. 1977; Howarth 1976; R. Loo 1979; Mehrabian 1977; Scarr et al. 1981; Spielberger & Jacobs 1982.

Psychoticism

Farley et al. 1977; R. Loo 1979; Spielberger & Jacobs 1982.

External Locus of Control

Dixon, McKee, & McRae 1976; Doherty & Ryder 1979; Falbo 1981; S. J. Johnson & Black 1981; Kestenbaum & Hammersla 1976; Kleiber & Hemmer 1981; Lamm, Schmidt, & Trommsdorff 1976; Naditch & DeMaio 1975; Nideffer 1976; Nisbett & Temoshok 1976; Ramanaiah & Adams 1981; Strickland & Haley 1980; Walkey 1979.

Extraversion

Farley et al. 1977; Howarth 1976; R. Loo 1979; Mehrabian 1977; Pilkonis 1977a, D. A. Rosenthal & Lines 1978; Scarr et al. 1981; Schaie & Parham 1976; Spielberger & Jacobs 1982.

Liking and Emotional Closeness

Filsinger 1981; Hill & Stull 1981; Miller & Lefcourt 1982; Scarr et al. 1981; Tesser 1980.

Self-disclosure

Bender et al. 1976; Carpenter & Freese 1979; J. D. Davis 1978; Derlega et al. 1981; Gerdes, Gehling, & Rapp 1981; S. S. Hendrick 1981; Hill & Stull 1981; Morgan 1976; Morton 1978; Rubin & Shenker 1978.

References

Abramovitch, R. 1977. Children's recognition of situational aspects of facial expression. *Child Development* 48:459–63.

Abramovitch, R., and Daly, E. M. 1978. Children's use of head orientation and eye contact in making attributions of affiliation. *Child Development* 49:519–22.

———. 1979. Inferring attributes of a situation from the facial expressions of peers. *Child Development* 50:586–89.

Achenbach, T. M., and Weisz, J. R. 1975. A longitudinal study of relations between outer-directedness and IQ changes in preschoolers. *Child Development* 46:650–57.

Adams, K. A. 1980. Who has the final word? Sex, race, and dominance behavior. *Journal of Personality and Social Psychology* 38:1–8.

Adams, K. A., and Landers, A. D. 1978. Sex differences in dominance behavior. *Sex Roles* 4:215–23.

Adams, R. M., and Kirkevold, B. 1978. Looking, smiling, laughing, and moving in restaurants: Sex and age differences. *Environmental Psychology and Nonverbal Behavior* 3:117–21.

Adler, L. L., and Iverson, M. A. 1974. Interpersonal distance as a function of task difficulty, praise, status orientation, and sex of partner. *Perceptual and Motor Skills* 39:683–92.

———. 1975. Projected social distance as a function of praise conditions and status orientation: Comparison with physical interpersonal spacing in the laboratory. *Perceptual and Motor Skills* 41:659–64.

Aiello, J. R. 1972. A test of equilibrium theory: Visual interaction in relation to orientation, distance and sex of interactants. *Psychonomic Science* 27:335–36.

———. 1977a. A further look at equilibrium theory: Visual interaction as a function of interpersonal distance. *Environmental Psychology and Nonverbal Behavior* 1:122–40.

———. 1977b. Visual interaction at extended distances. *Personality and Social Psychology Bulletin* 3:83–86.

Aiello, J. R., and Aiello, T. D. 1974. The development of personal space: Proxemic behavior of children 6 through 16. *Human Ecology* 2:177–89.

Aiello, J. R., and Jones, S. E. 1971. Field study of the proxemic behavior of young school children in three subcultural groups. *Journal of Personality and Social Psychology* 19:351–56.

Aiello, J. R., and Thompson, D. E. 1980. Personal space, crowding, and spatial behavior in a cultural context. In *Human behavior and environment: Advances in theory and research,* vol. 4. Ed. I. Altman, A. Rapoport, and J. F. Wohlwill. New York: Plenum.

Alagna, F. J.; Whitcher, S. J.; Fisher, J. D.; and Wicas, E. A. 1979. Evaluative reaction to interpersonal touch in a counseling interview. *Journal of Counseling Psychology* 26:465–72.

Allgeier, A. R., and Byrne, D. 1973. Attraction toward the opposite sex as a determinant of physical proximity. *Journal of Social Psychology* 90:213–19.

Allport, F. H. 1924. *Social psychology.* Boston: Houghton Mifflin.

Ames, L. B. 1949. Development of interpersonal smiling responses in the preschool years. *Journal of Genetic Psychology* 74:273–91.

Anderson, F. J., and Willis, F. N. 1976. Glancing at others in preschool children in relation to dominance. *Psychological Record* 26:467–72.

Archer, D., and Akert, R. M. 1977. Words and everything else: Verbal and nonverbal cues in social interpretation. *Journal of Personality and Social Psychology* 35:443–49.

Archer, J., and Westeman, K. 1981. Sex differences in the aggressive behaviour of schoolchildren. *British Journal of Social Psychology* 20:31–36.

Argyle, M., and Cook, M. 1976. *Gaze and mutual gaze.* Cambridge: Cambridge University Press.

Argyle, M., and Dean, J. 1965. Eye-contact, distance and affiliation. *Sociometry* 28:289–304.

Argyle, M., and Ingham, R. 1972. Gaze, mutual gaze, and proximity. *Semiotica* 6:32–49.

Argyle, M.; Ingham, R.; Alkema, F.; and McCallin, M. 1973. The different functions of gaze. *Semiotica* 7:19–32.

Argyle, M.; Lalljee, M.; and Cook, M. 1968. The effects of visibility on interaction in a dyad. *Human Relations* 21:3–17.

Argyle, M.; Salter, V.; Nicholson, H.; Williams, M.; and Burgess, P. 1970. The communication of inferior and superior attitudes by verbal and nonverbal signals. *British Journal of Social and Clinical Psychology* 9:222–31.

Aries, E. 1976. Interaction patterns and themes of male, female, and mixed groups. *Small Group Behavior* 7:7–18.

Aronoff, J., and Crano, W. D. 1977. Sex role differentiation. In *Woman in a man-made world.* Ed. N. Glazer and H. Y. Waehrer. Chicago: Rand-McNally.

Ashear, V., and Snortum, J. R. 1971. Eye contact in children as a function of age, sex, social and intellective variables. *Developmental Psychology* 4:479.

Ashton, N. L., and Shaw, M. E. 1980. Empirical investigations of a reconceptualized personal space. *Bulletin of the Psychonomic Society* 15:309–12.

Bailey, K. G.; Caffrey, J. V., III; and Hartnett, J. J. 1976. Body size as implied threat: Effects on personal space and person perception. *Perceptual and Motor Skills* 43:223–30.

Bailey, K. G.; Hartnett, J. J.; and Gibson, F. W., Jr. 1972. Implied threat and the territorial factor in personal space. *Psychological Reports* 30:263–70.

Bailey, K. G.; Hartnett, J. J.; and Glover, H. W. 1973. Modeling and personal space behavior in children. *Journal of Psychology* 85:143–50.

Ban, P. L., and Lewis, M. 1974. Mothers and fathers, girls and boys: Attachment behavior in the one-year-old. *Merrill-Palmer Quarterly* 20:195–204.

Barrios, B. A.; Corbitt, L. C.; Estes, J. P.; and Topping, J. S. 1976. Effect of a social stigma on interpersonal distance. *Psychological Record* 26:343–48.

Barrios, B., and Giesen, M. 1977. Getting what you expect: Effects of expectation on intragroup attraction and interpersonal distance. *Personality and Social Psychology Bulletin* 3:87–90.

Bass, M. H., and Weinstein, M. S. 1971. Early development of interpersonal distance in children. *Canadian Journal of Behavioural Science* 3:368–76.

Bassili, J. N. 1979. Emotion recognition: The role of facial movement and the relative importance of upper and lower areas of the face. *Journal of Personality and Social Psychology* 37:2049–58.

Batchelor, J. P., and Goethals, G. R. 1972. Spatial arrangements in freely formed groups. *Sociometry* 35:270–9.

Bates, J. E. 1976. Effects of children's nonverbal behavior upon adults. *Child Development* 47:1079–88.

Bauer, E. A. 1973. Personal space: A study of blacks and whites. *Sociometry* 36:402–8.

Baum, A., and Greenberg, C. I. 1975. Waiting for a crowd: The behavioral and perceptual effects of anticipated crowding. *Journal of Personality and Social Psychology* 32:671–79.

Baxter, J. C. 1970. Interpersonal spacing in natural settings. *Sociometry* 33:444–56.

Beach, D. R., and Sokoloff, M. J. 1974. Spatially dominated nonverbal communication of children: A methodological study. *Perceptual and Motor Skills* 38:1303–10.

Beckwith, L.; Cohen, S. E.; Kopp, C. B.; Parmelee, A. H.; and Marcy, T. G. 1976. Caregiver-infant interaction and early cognitive development in preterm infants. *Child Development* 47:579–87.

Beier, E. G., and Sternberg, D. P. 1977. Marital communication: Subtle cues between newlyweds. *Journal of Communication* 27 (Summer): 92–97.

Beldoch, M. 1964. Sensitivity to expression of emotional meaning in three modes of communication. In *The communication of emotional meaning*. Ed. J. R. Davitz. New York: McGraw-Hill.

Bem, S. L. 1974. The measurement of psychological androgyny. *Journal of Consulting and Clinical Psychology* 42:155–62.

Bem, S. L.; Martyna, W.; and Watson, C. 1976. Sex typing and androgyny: Further explorations of the expressive domain. *Journal of Personality and Social Psychology* 34:1016–23.

Bender, V. L.; Davis, Y.; Glover, O.; and Stapp, J. 1976. Patterns of self-disclosure in homosexual and heterosexual college students. *Sex Roles* 2:149–60.

Berkowitz, W. R. 1971. A cross-national comparison of some social patterns of urban pedestrians. *Journal of Cross-Cultural Psychology* 2:129–44.

Bernard, L. C. 1981. The multidimensional aspects of masculinity-femininity. *Journal of Personality and Social Psychology* 41:797–802.

Bever, T. G., and Chiarello, R. J. 1974. Cerebral dominance in musicians and nonmusicians. *Science* 185:537–39.

Birdwhistell, R. L. 1974. Masculinity and femininity as display. In *Nonverbal communication: Readings with commentary.* Ed. S. Weitz. New York: Oxford.

Blanck, P. D.; Rosenthal, R.; Snodgrass, S. E.; DePaulo, B. M.; and Zuckerman, M. 1981. Sex differences in eavesdropping on nonverbal cues: Developmental changes. *Journal of Personality and Social Psychology* 41:391–96.

Blaney, R. L., and Winograd, E. 1978. Developmental differences in children's recognition memory for faces. *Developmental Psychology* 14:441–42.

Bleda, P. R., and Bleda, S. E. 1978. Effects of sex and smoking on reactions to spatial invasion at a shopping mall. *Journal of Social Psychology* 104:311–12.

Blehar, M. C.; Lieberman, A. F.; and Ainsworth, M.D.S. 1977. Early face-to-face interaction and its relation to later infant-mother attachment. *Child Development* 48:182–94.

Bond, M. H., and Shiraishi, D. 1974. The effect of body lean and status of an interviewer on the non-verbal behavior of Japanese interviewees. *International Journal of Psychology* 9:117–28.

Borden, R. J., and Homleid, G. M. 1978. Handedness and lateral positioning in heterosexual couples: Are men still strong-arming women? *Sex Roles* 4:67–73.

Borges, M. A., and Vaughn, L. S. 1977. Cognitive differences between the sexes in memory for names and faces. *Perceptual and Motor Skills* 45:317–18.

Boulding, E.; Nuss, S. A.; Carson, D. L.; and Greenstein, M. A. 1976. *Handbook of international data on women.* New York: Halsted (Wiley).

Brackett, C. W. 1933. Laughing and crying of preschool children. *Journal of Experimental Education* 2:119–28.

Brady, A. T., and Walker, M. B. 1978. Interpersonal distance as a function of situationally induced anxiety. *British Journal of Social and Clinical Psychology* 17:127–33.

Bremer, T. H., and Wittig, M. A. 1980. Fear of success: A personality trait or a response to occupational deviance and role overload? *Sex Roles* 6:27–46.

Brend, R. M. 1975. Male-female intonation patterns in American English. In *Language and sex: Difference and dominance.* Ed. B. Thorne and N. Henley. Rowley, Mass.: Newbury House.

Bretherton, I. 1978. Making friends with one-year-olds: An experimental study of infant-stranger interaction. *Merrill-Palmer Quarterly* 24:29–51.

Bretherton, I.; Stolberg, U.; and Kreye, M. 1981. Engaging strangers in proximal interaction: Infants' social initiative. *Developmental Psychology* 17:746–55.

Brewer, M. B., and Blum, M. W. 1979. Sex-role androgyny and patterns of causal attribution for academic achievement. *Sex Roles* 5:783–96.

Brigham, J. C., and Barkowitz, P. 1978. Do "they all look alike?" The effect of race, sex, experience, and attitudes on the ability to recognize faces. *Journal of Applied Social Psychology* 8:306–18.

Britton, J. O., and Britton, J. H. 1969. Discrimination of age by preschool children. *Journal of Gerontology* 24:457–60.

Brodzinsky, D. M. 1977. Children's comprehension and appreciation of verbal jokes in relation to conceptual tempo. *Child Development* 48:960–67.

Brodzinsky, D. M.; Barnet, K.; and Aiello, J. R. 1981. Sex of subject and gender identity as factors in humor appreciation. *Sex Roles* 7:561–73.

Brooks, J., and Lewis, M. 1974. Attachment behavior in thirteen-month-old, opposite-sex twins. *Child Development* 45:243–47.

————. 1976. Infants' responses to strangers: Midget, adult, and child. *Child Development* 47:323–32.

Brooks, R.; Brandt, L.; and Wiener, M. 1969. Differential response to two communication channels: Socioeconomic class differences in response to verbal reinforcers communicated with and without tonal inflection. *Child Development* 40:453–70.

Brooks-Gunn, J., and Lewis, M. 1981. Infant social perception: Responses to pictures of parents and strangers. *Developmental Psychology* 17:647–49.

Brotherton, P. L., and Penman, R. A. 1977. A comparison of some characteristics of male and female speech. *Journal of Social Psychology* 103:161–62.

Broverman, I. K.; Vogel, S. R.; Broverman, D. M.; Clarkson, F. E.; and Rosenkrantz, P. S. 1972. Sex-role stereotypes: A current appraisal. *Journal of Social Issues* 28(2):59–78.

Brown, R., and Ford, M. 1961. Address in American English. *Journal of Abnormal and Social Psychology* 62:375–85.

Brownell, W., and Smith, D. R. 1973. Communication patterns, sex, and length of verbalization in speech of four-year-old children. *Speech Monographs* 40:310–16.

Buchanan, D. R.; Goldman, M.; and Juhnke, R. 1977. Eye contact, sex, and the violation of personal space. *Journal of Social Psychology* 103:19–25.

Buchanan, D. R.; Juhnke, R.; and Goldman, M. 1976. Violation of personal space as a function of sex. *Journal of Social Psychology* 99:187–92.

Buck, R. 1975. Nonverbal communication of affect in children. *Journal of Personality and Social Psychology* 31:644–53.

————. 1976. A test of nonverbal receiving ability: Preliminary studies. *Human Communication Research* 2:162–71.

————. 1977. Nonverbal communication of affect in preschool children: Relationships with personality and skin conductance. *Journal of Personality and Social Psychology* 35:225–36.

————. 1979. Individual differences in nonverbal sending accuracy and electrodermal responding: The externalizing-internalizing dimension. In *Skill in nonverbal communication: Individual differences*. Ed. R. Rosenthal. Cambridge: Oelgeschlager, Gunn & Hain.

————. 1983. Nonverbal receiving ability. In *Nonverbal interaction*. Ed. J. M. Wiemann and R. P. Harrison. Beverly Hills: Sage.

Buck, R.; Baron, R.; and Barrette, D. 1982. Temporal organization of spontaneous emotional expression: A segmentation analysis. *Journal of Personality and Social Psychology* 42:506–17.

Buck, R.; Baron, R.; Goodman, N.; and Shapiro, B. 1980. Unitization of spontaneous nonverbal behavior in the study of emotion communication. *Journal of Personality and Social Psychology* 39:522–29.

Buck, R.; Miller, R. E.; and Caul, W. F. 1974. Sex, personality, and physiological variables in the communication of affect via facial expression. *Journal of Personality and Social Psychology* 30:587–96.

Bugental, D. B.; Henker, B.; and Whalen, C. K. 1976. Attributional antecedents of verbal and vocal assertiveness. *Journal of Personality and Social Psychology* 34:405–11.

Bugental, D. E.; Kaswan, J. W.; Love, L. R.; and Fox, M. N. 1970. Child versus adult perception of evaluative messages in verbal, vocal, and visual channels. *Developmental Psychology* 2:367–75.

Bugental, D. E.; Love, L. R.; and Gianetto, R. M. 1971. Perfidious feminine faces. *Journal of Personality and Social Psychology* 17:314–18.

Bugental, D. E.; Love, L. R.; Kaswan, J. W.; and April, C. 1971. Verbal-nonverbal conflict in parental messages to normal and disturbed children. *Journal of Abnormal Psychology* 77:6–10.

Buzby, D. E. 1924. The interpretation of facial expression. *American Journal of Psychology* 35:602–4.

Byrne, D.; Baskett, G. D.; and Hodges, L. 1971. Behavioral indicators of interpersonal attraction. *Journal of Applied Social Psychology* 1:137–49.

Campos, J. J.; Emde, R. N.; Gaensbauer, T.; and Henderson, C. 1975. Cardiac and behavioral interrelationships in the reactions of infants to strangers. *Developmental Psychology* 11:589–601.

Camras, L. A. 1980. Children's understanding of facial expressions used during conflict encounters. *Child Development* 51:879–85.

Caplan, M. E., and Goldman, M. 1981. Personal space violations as a function of height. *Journal of Social Psychology* 114:167–71.

Carducci, B. J., and Webber, A. W. 1979. Shyness as a determinant of interpersonal distance. *Psychological Reports* 44:1075–78.

Carey, S.; Diamond, R.; and Woods, B. 1980. Development of face recognition — A maturational component? *Developmental Psychology* 16:257–69.

Carli, L. L. 1982. Are women more social and men more task oriented? A meta-analytic review of sex differences in group interaction, reward allocation, coalition formation, and cooperation in the Prisoner's Dilemma game. Unpublished manuscript. University of Massachusetts (Amherst).

Carlson, R., and Levy, N. 1973. Studies of Jungian typology: I. Memory, social perception, and social action. *Journal of Personality* 41:559–76.

Carmichael, L.; Roberts, S. O.; and Wessell, N. Y. 1937. A study of the judgment of manual expression as presented in still and motion pictures. *Journal of Social Psychology* 8:115–42.

Carpenter, J. C., and Freese, J. J. 1979. Three aspects of self-disclosure as they relate to quality of adjustment. *Journal of Personality Assessment* 43:78–85.

Cary, M. S. 1978. Does civil inattention exist in pedestrian passing? *Journal of Personality and Social Psychology* 36:1185–93.

————. 1979. Gaze and facial display in pedestrian passing. *Semiotica* 28:323–26.

Chaiken, S. 1979. Communicator physical attractiveness and persuasion. *Journal of Personality and Social Psychology* 37:1387–97.

Chaikin, A. L., and Derlega, V. J. 1978. Nonverbal mediators of expectancy effects in black and white children. *Journal of Applied Social Psychology* 8:117–25.

Chaikin, A. L.; Sigler, E.; and Derlega, V. J. 1974. Nonverbal mediators of teacher expectancy effects. *Journal of Personality and Social Psychology* 30:144–49.

Challman, R. C. 1932. Factors influencing friendships among preschool children. *Child Development* 3:146-58.

Chance, J.; Goldstein, A. G.; and McBride, L. 1975. Differential experience and recognition memory for faces. *Journal of Social Psychology* 97:243-53.

Chance, J. E.; Turner, A. L.; and Goldstein, A. G. 1982. Development of differential recognition for own- and other-race faces. *Journal of Psychology* 112:29-37.

Chapman, A. J. 1973a. Social facilitation of laughter in children. *Journal of Experimental Social Psychology* 9:528-41.

―――. 1973b. Funniness of jokes, canned laughter and recall performance. *Sociometry* 36:569-78.

―――. 1974. An experimental study of socially facilitated 'humorous laughter.' *Psychological Reports* 35:727-34.

―――. 1975. Humorous laughter in children. *Journal of Personality and Social Psychology* 31:42-49.

Chapman, A. J., and Chapman, W. A. 1974. Responsiveness to humor: Its dependency upon a companion's humorous smiling and laughter. *Journal of Psychology* 88:245-52.

Cherulnik, P. D. 1979. Sex differences in the expression of emotion in a structured social encounter. *Sex Roles* 5:413-24.

Cherulnik, P. D.; Neely, W. T.; Flanagan, M.; and Zachau, M. 1978. Social skill and visual interaction. *Journal of Social Psychology* 104:263-70.

Cheyne, J. A. 1976. Development of forms and functions of smiling in preschoolers. *Child Development* 47:820-23.

Cheyne, J. A., and Efran, M. G. 1972. The effect of spatial and interpersonal variables on the invasion of group controlled territories. *Sociometry* 35:477-89.

Coates, B.; Anderson, E. P.; and Hartup, W. W. 1972. Interrelations in the attachment behavior of human infants. *Developmental Psychology* 6:218-30.

Cohen, J. 1969. *Statistical power analysis for the behavioral sciences*. New York: Academic Press.

Cohen, L. J., and Campos, J. J. 1974. Father, mother, and stranger as elicitors of attachment behaviors in infancy. *Developmental Psychology* 10:146-54.

Coleman, J. C. 1949. Facial expressions of emotion. *Psychological Monographs* 63(1), Whole no. 296.

Coleman, R. O. 1971. Male and female voice quality and its relationship to vowel formant frequencies. *Journal of Speech and Hearing Research* 14:565-77.

―――. 1976. A comparison of the contributions of two voice quality characteristics to the perception of maleness and femaleness in the voice. *Journal of Speech and Hearing Research* 19:168-80.

Collett, P., and Marsh, P. 1974. Patterns of public behavior: Collision avoidance on a pedestrian crossing. *Semiotica* 12:281-99.

Conley, J. J. 1978. Sex differences and androgyny in fantasy content. *Journal of Personality Assessment* 42:604-10.

Constantinople, A. 1973. Masculinity-femininity: An exception to a famous dictum? *Psychological Bulletin* 80:389-407.

Cooley, R. S., and Seeman, J. 1979. Personality integration and social schemata. *Journal of Personality* 47:288–304.

Cornell, E. H. 1974. Infants' discrimination of photographs of faces following redundant presentations. *Journal of Experimental Child Psychology* 18:98–106.

Coutts, L. M., and Schneider, F. W. 1975. Visual behavior in an unfocused interaction as a function of sex and distance. *Journal of Experimental Social Psychology* 11:64–77.

Cozby, P. C. 1973. Effects of density, activity, and personality on environmental preferences. *Journal of Research in Personality* 7:45–60.

Craddock, A. E. 1977. Task and emotional behavior in the marital dyad. In *Woman in a man-made world*. Ed. N. Glazer and H. Y. Waehrer. Chicago: Rand-McNally.

Crawley, S. B.; Rogers, P. P.; Friedman, S.; Iacobbo, M.; Criticos, A.; Richardson, L.; and Thompson, M. A. 1978. Developmental changes in the structure of mother-infant play. *Developmental Psychology* 14:30–36.

Crosby, F.; Jose, P.; and Wong-McCarthy, W. 1981. Gender, androgyny, and conversational assertiveness. In *Gender and nonverbal behavior*. Ed. C. Mayo and N. M. Henley. New York: Springer-Verlag.

Cross, D. T.; Barclay, A.; and Burger, G. K. 1978. Differential effects of ethnic membership, sex, and occupation on the California Psychological Inventory. *Journal of Personality Assessment* 42:597–603.

Cross, J. F.; Cross, J.; and Daly, J. 1971. Sex, race, age, and beauty as factors in recognition of faces. *Perception & Psychophysics* 10:393–96.

Cunningham, M. R. 1977. Personality and the structure of the nonverbal communication of emotion. *Journal of Personality* 45:564–84.

Cupchik, G. C., and Leventhal, H. 1974. Consistency between expressive behavior and the evaluation of humorous stimuli: The role of sex and self-observation. *Journal of Personality and Social Psychology* 30:429–42.

Cutting, J. E.; Proffitt, D. R.; and Kozlowski, L. T. 1978. A biomechanical invariant for gait perception. *Journal of Experimental Psychology: Human Perception and Performance* 4:357–72.

Dabbs, J. M., Jr.; Evans, M. S.; Hopper, C. H.; and Purvis, J. A. 1980. Self-monitors in conversation: What do they monitor? *Journal of Personality and Social Psychology* 39:278–84.

Dabbs, J. M., Jr., and Stokes, N. A., III. 1975. Beauty is power: The use of space on the sidewalk. *Sociometry* 38:551–57.

Davis, J. D. 1978. When boy meets girl: Sex roles and the negotiation of intimacy in an acquaintance exercise. *Journal of Personality and Social Psychology* 36:684–92.

Davis, M., and Weitz, S. 1981. Sex differences in body movements and positions. In *Gender and nonverbal behavior*. Ed. C. Mayo and N. M. Henley. New York: Springer-Verlag.

Dean, L. M.; Willis, F. N.; and Hewitt, J. 1975. Initial interaction distance among individuals equal and unequal in military rank. *Journal of Personality and Social Psychology* 32:294–99.

Deaux, K. 1976. *The behavior of men and women*. Monterey: Brooks/Cole.

De LaCoste-Utamsing, C., and Holloway, R. L. 1982. Sexual dimorphism in the human corpus callosum. *Science* 216:1431–32.

DeGregorio, E., and Carver, C. S. 1980. Type A behavior pattern, sex role orientation, and psychological adjustment. *Journal of Personality and Social Psychology* 39:286–93.

DeJulio, S., and Duffy, K. 1977. Neuroticism and proxemic behavior. *Perceptual and Motor Skills* 45:51–55.

DePaulo, B. M.; Jordan, A.; Irvine, A.; and Laser, P. S. 1982. Age changes in the detection of deception. *Child Development* 53:701–9.

DePaulo, B. M., and Rosenthal, R. 1979. Ambivalence, discrepancy, and deception in nonverbal communication. In *Skill in nonverbal communication: Individual differences*. Ed. R. Rosenthal. Cambridge: Oelgeschlager, Gunn & Hain.

DePaulo, B. M.; Rosenthal, R.; Eisenstat, R. A.; Rogers, P. L.; and Finkelstein, S. 1978. Decoding discrepant nonverbal cues. *Journal of Personality and Social Psychology* 36:313–23.

Derlega, V. J.; Durham, B.; Gockel, B.; and Sholis, D. 1981. Sex differences in self-disclosure: Effects of topic content, friendship, and partner's sex. *Sex Roles* 7:433–47.

Diamond, E. L. 1982. The role of anger and hostility in essential hypertension and coronary heart disease. *Psychological Bulletin* 92:410–33.

Dickey, E. C., and Knower, F. H. 1941. A note on some ethnological differences in recognition of simulated expressions of the emotions. *American Journal of Sociology* 47:190–3.

Dies, R. R., and Greenberg, B. 1976. Effects of physical contact in an encounter group context. *Journal of Consulting and Clinical Psychology* 44:400–405.

DiMatteo, M. R., and Hall, J. A. 1979. Nonverbal decoding skill and attention to nonverbal cues: A research note. *Environmental Psychology and Nonverbal Behavior* 3:188–92.

Dimitrovsky, L. 1964. The ability to identify the emotional meaning of vocal expressions at successive age levels. In *The communication of emotional meaning*. Ed. J. R. Davitz. New York: McGraw-Hill.

Ding, G. F., and Jersild, A. T. 1932. A study of the laughing and smiling of preschool children. *Journal of Genetic Psychology* 40:452–72.

DiPietro, J. A. 1981. Rough and tumble play: A function of gender. *Developmental Psychology* 17:50–58.

Dittmann, A. T. 1972. Developmental factors in conversational behavior. *Journal of Communication* 22:404–23.

Dixon, D. N.; McKee, C. S.; and McRae, B. C. 1976. Dimensionality of three adult, objective locus of control scales. *Journal of Personality Assessment* 40:310–19.

Doherty, W. J., and Ryder, R. G. 1979. Locus of control, interpersonal trust, and assertive behavior among newlyweds. *Journal of Personality and Social Psychology* 37:2212–20.

Dosey, M. A., and Meisels, M. 1969. Personal space and self-protection. *Journal of Personality and Social Psychology* 11:93–97.

Drag, R. M., and Shaw, M. E. 1967. Factors influencing the communication of emotional intent by facial expressions. *Psychonomic Science* 8:137–38.

Duffy, R. J. 1970. Fundamental frequency characteristics of adolescent females. *Language and Speech* 13:14–24.

Duke, M. P., and Kiebach, C. 1974. A brief note on the validity of the Comfortable Interpersonal Distance Scale. *Journal of Social Psychology* 94:297–98.

Duke, M. P., and Nowicki, S., Jr. 1972. A new measure and social-learning model for interpersonal distance. *Journal of Experimental Research in Personality* 6:119–32.

Dusenbury, D., and Knower, F. H. 1938. Experimental studies of the symbolism of action and voice: I. A study of the specificity of meaning in facial expression. *Quarterly Journal of Speech* 24:424–35.

_____. 1939. Experimental studies of the symbolism of action and voice: II. A study of the specificity of meaning in abstract tonal symbols. *Quarterly Journal of Speech* 25:67–75.

Eagly, A. H., and Carli, L. L. 1981. Sex of researchers and sex-typed communications as determinants of sex differences in influenceability. *Psychological Bulletin* 90:1–20.

Eakins, B. W., and Eakins, R. G. 1978. *Sex differences in human communication.* Boston: Houghton Mifflin.

Eberts, E. H., and Lepper, M. R. 1975. Individual consistency in the proxemic behavior of preschool children. *Journal of Personality and Social Psychology* 32:841–49.

Eckerman, C. O., and Rheingold, H. L. 1974. Infants' exploratory responses to toys and people. *Developmental Psychology* 10:255–59.

Eckerman, C. O.; Whatley, J. L.; and Kutz, S. L. 1975. Growth of social play with peers during the second year of life. *Developmental Psychology* 11:42–49.

Edelsky, C. 1979. Question intonation and sex roles. *Language in Society* 8:15–32.

_____. 1981. Who's got the floor? *Language in Society* 10:383–421.

Edney, J. J., and Jordan-Edney, N. L. 1974. Territorial spacing on a beach. *Sociometry* 37:92–104.

Edney, J. J.; Walker, C. A.; and Jordan, N. L. 1976. Is there reactance in personal space? *Journal of Social Psychology* 100:207–17.

Edwards, D.J.A. 1977. Perception of crowding and personal space as a function of locus of control, arousal seeking, sex of experimenter, and sex of subject. *Journal of Psychology* 95:223–29.

_____. 1980. Perception of crowding and tolerance for interpersonal proximity and separation in South Africa. *Journal of Social Psychology* 110:19–28.

Efran, J. S. 1968. Looking for approval: Effects on visual behavior of approbation from persons differing in importance. *Journal of Personality and Social Psychology* 10:21–25.

Efran, J. S., and Broughton, A. 1966. Effect of expectancies for social approval on visual behavior. *Journal of Personality and Social Psychology* 4:103–7.

Eisenberg, N., and Lennon, R. 1983. Sex differences in empathy and related capacities. *Psychological Bulletin* 94:100–131.

Eisenberg, P., and Reichline, P. B. 1939. Judging expressive movement: II. Judgments of dominance-feeling from motion pictures of gait. *Journal of Social Psychology* 10:345–57.

Ekman, P., and Friesen, W. V. 1969a. The repertoire of nonverbal behavior: Categories, origins, usage, and coding. *Semiotica* 1:49–98.

————. 1969b. Nonverbal leakage and clues to deception. *Psychiatry* 32(1):88–105.

————. 1971. Constants across cultures in the face and emotion. *Journal of Personality and Social Psychology* 17:124–29.

————. 1974. Detecting deception from the body or face. *Journal of Personality and Social Psychology* 29:288–98.

Ellis, H.; Shepherd, J.; and Bruce, A. 1973. The effects of age and sex upon adolescents' recognition of faces. *Journal of Genetic Psychology* 123:173–74.

Ellsworth, P. C., and Ludwig, L. M. 1972. Visual behavior in social interaction. *Journal of Communication* 22:375–403.

Ellyson, S. L.; Dovidio, J. F.; and Fehr, B. J. 1981. Visual behavior and dominance in women and men. In *Gender and nonverbal behavior.* Ed. C. Mayo and N. M. Henley. New York: Springer-Verlag.

Engebretson, D., and Fullmer, D. 1970. Cross-cultural differences in territoriality: Interaction distances of native Japanese, Hawaii Japanese, and American Caucasians. *Journal of Cross-Cultural Psychology* 1:261–69.

English, P. W. 1972. Behavioral concomitants of dependent and subservient roles. Unpublished manuscript. Harvard University.

Evans, G. W., and Howard, R. B. 1973. Personal space. *Psychological Bulletin* 80:334–44.

Exline, R. V. 1963. Explorations in the process of person perception: Visual interaction in relation to competition, sex, and need for affiliation. *Journal of Personality* 31:1–20.

————. 1972. Visual interaction: The glances of power and preference. In *Nebraska Symposium on Motivation, 1971.* Ed. J. K. Cole. Lincoln: University of Nebraska Press.

Exline, R. V.; Ellyson, S. L.; and Long, B. 1975. Visual behavior as an aspect of power role relationships. In *Nonverbal communication of aggression.* Ed. P. Pliner, L. Krames, and T. Alloway. New York: Plenum.

Exline, R.; Gray, D.; and Schuette, D. 1965. Visual behavior in a dyad as affected by interview content and sex of respondent. *Journal of Personality and Social Psychology* 1:201–9.

Exline, R. V., and Winters, L. C. 1965. Affective relations and mutual glances in dyads. In *Affect, cognition, and personality: Empirical studies.* Ed. S. S. Tomkins and C. E. Izard. New York: Springer.

Fagan, J. F., III. 1972. Infants' recognition memory for faces. *Journal of Experimental Child Psychology* 14:453–76.

————. 1973. Infants' delayed recognition memory and forgetting. *Journal of Experimental Child Psychology* 16:424–50.

————. 1974. Infant recognition memory: The effects of length of familiarization and type of discrimination task. *Child Development* 45:351–56.

————. 1976. Infants' recognition of invariant features of faces. *Child Development* 47:627–38.

————. 1977. Infant recognition memory: Studies in forgetting. *Child Development* 48:68–78.

Falbo, T. 1981. Relationships between birth category, achievement, and interpersonal orientation. *Journal of Personality and Social Psychology* 41:121-31.

Farley, F. H.; Goh, D. S.; Sewell, T.; Davis, S. A.; and Dyer, M. 1977. American and British data on a three dimensional assessment of personality in college students. *Journal of Personality Assessment* 41:160-63.

Fay, P. J., and Middleton, W. C. 1939. Judgment of Spranger personality types from the voice as transmitted over a public address system. *Character and Personality* 8:144-55.

_____. 1940a. The ability to judge the rested or tired condition of a speaker from his voice as transmitted over a public address system. *Journal of Applied Psychology* 24:645-50.

_____. 1940b. Judgment of Kretschmerian body types from the voice as transmitted over a public address system. *Journal of Social Psychology* 12:151-62.

_____. 1940c. Judgment of intelligence from the voice as transmitted over a public address system. *Sociometry* 3:186-91.

_____. 1941a. The ability to judge sociability from the voice as transmitted over a public address system. *Journal of Social Psychology* 13:303-9.

_____. 1941b. The ability to judge truth-telling, or lying, from the voice as transmitted over a public address system. *Journal of General Psychology* 24:211-15.

Fein, G. G. 1975. Children's sensitivity to social contexts at 18 months of age. *Developmental Psychology* 11:853-54.

Feinman, S., and Entwisle, D. R. 1976. Children's ability to recognize other children's faces. *Child Development* 47:506-10.

Feldman, J. F.; Brody, N.; and Miller, S. A. 1980. Sex differences in non-elicited neonatal behaviors. *Merrill-Palmer Quarterly* 26:63-73.

Feldman, M., and Thayer, S. 1980. A comparison of three measures of nonverbal decoding ability. *Journal of Social Psychology* 112:91-97.

Feldman, S. S., and Ingham, M. E. 1975. Attachment behavior: A validation study in two age groups. *Child Development* 46:319-30.

Feldstein, J. H. 1976. Sex differences in social memory among preschool children. *Sex Roles* 2:75-79.

Feldstein, S.; Brenner, M. S.; and Jaffe, J. 1963. The effect of subject sex, verbal interaction and topical focus on speech disruption. *Language and Speech* 6:229-39.

Fernberger, S. W. 1927. Six more Piderit faces. *American Journal of Psychology* 39:162-66.

Field, T. M. 1977. Effects of early separation, interactive deficits, and experimental manipulations on infant-mother face-to-face interaction. *Child Development* 48:763-71.

Field, T. 1978. Interaction behaviors of primary versus secondary caretaker fathers. *Developmental Psychology* 14:183-84.

Fields, S. J. 1953. Discrimination of facial expression and its relation to personal adjustment. *Journal of Social Psychology* 38:63-71.

Filsinger, E. E. 1981. A measure of interpersonal orientation: The Liking People Scale. *Journal of Personality Assessment* 45:295-300.

Finley, G. E., and Layne, O., Jr. 1971. Play behavior in young children: A cross-cultural study. *Journal of Genetic Psychology* 119:203-10.

Fisher, J. D., and Byrne, D. 1975. Too close for comfort: Sex differences in response to invasions of personal space. *Journal of Personality and Social Psychology* 32:15–21.

Fisher, J. D.; Rytting, M.; and Heslin, R. 1976. Hands touching hands: Affective and evaluative effects of an interpersonal touch. *Sociometry* 39:416–21.

Flaherty, J. F., and Dusek, J. B. 1980. An investigation of the relationship between psychological androgyny and components of self-concept. *Journal of Personality and Social Psychology* 38:984–92.

Fleming, J. S., and Watts, W. A. 1980. The dimensionality of self-esteem: Some results for a college sample. *Journal of Personality and Social Psychology* 39:921–29.

Flin, R. H. 1980. Age effects in children's memory for unfamiliar faces. *Developmental Psychology* 16:373–74.

Foddy, M. 1978. Patterns of gaze in cooperative and competitive negotiation. *Human Relations* 31:925–38.

Foley, J. P., Jr. 1935. Judgment of facial expression of emotion in the chimpanzee. *Journal of Social Psychology* 6:31–67.

Foot, H. C.; Chapman, A. J.; and Smith, J. R. 1977. Friendship and social responsiveness in boys and girls. *Journal of Personality and Social Psychology* 35:401–11.

Foot, H. C.; Smith, J. R.; and Chapman, A. J. 1979. Non-verbal expressions of intimacy in children. In *Love and attraction*. Ed. M. Cook and G. Wilson. Oxford: Pergamon.

Ford, J. G.; Cramer, R. E.; and Owens, G. 1977. A paralinguistic consideration of proxemic behavior. *Perceptual and Motor Skills* 45:487–93.

Ford, J. G., and Graves, J. R. 1977. Differences between Mexican-American and white children in interpersonal distance and social touching. *Perceptual and Motor Skills* 45:779–85.

Forden, C. 1981. The influence of sex-role expectations on the perception of touch. *Sex Roles* 7:889–94.

Frances, S. J. 1979. Sex differences in nonverbal behavior. *Sex Roles* 5:519–35.

Frankel, A. S., and Barrett, J. 1971. Variations in personal space as a function of authoritarianism, self-esteem, and racial characteristics of a stimulus situation. *Journal of Consulting and Clinical Psychology* 37:95–98.

Friedman, H. S.; DiMatteo, M. R.; and Taranta, A. 1980. A study of the relationship between individual differences in nonverbal expressiveness and factors of personality and social interaction. *Journal of Research in Personality* 14:351–64.

Friedman, H. S.; Prince, L. M.; Riggio, R. E.; and DiMatteo, M. R. 1980. Understanding and assessing nonverbal expressiveness: The Affective Communication Test. *Journal of Personality and Social Psychology* 39:333–51.

Frieze, I. H., and Ramsey, S. J. 1976. Nonverbal maintenance of traditional sex roles. *Journal of Social Issues* 32(3):133–41.

Frieze, I. H.; Whitley, B. E.; Hanusa, B. H.; and McHugh, M. C. 1982. Assessing the theoretical models for sex differences in causal attributions for success and failure. *Sex Roles* 8:333–43.

Frijda, N. H. 1953. The understanding of facial expression of emotion. *Acta Psychologica* 9:294–362.

Fromme, D. K., and Beam, D. C. 1974. Dominance and sex differences in nonverbal responses to differential eye contact. *Journal of Research in Personality* 8:76–87.

Fugita, S. S. 1974. Effects of anxiety and approval on visual interaction. *Journal of Personality and Social Psychology* 29:586–92.

Fujita, B. N.; Harper, R. G.; and Wiens, A. N. 1980. Encoding-decoding of nonverbal emotional messages: Sex differences in spontaneous and enacted expressions. *Journal of Nonverbal Behavior* 4:131–45.

Fuller, R.G.C., and Sheehy-Skeffington, A. 1974. Effects of group laughter on responses to humourous material, a replication and extension. *Psychological Reports* 35:531–34.

Galassi, J. P.; Galassi, M. D.; and Litz, M. C. 1974. Assertive training in groups using video feedback. *Journal of Counseling Psychology* 21:390–94.

Gall, M. D.; Hobby, A. K.; and Craik, K. H. 1969. Non-linguistic factors in oral language productivity. *Perceptual and Motor Skills* 29:871–74.

Gallagher, D., and Shuntich, R. J. 1981. Encoding and decoding of nonverbal behavior through facial expressions. *Journal of Research in Personality* 15:241–52.

Garai, J. E., and Scheinfeld, A. 1968. Sex differences in mental and behavioral traits. *Genetic Psychology Monographs* 77:169–299.

Gates, G. S. 1923. An experimental study of the growth of social perception. *Journal of Educational Psychology* 14:449–61.

Gerber, W. S., and Routh, D. K. 1975. Humor response as related to violation of expectancies and to stimulus intensity in a weight-judgment task. *Perceptual and Motor Skills* 41:673–74.

Gerdes, E. P., Gehling, J. D.; and Rapp, J. N. 1981. The effects of sex and sex-role concept on self-disclosure. *Sex Roles* 7:989–98.

Giesen, M., and McClaren, H. A. 1976. Discussion, distance and sex: Changes in impressions and attraction during small group interaction. *Sociometry* 39:60–70.

Gifford, R. 1982. Projected interpersonal distance and orientation choices: Personality, sex, and social situation. *Social Psychology Quarterly* 45:145–52.

Gifford, R., and Price, J. 1979. Personal space in nursery school children. *Canadian Journal of Behavioural Science* 11:318–26.

Gitter, A. G.; Black, H.; and Mostofsky, D. 1972a. Race and sex in the communication of emotion. *Journal of Social Psychology* 88:273–76.

————. 1972b. Race and sex in the perception of emotion. *Journal of Social Issues* 28(4):63–78.

Gitter, A. G.; Kozel, N. J.; and Mostofsky, D. I. 1972. Perception of emotion: The role of race, sex, and presentation mode. *Journal of Social Psychology* 88:213–22.

Gitter, A. G.; Mostofsky, D.; and Guichard, M. 1972. Some parameters in the perception of gaze. *Journal of Social Psychology* 88:115–21.

Gitter, A. G.; Mostofsky, D. I.; and Quincy, A. J., Jr. 1971. Race and sex differences in the child's perception of emotion. *Child Development* 42:2071–75.

Gladding, S. T. 1978. Empathy, gender, and training as factors in the identification of infant cry-signals. *Perceptual and Motor Skills* 47:267–70.

Glass, G. V.; McGaw, B.; and Smith, M. L. 1981. *Meta-analysis in social research.* Beverly Hills: Sage.

Goffman, E. 1967. *Interaction ritual.* Chicago: Aldine.

Going, M., and Read, J. D. 1974. Effects of uniqueness, sex of subject, and sex of photograph on facial recognition. *Perceptual and Motor Skills* 39:109–10.

Goldberg, S., and Lewis, M. 1969. Play behavior in the year-old infant: Early sex differences. *Child Development* 40:21–31.

Goldman, J.; Belser, J. L.; Kemp, M. M.; Maitland, K. A.; and Suarez, L. B. 1977. Activity and attachment in 10-month-old infants. *Journal of Genetic Psychology* 130:169–79.

Goldstein, A. G., and Chance, J. E. 1964. Recognition of children's faces. *Child Development* 35:129–36.

———. 1970. Visual recognition memory for complex configurations. *Perception & Psychophysics* 9:237–41.

Goldstein, A. G., and Jeffords, J. 1981. Status and touching behavior. *Bulletin of the Psychonomic Society* 17:79–81.

Goodenough, F. L. 1930. Inter-relationships in the behavior of young children. *Child Development* 1:29–47.

Gottfried, N. W., and Seay, B. 1974. Early social behavior: Age and sex baseline data from a hidden population. *Journal of Genetic Psychology* 125:61–69.

Gottheil, E.; Corey, J.; and Paredes, A. 1968. Psychological and physical dimensions of personal space. *Journal of Psychology* 69:7–9.

Graves, E. A. 1937. A study of competitive and cooperative behavior by the short sample technique. *Journal of Abnormal and Social Psychology* 32:343–51.

Green, B. F., and Hall, J. A. 1984. Quantitative methods for literature reviews. *Annual Review of Psychology* 35:37–53.

Greenbaum, P. E.; and Rosenfeld, H. M. 1980. Varieties of touching in greetings: Sequential structure and sex-related differences. *Journal of Nonverbal Behavior* 5:13–25.

Griffitt, W.; May, J.; and Veitch, R. 1974. Sexual stimulation and interpersonal behavior: Heterosexual evaluative responses, visual behavior, and physical proximity. *Journal of Personality and Social Psychology* 30:367–77.

Griffore, R. J., and Lewis, J. 1978. The Mehrabian Measures of Achieving Tendency: Are separate male and female scales necessary? *Journal of Personality Assessment* 42:621–25.

Guardo, C. J. 1969. Personal space in children. *Child Development* 40:143–51.

———. 1976. Personal space, sex differences, and interpersonal attraction. *Journal of Psychology* 92:9–14.

Guilford, J. P. 1929. An experiment in learning to read facial expression. *Journal of Abnormal and Social Psychology* 24:191–202.

Gunnar, M. R., and Donahue, M. 1980. Sex differences in social responsiveness between six months and twelve months. *Child Development* 51:262–65.

Haas, A. 1981. Partner influences on sex-associated spoken language of children. *Sex Roles* 7:925–35.

Halberstadt, A. G. Race, socioeconomic status, and nonverbal behavior. In *Nonverbal behavior in interpersonal relations.* Ed. A. W. Siegman and S. Feldstein. Hillsdale, NJ: Erlbaum, in press.

Halberstadt, A. G., and Hall, J. A. 1980. Who's getting the message? Children's nonverbal skill and their evaluation by teachers. *Developmental Psychology* 16:564–73.

Hall, J. A. 1976. Sex-role-related correlates of sensitivity to nonverbal cues. Doctoral dissertation, Harvard University.

_____. 1978. Gender effects in decoding nonverbal cues. *Psychological Bulletin* 85:845–57.

_____. 1979. Gender, gender roles, and nonverbal communication skills. In *Skill in nonverbal communication: Individual differences*. Ed. R. Rosenthal. Cambridge: Oelgeschlager, Gunn & Hain.

_____. 1980. Gender differences in nonverbal communication skills. In *Quantitative assessment of research domains*. Ed. R. Rosenthal. San Francisco: Jossey-Bass.

_____. Male and female nonverbal behavior. In *Nonverbal behavior in interpersonal relations*. Ed. A. W. Siegman and S. Feldstein. Hillsdale, NJ: Erlbaum, in press.

Hall, J. A.; Aist, M. B.; and Pike, K. M. 1983. Nonverbal behavior and person description in men's and women's prose. *Journal of Nonverbal Behavior* 7:213–22.

Hall, J. A., and Braunwald, K. G. 1981. Gender cues in conversations. *Journal of Personality and Social Psychology* 40:99–110.

Hall, J. A.; Braunwald, K. G.; and Mroz, B. J. 1982. Gender, affect, and influence in a teaching situation. *Journal of Personality and Social Psychology* 43:270–80.

Hall, J. A., and Halberstadt, A. G. 1980. Masculinity and femininity in children: Development of the Children's Personal Attributes Questionnaire. *Developmental Psychology* 16:270–80.

_____. 1981. Sex roles and nonverbal communication skills. *Sex Roles* 7:273–87.

_____. Smiling and gazing. In *The psychology of gender: Advances through meta-analysis*. Ed. J. S. Hyde and M. Linn. Baltimore: The Johns Hopkins University Press, forthcoming.

Hall, J. A.; Halberstadt, A. G.; Rosenthal, R.; and Zuckerman, M. 1977. Encoding and decoding vocal communication and inhibition of affect in childhood. Unpublished manuscript. Johns Hopkins University.

Hall, J. A., and Levin, S. 1980. Affect and verbal-nonverbal discrepancy in schizophrenic and non-schizophrenic family communication. *British Journal of Psychiatry* 137:78–92.

Hall, J. A.; Roter, D. L.; and Rand, C. S. 1981. Communication of affect between patient and physician. *Journal of Health and Social Behavior* 22:18–30.

Hamilton, M. L. 1973. Imitative behavior and expressive ability in facial expression of emotion. *Developmental Psychology* 8:138.

Hammen, C. L., and Peplau, L. A. 1978. Brief encounters: Impact of gender, sex-role attitudes, and partner's gender on interaction and cognition. *Sex Roles* 4:75–90.

Hammer, M., and Kaplan, A. M. 1964. Reliability of profile and front-facing directions in children's drawings. *Child Development* 35:973–77.

Hanaway, T., and Burghardt, G. 1976. The development of sexually dimorphic book-carrying behavior. *Bulletin of the Psychonomic Society* 7:267–70.

Harper, R. G.; Wiens, A. N.; and Matarazzo, J. D. 1978. *Nonverbal communication: The state of the art.* New York: Wiley-Interscience.

Harris, L. 1968. Looks by preschoolers at the experimenter in a choice-of-toys game: Effects of experimenter and age of child. *Journal of Experimental Child Psychology* 6:493–500.

Harter, S. 1974. Pleasure derived by children from cognitive challenge and mastery. *Child Development* 45:661–69.

Harter, S.; Shultz, T. R.; and Blum, B. 1971. Smiling in children as a function of their sense of mastery. *Journal of Experimental Child Psychology* 12:396–404.

Hartnett, J. J.; Bailey, K. G.; and Gibson, F. W., Jr. 1970. Personal space as influenced by sex and type of movement. *Journal of Psychology* 76:139–44.

Hartnett, J. J.; Bailey, K. G.; and Hartley, C. S. 1974. Body height, position, and sex as determinants of personal space. *Journal of Psychology* 87:129–36.

Hattie, J. 1979. Stability of results across many studies: Sex differences on the Personal Orientation Inventory. *Journal of Personality Assessment* 43:627–28.

Haviland, J. J., and Malatesta, C. Z. 1981. The development of sex differences in nonverbal signals: Fallacies, facts, and fantasies. In *Gender and nonverbal behavior.* Ed. C. Mayo and N. M. Henley. New York: Springer-Verlag.

Hayduk, L. A. 1978. Personal space: An evaluative and orienting overview. *Psychological Bulletin* 85:117–34.

———. 1983. Personal space: Where we now stand. *Psychological Bulletin* 94:293–335.

Heiss, J. S. 1962. Degree of intimacy and male-female interaction. *Sociometry* 25:197–208.

Helmreich, R. L.; Spence, J. T.; Beane, W. E.; Lucker, G. W.; and Matthews, K. A. 1980. Making it in academic psychology: Demographic and personality correlates of attainment. *Journal of Personality and Social Psychology* 39:896–908.

Helmreich, R. L.; Spence, J. T.; and Holahan, C. K. 1979. Psychological androgyny and sex role flexibility: A test of two hypotheses. *Journal of Personality and Social Psychology* 37:1631–44.

Hendrick, C.; Giesen, M.; and Coy, S. 1974. The social ecology of free seating arrangements in a small group interaction context. *Sociometry* 37:262–74.

Hendrick, S. S. 1981. Self-disclosure and marital satisfaction. *Journal of Personality and Social Psychology* 40:1150–59.

Hendricks, M., and Bootzin, R. 1976. Race and sex as stimuli for negative affect and physical avoidance. *Journal of Social Psychology* 98:111–120.

Henley, N. M. 1973. Status and sex: Some touching observations. *Bulletin of the Psychonomic Society* 2:91–93.

———. 1977. *Body politics: Power, sex, and nonverbal communication.* Englewood Cliffs: Prentice-Hall.

Hershey, S., and Werner, E. 1975. Dominance in marital decision making in women's liberation and non-women's liberation families. *Family Process* 14:223–33.

Heshka, S., and Nelson, Y. 1972. Interpersonal speaking distance as a function of age, sex, and relationship. *Sociometry* 35:491–98.

Heslin, R., and Boss, D. 1980. Nonverbal intimacy in airport arrival and departure. *Personality and Social Psychology Bulletin* 6:248–52.

Hess, E. H. 1975. *The tell-tale eye: How your eyes reveal hidden thoughts and emotions.* New York: Van Nostrand Reinhold.

Hewes, G. W. 1957. The anthropology of posture. *Scientific American* 196(February):122-32.

Hiatt, M. 1977. *The way women write.* New York: Teachers College Press.

Hill, C. T., and Stull, D. E. 1981. Sex differences in effects of social and value similarity in same-sex friendship. *Journal of Personality and Social Psychology* 41:488-502.

Hittelman, J. H., and Dickes, R. 1979. Sex differences in neonatal eye contact time. *Merrill-Palmer Quarterly* 25:171-84.

Hoffman, M. L. 1975. Sex differences in moral internalization and values. *Journal of Personality and Social Psychology* 32:720-29.

————. 1977. Sex differences in empathy and related behaviors. *Psychological Bulletin* 84:712-22.

Holahan, C. K., and Stephan, C. W. 1981. When beauty isn't talent: The influence of physical attractiveness, attitudes toward women, and competence on impression formation. *Sex Roles* 7:867-76.

Horowitz, L. M.; Weckler, D.; Saxon, A.; Livaudais, J. D.; and Boutacoff, L. I. 1977. Discomforting talk and speech disruptions. *Journal of Consulting and Clinical Psychology* 45:1036-42.

Horowitz, M. J.; Duff, D. F.; and Stratton, L. O. 1964. Personal space and the body-buffer zone. *Archives of General Psychiatry* 11:651-56.

Howarth, E. 1976. A psychometric investigation of Eysenck's personality inventory. *Journal of Personality Assessment* 40:173-85.

Howells, T. H. 1938. A study of the ability to recognize faces. *Journal of Abnormal and Social Psychology* 33:124-27.

Hrdy, S. B. 1977. *The langurs of Abu: Female and male strategies of reproduction.* Cambridge: Harvard University Press.

Hunt, T. 1928. The measurement of social intelligence. *Journal of Applied Psychology* 12:317-34.

Hyde, J. S. 1981. How large are cognitive gender differences? A meta-analysis using ω^2 and *d. American Psychologist* 36:892-901.

————. How large are gender differences in aggression? A developmental meta-analysis. *Developmental Psychology,* in press.

Ickes, W., and Barnes, R. D. 1977. The role of sex and self-monitoring in unstructured dyadic interactions. *Journal of Personality and Social Psychology* 35:315-30.

————. 1978. Boys and girls together — and alienated: On enacting stereotyped sex roles in mixed-sex dyads. *Journal of Personality and Social Psychology* 36:669-83.

Ickes, W.; Schermer, B.; and Steeno, J. 1979. Sex and sex-role influences in same-sex dyads. *Social Psychology Quarterly* 42:373-85.

Ihara, N. 1978. The development of personal space in Japanese children. *Journal of Child Development* 14:42-51.

Isenhart, M. W. 1980. An investigation of the relationship of sex and sex role to the ability to decode nonverbal cues. *Human Communication Research* 6:309-18.

Izard, C. E. 1971. *The face of emotion.* New York: Appleton-Century-Crofts.

Jackaway, R., and Teevan, R. 1976. Fear of failure and fear of success: Two dimensions of the same motive. *Sex Roles* 2:283-93.

Janda, L. H.; O'Grady, K. E.; and Capps, C. F. 1978. Fear of success in males and females in sex-linked occupations. *Sex Roles* 4:43-50.

Jay, T. B. 1980. Sex roles and dirty word usage: A review of the literature and a reply to Haas. *Psychological Bulletin* 88:614-21.

Jenness, A. 1932. Differences in the recognition of facial expression of emotion. *Journal of General Psychology* 7:192-96.

Jenni, D. A., and Jenni, M. A. 1976. Carrying behavior in humans: Analysis of sex differences. *Science* 194:859-60.

Jenni, M. A. 1976. Sex differences in carrying behavior. *Perceptual and Motor Skills* 43:323-30.

Johnson, H. G.; Ekman, P.; and Friesen, W. V. 1975. Communicative body movements: American emblems. *Semiotica* 15:335-53.

Johnson, S. J., and Black, K. N. 1981. The relationship between sex-role identity and beliefs in personal control. *Sex Roles* 7:425-31.

Jones, E. E. 1978. Black-White personality differences: Another look. *Journal of Personality Assessment* 42:244-52.

Jones, S. E. 1971. A comparative proxemics analysis of dyadic interaction in selected subcultures of New York City. *Journal of Social Psychology* 84:35-44.

Jones, S. E., and Aiello, J. R. 1973. Proxemic behavior of black and white first-, third-, and fifth-grade children. *Journal of Personality and Social Psychology* 25:21-27.

———. 1979. A test of the validity of projective and quasi-projective measures of interpersonal distance. *Western Journal of Speech Communication* 43(Spring):143-52.

Jorgenson, D. O. 1975. Field study of the relationship between status discrepancy and proxemic behavior. *Journal of Social Psychology* 97:173-79.

———. 1978. Nonverbal assessment of attitudinal affect with the smile-return technique. *Journal of Social Psychology* 106:173-79.

Jourard, S. M. 1966. An exploratory study of body accessibility. *British Journal of Social and Clinical Psychology* 5:221-31.

Juni, S., and Brannon, R. 1981. Interpersonal touching as a function of status and sex. *Journal of Social Psychology* 114:135-36.

Justin, F. 1932. A genetic study of laughter provoking stimuli. *Child Development* 3:114-36.

Kagan, J.; Henker, B. A.; Hen-Tov, A; Levine, J.; and Lewis, M. 1966. Infants' differential reactions to familiar and distorted faces. *Child Development* 37:519-32.

Kanner, L. 1931. Judging emotions from facial expressions. *Psychological Monographs* 41(3), Whole no. 186.

Kasl, S. V., and Mahl, G. F. 1965. The relationship of disturbances and hesitations in spontaneous speech to anxiety. *Journal of Personality and Social Psychology* 1:425-33.

Kellogg, W. N., and Eagleson, B. M. 1931. The growth of social perception in different racial groups. *Journal of Educational Psychology* 22:367-75.

Kendon, A. 1967. Some functions of gaze-direction in social interaction *Acta Psychologica* 26:22–63.

Kendon, A., and Cook, M. 1969. The consistency of gaze patterns in social interaction. *British Journal of Psychology* 60:481–94.

Kendon, A., and Ferber, A. 1973. A description of some human greetings. In *Comparative ecology and behaviour of primates*. Ed. R. P. Michael and J. H. Crook. London: Academic Press.

Kendrick, C., and Dunn, J. 1980. Caring for a second baby: Effects on interaction between mother and firstborn. *Developmental Psychology* 16:303–11.

Kenkel, W. F. 1957. Influence differentiation in family decision making. *Sociology and Social Research* 42:18–25.

Kestenbaum, J. M., and Hammersla, J. 1976. Filler items and social desirability in Rotter's locus of control scale. *Journal of Personality Assessment* 40:162–68.

Kirouac, G., and Doré, F. Y. 1983. Accuracy and latency of judgment of facial expressions of emotions. *Perceptual and Motor Skills* 57:683–86.

Kleck, R. E., and Nuessle, W. 1968. Congruence between the indicative and communicative functions of eye contact in interpersonal relations. *British Journal of Social and Clinical Psychology* 7:241–46.

Kleiber, D. A., and Hemmer, J. D. 1981. Sex differences in the relationship of locus of control and recreational sport participation. *Sex Roles* 7:801–10.

Kleinke, C. L.; Desautels, M. S.; and Knapp, B. E. 1977. Adult gaze and affective and visual responses of preschool children. *Journal of Genetic Psychology* 131:321–22.

Knower, F. H. 1941. Analysis of some experimental variations of simulated vocal expressions of the emotions. *Journal of Social Psychology* 14:369–72.

Knowles, E. S. 1980. Convergent validity of personal space measures: Consistent results with low intercorrelations. *Journal of Nonverbal Behavior* 4:240–48.

Koch, H. L. 1935. An analysis of certain forms of so-called "nervous habits" in young children. *Journal of Genetic Psychology* 46:139–69.

Kohlberg, L. 1966. A cognitive-developmental analysis of children's sex-role concepts and attitudes. In *The development of sex differences*. Ed. E. E. Maccoby. Stanford: Stanford University Press.

Koivumaki, J. H. 1975. "Body language taught here": Critique of popular books on nonverbal communication. *Journal of Communication* 25(Winter):26–30.

Korner, A. F. 1969. Neonatal startles, smiles, erections, and reflex sucks as related to state, sex, and individuality. *Child Development* 40:1039–53.

Krail, K. A., and Leventhal, G. 1976. The sex variable in the intrusion of personal space. *Sociometry* 39:170–73.

Kramer, C. 1977. Perceptions of female and male speech. *Language and Speech* 20:151–61.

Kramer, C.; Thorne, B.; and Henley, N. 1978. Perspectives on language and communication. *Signs* 3:638–51.

Krasnoff, A. G. 1981. The sex difference in self-assessed fears. *Sex Roles* 7:19–23.

Kratochwill, T. R., and Goldman, J. A. 1973. Developmental changes in children's judgments of age. *Developmental Psychology* 9:358–62.

Krout, M. H. 1954. An experimental attempt to determine the significance of unconscious manual symbolic movements. *Journal of General Psychology* 51:121-52.

LaFrance, M., and Carmen, B. 1980. The nonverbal display of psychological androgyny. *Journal of Personality and Social Psychology* 38:36-49.

LaFrance, M., and Mayo, C. 1976. Racial differences in gaze behavior during conversations: Two systematic observational studies. *Journal of Personality and Social Psychology* 33:547-52.

_____. 1978. *Moving bodies: Nonverbal communication in social relationships.* Monterey: Brooks/Cole.

Lakoff, R. 1973. Language and woman's place. *Language in Society* 2:45-79.

Lallgee, M. G., and Cook, M. 1969. An experimental investigation of the function of filled pauses in speech. *Language and Speech* 12:24-28.

Lalljee, M., and Cook, M. 1973. Uncertainty in first encounters. *Journal of Personality and Social Psychology* 26:137-41.

Lamb, M. E. 1976. Twelve-month-olds and their parents: Interaction in a laboratory playroom. *Developmental Psychology* 12:237-44.

_____. 1977a. Father-infant and mother-infant interaction in the first year of life. *Child Development* 48:167-81.

_____. 1977b. The development of mother-infant and father-infant attachments in the second year of life. *Developmental Psychology* 13:637-48.

_____. 1978a. Interactions between eighteen-month-olds and their preschool-aged siblings. *Child Development* 49:51-59.

_____. 1978b. The development of sibling relationships in infancy: A short-term longitudinal study. *Child Development* 49:1189-96.

Lamm, H.; Schmidt, R. W.; and Trommsdorff, G. 1976. Sex and social class as determinants of future orientation (time perspective) in adolescents. *Journal of Personality and Social Psychology* 34:317-26.

Langer, E. J.; Fiske, S.; Taylor, S. E.; and Chanowitz, B. 1976. Stigma, staring, and discomfort: A novel-stimulus hypothesis. *Journal of Experimental Social Psychology* 12:451-63.

Langlois, J. H.; Gottfried, N. W.; and Seay, B. 1973. The influence of sex of peer on the social behavior of preschool children. *Developmental Psychology* 8:93-98.

Lasky, R. E., and Klein, R. E. 1979. The reactions of five-month-old infants to eye contact of the mother and of a stranger. *Merrill-Palmer Quarterly* 25:163-70.

Lass, N. J.; Hughes, K. R.; Bowyer, M. D.; Waters, L. T.; and Bourne, V. T. 1976. Speaker sex identification from voiced, whispered, and filtered isolated vowels. *Journal of the Acoustical Society of America* 59:675-78.

Latta, R. M. 1978. Relation of status incongruence to personal space. *Personality and Social Psychology Bulletin* 4:143-46.

Laughery, K. R.; Alexander, J. F.; and Lane, A. B. 1971. Recognition of human faces: Effects of target exposure time, target position, pose position, and type of photograph. *Journal of Applied Psychology* 55:477-83.

Leathers, D. G., and Emigh, T. H. 1980. Decoding facial expressions: A new test with decoding norms. *Quarterly Journal of Speech* 66:418-36.

Leckart, B. T.; Keeling, K. R.; and Bakan, P. 1966. Sex differences in the duration of visual attention. *Perception & Psychophysics* 1:374-76.

Leginski, W., and Izzett, R. R. 1976. The selection and evaluation of interpersonal distances as a function of linguistic styles. *Journal of Social Psychology* 99:125-37.

Lerner, R. M. 1973. The development of personal space schemata toward body build. *Journal of Psychology* 84:229-35.

Lerner, R. M.; Iwawaki, S.; and Chihara, T. 1976. Development of personal space schemata among Japanese children. *Developmental Psychology* 12:466-67.

Lerner, R. M.; Karabenick, S. A.; and Meisels, M. 1975. Effects of age and sex on the development of personal space schemata towards body build. *Journal of Genetic Psychology* 127:91-101.

Lerner, R. M.; Sorell, G. T.; and Brackney, B. E. 1981. Sex differences in self-concept and self-esteem of late adolescents: A time-lag analysis. *Sex Roles* 7:709-22.

Lerner, R. M.; Venning, J.; and Knapp, J. R. 1975. Age and sex effects on personal space schemata toward body build in late childhood. *Developmental Psychology* 11:855-56.

Lester, B. M.; Kotelchuck, M.; Spelke, E.; Sellers, M. J.; and Klein, R. E. 1974. Separation protest in Guatemalan infants: Cross-cultural and cognitive findings. *Developmental Psychology* 10:79-85.

Leung, E.H.L., and Rheingold, H. L. 1981. Development of pointing as a social gesture. *Developmental Psychology* 17:215-20.

Leventhal, G.; Lipshultz, M.; and Chiodo, A. 1978. Sex and setting effects on seating arrangement. *Journal of Psychology* 100:21-26.

Leventhal, G.; Matturro, M.; and Schanerman, J. 1978. Effects of attitude, sex, and approach on nonverbal, verbal and projective measures of personal space. *Perceptual and Motor Skills* 47:107-18.

Leventhal, G.; Schanerman, J.; and Matturro, M. 1978. Effect of room size, initial approach distance and sex on personal space. *Perceptual and Motor Skills* 47:792-94.

Leventhal, H., and Cupchik, G. C. 1975. The informational and facilitative effects of an audience upon expression and the evaluation of humorous stimuli. *Journal of Experimental Social Psychology* 11:363-80.

Leventhal, H., and Mace, W. 1970. The effect of laughter on evaluation of a slapstick movie. *Journal of Personality* 38:16-30.

Levin, H., and Hunter, W. A. 1982. Children's use of a social speech register: Age and sex differences. *Journal of Language and Social Psychology* 1:63-72.

Levin, H., and Silverman, I. 1965. Hesitation phenomena in children's speech. *Language and Speech* 8:67-85.

Levine, M. H., and Sutton-Smith, B. 1973. Effects of age, sex, and task on visual behavior during dyadic interaction. *Developmental Psychology* 9:400-405.

Levitt, E. A. 1964. The relationship between abilities to express emotional meanings vocally and facially. In *The communication of emotional meaning*. Ed. J. R. Davitz. New York: McGraw-Hill.

Levy, N., and Schlosberg, H. 1960. Woodworth scale values of the Lightfoot pictures of facial expression. *Journal of Experimental Psychology* 60:121-25.

Levy, P. K. 1964. The ability to express and perceive vocal communications of feeling. In *The communication of emotional meaning*. Ed. J. R. Davitz. New York: McGraw-Hill.

Lewis, M. 1969. Infants' responses to facial stimuli during the first year of life. *Developmental Psychology* 1:75-86.

————. 1972. State as an infant-environment interaction: An analysis of mother-infant interaction as a function of sex. *Merrill-Palmer Quarterly* 18:95-121.

Lewis, M.; Kagan, J.; and Kalafat, J. 1966. Patterns of fixation in the young infant. *Child Development* 37:331-41.

Lewis, M., and Kreitzberg, V. S. 1979. Effects of birth order and spacing on mother-infant interactions. *Developmental Psychology* 15:617-25.

Lewis, M., and Weinraub, M. 1974. Sex of parent × sex of child: Socioemotional development. In *Sex differences in behavior*. Ed. R. C. Friedman, R. M. Richart, and R. L. Vande Wiele. New York: Wiley.

Libby, W. L., Jr. 1970. Eye contact and direction of looking as stable individual differences. *Journal of Experimental Research in Personality* 4:303-12.

Libby, W. L., Jr., and Yaklevich, D. 1973. Personality determinants of eye contact and direction of gaze aversion. *Journal of Personality and Social Psychology* 27:197-206.

Ling, D., and Ling, A. H. 1974. Communication development in the first three years of life. *Journal of Speech and Hearing Research* 17:146-59.

Little, K. B. 1968. Cultural variations in social schemata. *Journal of Personality and Social Psychology* 10:1-7.

Lochman, J. E., and Allen, G. 1981. Nonverbal communication of couples in conflict. *Journal of Research in Personality* 15:253-69.

Lomranz, J.; Shapira, A.; Choresh, N.; and Gilat, Y. 1975. Children's personal space as a function of age and sex. *Developmental Psychology* 11:541-45.

Loo, C., and Kennelly, D. 1979. Social density: Its effects on behaviors and perceptions of preschoolers. *Environmental Psychology and Nonverbal Behavior* 3:131-46.

Loo, R. 1979. A psychometric investigation of the Eysenck Personality Inventory. *Journal of Personality Assessment* 43:54-58.

Lott, A. J.; Lott, B. E.; Reed, T.; and Crow, T. 1970. Personality-trait descriptions of differentially liked persons. *Journal of Personality and Social Psychology* 16:284-90.

Lott, B. 1978. Behavioral concordance with sex role ideology related to play areas, creativity, and parental sex typing of children. *Journal of Personality and Social Psychology* 36:1087-1110.

Lott, D. F., and Sommer, R. 1967. Seating arrangements and status. *Journal of Personality and Social Psychology* 7:90-95.

Loucks, S. 1980. Loneliness, affect, and self-concept: Construct validity of the Bradley Loneliness Scale. *Journal of Personality Assessment* 44:142-47.

Loveday, L. 1981. Pitch, politeness and sexual role: An exploratory investigation into the pitch correlates of English and Japanese politeness formulae. *Language and Speech* 24:71-89.

Lyons, J., and Goldman, S. 1966. An experimentally generated set of expressive photographs. *Journal of Psychology* 62:67-82.

Maccoby, E. E., and Feldman, S. S. 1972. Mother-attachment and stranger-reactions in the third year of life. *Monographs of the Society for Research in Child Development* 37(1), Ser. no. 146.

Maccoby, E. E., and Jacklin, C. N. 1973. Stress, activity, and proximity seeking: Sex differences in the year-old child. *Child Development* 44:34–42.

———. 1974. *The psychology of sex differences.* Stanford: Stanford University Press.

———. 1980. Sex differences in aggression: A rejoinder and reprise. *Child Development* 51:964–80.

Macdonald, N. E., and Hyde, J. S. 1980. Fear of success, need achievement, and fear of failure: A factor analytic study. *Sex Roles* 6:695–711.

Mackey, W. C. 1976. Parameters of the smile as a social signal. *Journal of Genetic Psychology* 129:125–30.

Mahl, G. F. 1956. Disturbances and silences in the patient's speech in psychotherapy. *Journal of Abnormal and Social Psychology* 53:1–15.

Mahoney, E. R. 1974. Compensatory reactions to spatial immediacy. *Sociometry* 37:423–31.

Maines, D. R. 1977. Tactile relationships in the subway as affected by racial, sexual, and crowded seating conditions. *Environmental Psychology and Nonverbal Behavior* 2:100–108.

Major, B. 1981. Gender patterns in touching behavior. In *Gender and nonverbal behavior.* Ed. C. Mayo and N. M. Henley. New York: Springer-Verlag.

Major, B., and Heslin, R. 1982. Perceptions of cross-sex and same-sex nonreciprocal touch: It is better to give than to receive. *Journal of Nonverbal Behavior* 6:148–62.

Major, B., and Williams, L. 1980. Frequency of touch by sex and race: A replication of some touching observations. Unpublished manuscript. State University of New York at Buffalo.

Markel, N. N.; Prebor, L. D.; and Brandt, J. F. 1972. Biosocial factors in dyadic communication: Sex and speaking intensity. *Journal of Personality and Social Psychology* 23:11–13.

Mattingly, I. G. 1966. Speaker variation and vocal-tract size. *Journal of the Acoustical Society of America* 39:1219.

Mazanec, N., and McCall, G. J. 1976. Sex factors and allocation of attention in observing persons. *Journal of Psychology* 93:175–80.

McCall, R. B. 1974. Exploratory manipulation and play in the human infant. *Monographs of the Society for Research in Child Development* 39(2), Ser. no. 155.

McCauley, C.; Coleman, G.; and DeFusco, P. 1978. Commuters' eye contact with strangers in city and suburban train stations: Evidence of short-term adaptation to interpersonal overload in the city. *Environmental Psychology and Nonverbal Behavior* 2:215–25.

McClintock, C. C., and Hunt, R. G. 1975. Nonverbal indicators of affect and deception in an interview setting. *Journal of Applied Social Psychology* 5:54–67.

McDowell, K. V. 1972. Violations of personal space. *Canadian Journal of Behavioural Science* 4:210–17.

McGee, M. G. 1979. Human spatial abilities: Psychometric studies and environmental, genetic, hormonal, and neurological influences. *Psychological Bulletin* 86:889–918.

McGehee, F. 1937. The reliability of the identification of the human voice. *Journal of General Psychology* 17:249–71.

McGhee, P. E. 1974. Moral development and children's appreciation of humor. *Developmental Psychology* 10:514–25.

———. 1976. Sex differences in children's humor. *Journal of Communication* 26(Summer):176–89.

McKelvie, S. J. 1978. Sex differences in facial memory. In *Practical aspects of memory.* Ed. M. M. Gruneberg, P. E. Morris, and R. N. Sykes. London: Academic Press.

———. 1981. Sex differences in memory for faces. *Journal of Psychology* 107:109–25.

McMillan, J. R.; Clifton, A. K.; McGrath, D.; and Gale, W. S. 1977. Women's language: Uncertainty or interpersonal sensitivity and emotionality? *Sex Roles* 3:545–59.

Meditch, A. 1975. The development of sex-specific speech patterns in young children. *Anthropological Linguistics* 17:421–33.

Mehrabian, A. 1968. Inference of attitudes from the posture, orientation, and distance of a communicator. *Journal of Consulting and Clinical Psychology* 32:296–308.

———. 1971a. Nonverbal betrayal of feeling. *Journal of Experimental Research in Personality* 5:64–73.

———. 1971b. Verbal and nonverbal interaction of strangers in a waiting situation. *Journal of Experimental Research in Personality* 5:127–38.

———. 1977. Individual differences in stimulus screening and arousability. *Journal of Personality* 45:237–50.

Mehrabian, A., and Diamond, S. G. 1971. Seating arrangement and conversation. *Sociometry* 34:281–89.

Mehrabian, A., and Williams, M. 1969. Nonverbal concomitants of perceived and intended persuasiveness. *Journal of Personality and Social Psychology* 13:37–58.

Meisels, M., and Dosey, M. A. 1971. Personal space, anger-arousal, and psychological defense. *Journal of Personality* 39:333–44.

Meisels, M., and Guardo, C. J. 1969. Development of personal space schemata. *Child Development* 40:1167–78.

Melson, G. F. 1976. Determinants of personal space in young children: Perception of distance cues. *Perceptual and Motor Skills* 43:107–14.

———. 1977. Sex differences in proxemic behavior and personal space schemata in young children. *Sex Roles* 3:81–89.

Messer, S. B., and Lewis, M. 1972. Social class and sex differences in the attachment and play behavior of the year-old infant. *Merrill-Palmer Quarterly* 18:295–306.

Michael, G., and Willis, F. N., Jr. 1968. The development of gestures as a function of social class, education, and sex. *Psychological Record* 18:515–19.

———. 1969. The development of gestures in three subcultural groups. *Journal of Social Psychology* 79:35–41.

Miller, R. S., and Lefcourt, H. M. 1982. The assessment of social intimacy. *Journal of Personality Assessment* 46:514–18.

Morgan, B. S. 1976. Intimacy of disclosure topics and sex differences in self-disclosure. *Sex Roles* 2:161–66.

Morse, C. 1982. College yearbook pictures: More females smile than males. *Journal of Psychology* 110:3–6.

Morton, T. L. 1978. Intimacy and reciprocity of exchange: A comparison of spouses and strangers. *Journal of Personality and Social Psychology* 36:72–81.

Moskowitz, D. S.; Schwarz, J. C.; and Corsini, D. A. 1977. Initiating day care at three years of age: Effects on attachment. *Child Development* 48:1271–76.

Moss, F. A. 1929. *Your mind in action: Applications of psychology.* Boston: Houghton Mifflin.

Moss, H. A. 1967. Sex, age, and state as determinants of mother-infant interaction. *Merrill-Palmer Quarterly* 13:19–36.

Muirhead, R. D., and Goldman, M. 1979. Mutual eye contact as affected by seating position, sex, and age. *Journal of Social Psychology* 109:201–6.

Murry, T.; Amundson, P.; and Hollien, H. 1977. Acoustical characteristics of infant cries: Fundamental frequency. *Journal of Child Language* 4:321–28.

Naditch, M. P., and DeMaio, T. 1975. Locus of control and competence. *Journal of Personality* 43:541–59.

Natale, M.; Entin, E.; and Jaffe, J. 1979. Vocal interruptions in dyadic communication as a function of speech and social anxiety. *Journal of Personality and Social Psychology* 37:865–78.

Naus, P. J., and Eckenrode, J. J. 1974. Age differences and degree of acquaintance as determinants of interpersonal distance. *Journal of Social Psychology* 93:133–34.

Nemeth, C.; Endicott, J.; and Wachtler, J. 1976. From the '50s to the '70s: Women in jury deliberations. *Sociometry* 39:293–304.

Nesbitt, P. D., and Steven, G. 1974. Personal space and stimulus intensity at a Southern California amusement park. *Sociometry* 37:105–15.

Nevill, D. 1974. Experimental manipulation of dependency motivation and its effects on eye contact and measures of field dependency. *Journal of Personality and Social Psychology* 29:72–79.

Nideffer, R. M. 1976. Test of Attentional and Interpersonal Style. *Journal of Personality and Social Psychology* 34:394–404.

Nisbett, R. E., and Temoshok, L. 1976. Is there an "external" cognitive style? *Journal of Personality and Social Psychology* 33:36–47.

Noesjirwan, J. 1977. Contrasting cultural patterns of interpersonal closeness in doctors' waiting rooms in Sydney and Jakarta. *Journal of Cross-Cultural Psychology* 8:357–68.

Noller, P. 1980a. Misunderstandings in marital communication: A study of couples' nonverbal communication. *Journal of Personality and Social Psychology* 39:1135–48.

———. 1980b. Cross-gender effect in two-child families. *Developmental Psychology* 16:159–60.

———. 1981. Gender and marital adjustment level differences in decoding messages from spouses and strangers. *Journal of Personality and Social Psychology* 41:272-78.

_____. 1982. Channel consistency and inconsistency in the communications of married couples. *Journal of Personality and Social Psychology* 43:732-41.

Norum, G. A.; Russo, N. J.; and Sommer, R. 1967. Seating patterns and group task. *Psychology in the Schools* 4:276-80.

Nowicki, S., Jr., and Duke, M. P. 1972. Use of Comfortable Interpersonal Distance Scale in high school students: Replication. *Psychological Reports* 30:182.

Nowicki, S., Jr.; Winograd, E.; and Millard, B. A. 1979. Memory for faces: A social learning analysis. *Journal of Research in Personality* 13:460-68.

Olds, D. E., and Shaver, P. 1980. Masculinity, femininity, academic performance, and health: Further evidence concerning the androgyny controversy. *Journal of Personality* 48:323-41.

O'Malley, P. M., and Bachman, J. G. 1979. Self-esteem and education: Sex and cohort comparisons among high school seniors. *Journal of Personality and Social Psychology* 37:1153-59.

Orlofsky, J. L. 1981a. A comparison of projective and objective fear-of-success and sex-role orientation measures as predictors of women's performance on masculine and feminine tasks. *Sex Roles* 7:999-1018.

_____. 1981b. Relationship between sex role attitudes and personality traits and the Sex Role Behavior Scale-1: A new measure of masculine and feminine role behaviors and interests. *Journal of Personality and Social Psychology* 40:927-40.

Orlofsky, J. L.; Ramsden, M. W.; and Cohen, R. S. 1982. Development of the Revised Sex-role Behavior Scale. *Journal of Personality Assessment* 46:632-38.

Orlofsky, J. L., and Windle, M. T. 1978. Sex-role orientation, behavioral adaptability and personal adjustment. *Sex Roles* 4:801-11.

Padesky, C. A., and Hammen, C. L. 1981. Sex differences in depressive symptom expression and help-seeking among college students. *Sex Roles* 7:309-20.

Pagán, G., and Aiello, J. R. 1982. Development of personal space among Puerto Ricans. *Journal of Nonverbal Behavior* 7:59-68.

Parke, R. D., and O'Leary, S. E. 1976. Family interaction in the newborn period: Some findings, some observations, and some unresolved issues. In *The developing individual in a changing world,* vol. 2. Ed. K. F. Riegel and J. A. Meacham. The Hague: Mouton.

Parsons, T., and Bales, R. F. 1955. *Family, socialization and interaction process.* Glencoe, Ill.: The Free Press.

Patterson, A. H., and Boles, W. E. 1974. The effects of personal space variables upon approach and attitudes toward the other in a prisoner's dilemma game. *Personality and Social Psychology Bulletin* 1:364-66.

Patterson, M. L. 1973. Stability of nonverbal immediacy behaviors. *Journal of Experimental Social Psychology* 9:97-109.

_____. 1977. Interpersonal distance, affect, and equilibrium theory. *Journal of Social Psychology* 101:205-14.

Patterson, M. L.; Mullens, S.; and Romano, J. 1971. Compensatory reactions to spatial intrusion. *Sociometry* 34:114-21.

Pedersen, D. M. 1973. Developmental trends in personal space. *Journal of Psychology* 83:3-9.

————. 1977. Factors affecting personal space toward a group. *Perceptual and Motor Skills* 45:735-43.

Pedersen, D. M., and Heaston, A. B. 1972. The effects of sex of subject, sex of approaching person, and angle of approach upon personal space. *Journal of Psychology* 82:277-86.

Pedersen, F. A., and Bell, R. Q. 1970. Sex differences in preschool children without histories of complications of pregnancy and delivery. *Developmental Psychology* 3:10-15.

Pellegrini, R. J., and Empey, J. 1970. Interpersonal spatial orientation in dyads. *Journal of Psychology* 76:67-70.

Pellowe, J., and Jones, V. 1978. On intonational variability in Tyneside speech. In *Sociolinguistic patterns in British English*. Ed. P. Trudgill. London: Edward Arnold.

Perdue, V. P., and Connor, J. M. 1978. Patterns of touching between preschool children and male and female teachers. *Child Development* 49:1258-62.

Petri, H. L.; Huggins, R. G.; Mills, C. J.; and Barry, L. S. 1974. Variables influencing the shape of personal space. *Personality and Social Psychology Bulletin* 1:360-61.

Pfaff, P. L. 1954. An experimental study of the communication of feeling without contextual material. *Speech Monographs* 21:155-56.

Phillips, J. R. 1979. An exploration of perception of body boundary, personal space, and body size in elderly persons. *Perceptual and Motor Skills* 48:299-308.

Phillips, S.; King, S.; and DuBois, L. 1978. Spontaneous activities of female versus male newborns. *Child Development* 49:590-97.

Pien, D., and Rothbart, M. K. 1976. Incongruity and resolution in children's humor: A reexamination. *Child Development* 47:966-71.

Piliavin, J. A., and Martin, R. R. 1978. The effects of the sex composition of groups on style of social interaction. *Sex Roles* 4:281-96.

Pilkonis, P. A. 1977a. Shyness, public and private, and its relationship to other measures of social behavior. *Journal of Personality* 45:585-95.

————. 1977b. The behavioral consequences of shyness. *Journal of Personality* 45:596-611.

Poling, T. H. 1978. Sex differences, dominance, and physical attractiveness in the use of nonverbal emblems. *Psychological Reports* 43:1087-92.

Polit, D., and LaFrance, M. 1977. Sex differences in reaction to spatial invasion. *Journal of Social Psychology* 102:59-60.

Post, B., and Hetherington, E. M. 1974. Sex differences in the use of proximity and eye contact in judgments of affiliation in preschool children. *Developmental Psychology* 10:881-89.

Powell, P. H., and Dabbs, J. M., Jr. 1976. Physical attractiveness and personal space. *Journal of Social Psychology* 100:59-64.

Price, G. H., and Dabbs, J. M., Jr. 1974. Sex, setting, and personal space: Changes as children grow older. *Personality and Social Psychology Bulletin* 1:362-63.

Prociuk, T. J., and Breen, L. J. 1975. Defensive externality and its relation to academic performance. *Journal of Personality and Social Psychology* 31:549–56.

Radecki, C., and Jennings (Walstedt), J. 1980. Sex as a status variable in work settings: Female and male reports of dominance behavior. *Journal of Applied Social Psychology* 10:71–85.

Radloff, L. 1975. Sex differences in depression: The effects of occupation and marital status. *Sex Roles* 1:249–65.

Ragan, J. M. 1982. Gender displays in portrait photographs. *Sex Roles* 8:33–43.

Rago, W. V., Jr., and Cleland, C. C. 1978. Relationship between the frequency of touching and status in institutionalized profoundly retarded. *Bulletin of the Psychonomic Society* 11:249–50.

Ramanaiah, N. V., and Adams, M. L. 1981. Locus of control and attribution of responsibility for academic performance. *Journal of Personality Assessment* 45:309–13.

Rekers, G. A.; Amaro-Plotkin, H. D.; and Low, B. P. 1977. Sex-typed mannerisms in normal boys and girls as a function of sex and age. *Child Development* 48:275–78.

Rekers, G. A., and Mead, S. 1979. Human sex differences in carrying behaviors: A replication and extension. *Perceptual and Motor Skills* 48:625–26.

Rekers, G. A., and Rudy, J. P. 1978. Differentiation of childhood body gestures. *Perceptual and Motor Skills* 46:839–45.

Rekers, G. A.; Sanders, J. A.; and Strauss, C. C. 1981. Developmental differentiation of adolescent body gestures. *Journal of Genetic Psychology* 138:123–31.

Rheingold, H. L., and Samuels, H. R. 1969. Maintaining the positive behavior of infants by increased stimulation. *Developmental Psychology* 1:520–27.

Riggio, R. E.; Friedman, H. S.; and DiMatteo, M. R. 1981. Nonverbal greetings: Effects of the situation and personality. *Personality and Social Psychology Bulletin* 7:682–89.

Rinck, C. M.; Willis, F. N., Jr.; and Dean, L. M. 1980. Interpersonal touch among residents of homes for the elderly. *Journal of Communication* 30(Spring): 44–47.

Rios-Garcia, L. R., and Cook, P. E. 1975. Self-derogation and defense style in college students. *Journal of Personality Assessment* 39:273–81.

Robson, K. S.; Pedersen, F. A.; and Moss, H. A. 1969. Developmental observations of diadic gazing in relation to the fear of strangers and social approach behavior. *Child Development* 40:619–27.

Rogers, P. L.; Scherer, K. R.; and Rosenthal, R. 1971. Content filtering human speech: A simple electronic system. *Behavior Research Methods and Instrumentation* 3:16–18.

Rosenblum, L. A.; Coe, C. L.; and Bromley, L. J. 1975. Peer relations in monkeys: The influence of social structure, gender, and familiarity. In *Friendship and peer relations*. Ed. M. Lewis and L. A. Rosenblum. New York: Wiley.

Rosenfeld, H. M. 1966. Approval-seeking and approval-inducing functions of verbal and nonverbal responses in the dyad. *Journal of Personality and Social Psychology* 4:597–605.

Rosenfeld, H. M.; Shea, M.; and Greenbaum, P. 1979. Facial emblems of 'right' and 'wrong': Topographical analysis and derivation of a recognition test. *Semiotica* 26:15-34.

Rosenhan, D., and Messick, S. 1966. Affect and expectation. *Journal of Personality and Social Psychology* 3:38-44.

Rosenthal, D. A., and Lines, R. 1978. Handwriting as a correlate of extraversion. *Journal of Personality Assessment* 42:45-48.

Rosenthal, R. 1976. *Experimenter effects in behavioral research,* enlarged edition. New York: Irvington.

_____. 1978. Combining results of independent studies. *Psychological Bulletin* 85:185-93.

_____, ed. 1980. *Quantitative assessment of research domains.* San Francisco: Jossey-Bass.

Rosenthal, R., and DePaulo, B. M. 1979a. Sex differences in eavesdropping on nonverbal cues. *Journal of Personality and Social Psychology* 37:273-85.

_____. 1979b. Sex differences in accommodation in nonverbal communication. In *Skill in nonverbal communication: Individual differences.* Ed. R. Rosenthal. Cambridge: Oelgeschlager, Gunn & Hain.

Rosenthal, R.; Hall, J. A.; DiMatteo, M. R.; Rogers, P. L.; and Archer, D. 1979. *Sensitivity to nonverbal communication: The PONS test.* Baltimore: The Johns Hopkins University Press.

Rosenthal, R., and Rubin, D. B. 1978. Interpersonal expectancy effects: The first 345 studies. *Brain and Behavioral Sciences* 3:377-415.

Ross, H. S., and Goldman, B. D. 1977. Infants' sociability toward strangers. *Child Development* 48:638-42.

Ross, M.; Layton, B.; Erickson, B.; and Schopler, J. 1973. Affect, facial regard, and reactions to crowding. *Journal of Personality and Social Psychology* 28:69-76.

Rubin, Z. 1970. Measurement of romantic love. *Journal of Personality and Social Psychology* 16:265-73.

Rubin, Z., and Shenker, S. 1978. Friendship, proximity, and self-disclosure. *Journal of Personality* 46:1-22.

Ruble, D. N. 1975. Visual orientation and self-perceptions of children in an external-cue-relevant or cue-irrelevant task situation. *Child Development* 46:669-76.

Ruble, D. N., and Nakamura, C. Y. 1972. Task orientation versus social orientation in young children and their attention to relevant social cues. *Child Development* 43:471-80.

_____. 1973. Outerdirectedness as a problem-solving approach in relation to developmental level and selected task variables. *Child Development* 44:519-28.

Russell, D.; Peplau, L. A.; and Cutrona, C. E. 1980. The Revised UCLA Loneliness Scale: Concurrent and discriminant validity evidence. *Journal of Personality and Social Psychology* 39:472-80.

Russell, D.; Peplau, L. A.; and Ferguson, M. L. 1978. Developing a measure of loneliness. *Journal of Personality Assessment* 42:290-94.

Russo, N. F. 1975. Eye contact, interpersonal distance, and the equilibrium theory. *Journal of Personality and Social Psychology* 31:497-502.

Rutter, D. R.; Morley, I. E.; and Graham, J. C. 1972. Visual interaction in a group of introverts and extraverts. *European Journal of Social Psychology* 2:371-84.

Rutter, D. R., and Stephenson, G. M. 1977. The role of visual communication in synchronising conversation. *European Journal of Social Psychology* 7:29-37.

Sabatelli, R. M.; Dreyer, A. S.; and Buck, R. 1979. Cognitive style and sending and receiving of facial cues. *Perceptual and Motor Skills* 49:203-12.

Sachs, J. 1975. Cues to the identification of sex in children's speech. In *Language and sex: Difference and dominance.* Ed. B. Thorne and N. Henley. Rowley, Mass.: Newbury House.

Safer, M. A. 1981. Sex and hemisphere differences in access to codes for processing emotional expressions and faces. *Journal of Experimental Psychology: General* 110:86-100.

Samuels, M. R. 1939. Judgments of faces. *Character and Personality* 8:18-27.

Sanders, J. L. 1976. Relationship of personal space to body-image boundary definiteness. *Journal of Research in Personality* 10:478-81.

Sarafino, E. P., and Helmuth, H. 1981. Development of personal space in pre-school children as a function of age and day-care experience. *Journal of Social Psychology* 115:59-63.

Sarason, I. G., and Winkel, G. H. 1966. Individual differences among subjects and experimenters and subjects' self-descriptions. *Journal of Personality and Social Psychology* 3:448-57.

Savitsky, J. C., and Izard, C. E. 1970. Developmental changes in the use of emotion cues in a concept-formation task. *Developmental Psychology* 3:350-57.

Savitsky, J. C., and Watson, M. J. 1975. Patterns of proxemic behavior among preschool children. *Representative Research in Social Psychology* 6:109-13.

Scarr, S.; Webber, P. L.; Weinberg, R. A.; and Wittig, M. A. 1981. Personality resemblance among adolescents and their parents in biologically related and adoptive families. *Journal of Personality and Social Psychology* 40:885-98.

Schaible, M. 1975. An analysis of noncontent TAT variables in a longitudinal sample. *Journal of Personality Assessment* 39:480-85.

Schaie, K. W., and Parham, I. A. 1976. Stability of adult personality: Fact or fable? *Journal of Personality and Social Psychology* 34:146-58.

Scheflen, A. E. 1973. *Communicational structure: Analysis of a psychotherapy transaction.* Bloomington: Indiana University Press.

Scheman, J. D., and Lockard, J. S. 1979. Development of gaze aversion in children. *Child Development* 50:594-96.

Scheman, J. D.; Lockard, J. S.; and Mehler, B. L. 1978. Influences of anatomical differences on gender-specific book-carrying behavior. *Bulletin of the Psychonomic Society* 11:17-20.

Scherer, K. R. 1971. Randomized splicing: A note on a simple technique for masking speech content. *Journal of Experimental Research in Personality* 5:155-59.

Schneider, F. W.; Coutts, L. M.; and Garrett, W. A. 1977. Interpersonal gaze in a triad as a function of sex. *Perceptual and Motor Skills* 44:184.

Schneider, S. M., and Kintz, B. L. 1977. The effect of lying upon foot and leg movement. *Bulletin of the Psychonomic Society* 10:451-53.

Schwarz, J. C. 1972. Effects of peer familiarity on the behavior of preschoolers in a novel situation. *Journal of Personality and Social Psychology* 24:276-84.

Schwarzwald, J.; Kavish, N.; Shoham, M.; and Waysman, M. 1977. Fear and sex-similarity as determinants of personal space. *Journal of Psychology* 96:55–61.

Scott, J. A. 1974. Awareness of informal space: A longitudinal analysis. *Perceptual and Motor Skills* 39:735–38.

Sechrest, L.; Flores, L.; and Arellano, L. 1968. Language and social interaction in a bilingual culture. *Journal of Social Psychology* 76:155–61.

Seham, M., and Boardman, D. V. 1934. A study of motor automatisms. *Archives of Neurology and Psychiatry* 32:154–73.

Serbin, L. A.; O'Leary, K. D.; Kent, R. N.; and Tonick, I. J. 1973. A comparison of teacher response to the preacademic and problem behavior of boys and girls. *Child Development* 44:796–804.

Severy, L. J.; Forsyth, D. R.; and Wagner, P. J. 1979. A multimethod assessment of personal space development in female and male, black and white children. *Journal of Nonverbal Behavior* 4:68–86.

Shaw, M. E., and Sadler, O. W. 1965. Interaction patterns in heterosexual dyads varying in degree of intimacy. *Journal of Social Psychology* 66:345–51.

Shepherd, J. W.; Deregowski, J. B.; and Ellis, H. D. 1974. A cross-cultural study of recognition memory for faces. *International Journal of Psychology* 9:205–11.

Shepherd, J. W., and Ellis, H. D. 1973. The effect of attractiveness on recognition memory for faces. *American Journal of Psychology* 86:627–33.

Shrout, P. E., and Fiske, D. W. 1981. Nonverbal behaviors and social evaluation. *Journal of Personality* 49:115–28.

Shultz, T. R., and Horibe, F. 1974. Development of the appreciation of verbal jokes. *Developmental Psychology* 10:13–20.

Shuter, R. 1976. Proxemics and tactility in Latin America. *Journal of Communication* 26(Summer):46–52.

————. 1979. A study of nonverbal communication among Jews and Protestants. *Journal of Social Psychology* 109:31–41.

Silverthorne, C.; Micklewright, J.; O'Donnell, M.; and Gibson, R. 1976. Attribution of personal characteristics as a function of the degree of touch on initial contact and sex. *Sex Roles* 2:185–93.

Skarin, K. 1977. Cognitive and contextual determinants of stranger fear in six- and eleven-month-old infants. *Child Development* 48:537–44.

Skotko, V. P., and Langmeyer, D. 1977. The effects of interaction distance and gender on self-disclosure in the dyad. *Sociometry* 40:178–82.

Slane, S.; Dragan, W.; Crandall, C. J.; and Payne, P. 1980. Stress effects on the nonverbal behavior of repressors and sensitizers. *Journal of Psychology* 106:101–9.

Slane, S.; Petruska, R.; and Cheyfitz, S. 1981. Personal space measurement: A validational comparison. *Psychological Record* 31:145–51.

Smetana, J.; Bridgeman, D. L.; and Bridgeman, B. 1978. A field study of interpersonal distance in early childhood. *Personality and Social Psychology Bulletin* 4:309–13.

Smith, D. E.; Willis, F. N.; and Gier, J. A. 1980. Success and interpersonal touch in a competitive setting. *Journal of Nonverbal Behavior* 5:26–34.

Smith, H. W. 1981. Territorial spacing on a beach revisited: A cross-national exploration. *Social Psychology Quarterly* 44:132–37.

Smith, M. L.; Glass, G. V.; and Miller, T. I. 1980. *The benefits of psychotherapy.* Baltimore: The Johns Hopkins University Press.

Smith, P. M. 1979. Sex markers in speech. In *Social markers in speech.* Ed. K. R. Scherer and H. Giles. Cambridge: Cambridge University Press.

Sobel, R. S., and Lillith, N. 1975. Determinants of nonstationary personal space invasion. *Journal of Social Psychology* 97:39–45.

Sommer, R. 1967. Sociofugal space. *American Journal of Sociology* 72:654–60.

Sparacino, J., and Hansell, S. 1979. Physical attractiveness and academic performance: Beauty is not always talent. *Journal of Personality* 47:449–69.

Spelke, E.; Zelazo, P.; Kagan, J.; and Kotelchuck, M. 1973. Father interaction and separation protest. *Developmental Psychology* 9:83–90.

Spence, J. T., and Helmreich, R. 1978. *Masculinity and femininity: Their psychological dimensions, correlates, and antecedents.* Austin: University of Texas Press.

Spence, J. T.; Helmreich, R. L.; and Holahan, C. K. 1979. Negative and positive components of psychological masculinity and femininity and their relationships to self-reports of neurotic and acting out behaviors. *Journal of Personality and Social Psychology* 37:1673–82.

Spence, J. T.; Helmreich, R.; and Stapp, J. 1973. A short version of the Attitudes toward Women Scale (AWS). *Bulletin of the Psychonomic Society* 2:219–20.

————. 1975. Ratings of self and peers on sex role attributes and their relation to self-esteem and conceptions of masculinity and femininity. *Journal of Personality and Social Psychology* 32:29–39.

Spielberger, C. D., and Jacobs, G. A. 1982. Personality and smoking behavior. *Journal of Personality Assessment* 46:396–403.

Spottswood, P. J., and Burghardt, G. M. 1976. The effects of sex, book weight, and grip strength on book-carrying styles. *Bulletin of the Psychonomic Society* 8:150–52.

Staffieri, J. R., and Bassett, J. E. 1970. Birth order and perception of facial expressions. *Perceptual and Motor Skills* 30:606.

Statistical yearbook 1974. Paris: UNESCO Press, 1975.

Stericker, A. B., and Johnson, J. E. 1977. Sex-role identification and self-esteem in college students: Do men and women differ? *Sex Roles* 3:19–26.

Stern, D. N., and Bender, E. P. 1974. An ethological study of children approaching a strange adult: Sex differences. In *Sex differences in behavior.* Ed. R. C. Friedman, R. M. Richart, and R. L. Vande Wiele. New York: Wiley.

Stier, D. S., and Hall, J. A. 1984. Gender differences in touch: An empirical and theoretical review. *Journal of Personality and Social Psychology* 47:440–59.

Stone, L. 1979. *The family, sex and marriage in England 1550–1800,* abridged ed. New York: Harper & Row.

Storms, M. D. 1979. Sex role identity and its relationships to sex role attributes and sex role stereotypes. *Journal of Personality and Social Psychology* 37:1779–89.

Stratton, L. O.; Tekippe, D. J.; and Flick, G. L. 1973. Personal space and self-concept. *Sociometry* 36:424–29.

Strickland, B. R., and Haley, W. E. 1980. Sex differences on the Rotter I-E Scale. *Journal of Personality and Social Psychology* 39:930–39.

Strodtbeck, F. L.; James, R. M.; and Hawkins, C. 1957. Social status in jury deliberations. *American Sociological Review* 22:713–19.

Strodtbeck, F. L., and Mann, R. D. 1956. Sex role differentiation in jury deliberations. *Sociometry* 19:3–11.

Strongman, K. T., and Champness, B. G. 1968. Dominance hierarchies and conflict in eye contact. *Acta Psychologica* 28:376–86.

Summerhayes, D. L., and Suchner, R. W. 1978. Power implications of touch in male-female relationships. *Sex Roles* 4:103–10.

Sussman, N. M., and Rosenfeld, H. M. 1978. Touch, justification, and sex: Influences on the aversiveness of spatial violations. *Journal of Social Psychology* 106:215–25.

_____. 1982. Influence of culture, language, and sex on conversational distance. *Journal of Personality and Social Psychology* 42:66–74.

Swacker, M. 1975. The sex of the speaker as a sociolinguistic variable. In *Language and sex: Difference and dominance.* Ed. B. Thorne and N. Henley. Rowley, Mass.: Newbury House.

Sweeney, M. A., and Cottle, W. C. 1976. Nonverbal acuity: A comparison of counselors and noncounselors. *Journal of Counseling Psychology* 23:394–97.

Sweeney, M. A.; Cottle, W. C.; and Kobayashi, M. J. 1980. Nonverbal communication: A cross-cultural comparison of American and Japanese counseling students. *Journal of Counseling Psychology* 27:150–56.

Tauber, M. A. 1979. Parental socialization techniques and sex differences in children's play. *Child Development* 50:225–34.

Taylor, M. C. 1979. Race, sex, and the expression of self-fulfilling prophecies in a laboratory teaching situation. *Journal of Personality and Social Psychology* 37:897–912.

Taylor, M. C., and Hall, J. A. 1982. Psychological androgyny: Theories, methods, and conclusions. *Psychological Bulletin* 92:347–66.

Taylor, S. E., and Langer, E. J. 1977. Pregnancy: A social stigma? *Sex Roles* 3:27–35.

Tennis, G. H., and Dabbs, J. M., Jr. 1975. Sex, setting and personal space: First grade through college. *Sociometry* 38:385–94.

Tesser, A. 1980. Self-esteem maintenance in family dynamics. *Journal of Personality and Social Psychology* 39:77–91.

Thoman, E. B.; Leiderman, P. H.; and Olson, J. P. 1972. Neonate-mother interaction during breast-feeding. *Developmental Psychology* 6:110–18.

Thomas, D. L.; Franks, D. D.; and Calonico, J. M. 1972. Role-taking and power in social psychology. *American Sociological Review* 37:605–14.

Thomas, D. R. 1973. Interaction distances in same-sex and mixed-sex groups. *Perceptual and Motor Skills* 36:15–18.

Thompson, D. F., and Meltzer, L. 1964. Communication of emotional intent by facial expression. *Journal of Abnormal and Social Psychology* 68:129–35.

Tidd, K. L., and Lockard, J. S. 1978. Monetary significance of the affiliative smile: A case for reciprocal altruism. *Bulletin of the Psychonomic Society* 11:344–46.

Tieger, T. 1980. On the biological basis of sex differences in aggression. *Child Development* 51:943–63.

Tolor, A. 1975. Effects of procedural variations in measuring interpersonal distance by means of representational space. *Psychological Reports* 36:475–91.

Tolor, A., and LeBlanc, R. F. 1974. An attempted clarification of the psychological distance construct. *Journal of Social Psychology* 92:259–67.

Tolor, A., and Orange, S. 1969. An attempt to measure psychological distance in advantaged and disadvantaged children. *Child Development* 40:407–20.

Tracy, R. L.; Lamb, M. E.; and Ainsworth, M.D.S. 1976. Infant approach behavior as related to attachment. *Child Development* 47:571–78.

Tresemer, D. E. 1977. Assumptions about gender role. In *Woman in a man-made world: A socioeconomic handbook,* 2d ed. Ed. N. Glazer and H. Y. Waehrer. Chicago: Rand-McNally.

Tyler, A. I.; Waag, W. L.; and George, C. E. 1972. Determinants of the ecology of the dyad: The effects of age and sex. *Journal of Psychology* 81:117–20.

Underwood, B.; Froming, W. J.; and Moore, B. S. 1980. Mood and personality: A search for the causal relationship. *Journal of Personality* 48:15–23.

Van Lieshout, C.F.M. 1975. Young children's reactions to barriers placed by their mothers. *Child Development* 46:879–86.

Van Rooijen, L. 1973. Talking about the bright side . . . Pleasantness of the referent as a determinant of communication accuracy. *European Journal of Social Psychology* 3:473–78.

Veitch, R.; Getsinger, A.; and Arkkelin, D. 1976. A note on the reliability and validity of the Comfortable Interpersonal Distance Scale. *Journal of Psychology* 94:163–65.

Vinacke, W. E. 1949. The judgment of facial expressions by three national-racial groups in Hawaii: I. Caucasian faces. *Journal of Personality* 17:407–29.

Vinacke, W. E., and Fong, R. W. 1955. The judgment of facial expressions by three national-racial groups in Hawaii: II. Oriental faces. *Journal of Social Psychology* 41:185–95.

Vleeming, R. G., and Engelse, J. A. 1981. Assessment of private and public self-consciousness: A Dutch replication. *Journal of Personality Assessment* 45:385–89.

Walker, J. W., and Borden, R. J. 1976. Sex, status, and the invasion of shared space. *Representative Research in Social Psychology* 7:28–34.

Walkey, F. H. 1979. Internal control, powerful others, and chance: A confirmation of Levenson's factor structure. *Journal of Personality Assessment* 43:532–35.

Warr, P. B. 1971. Pollyanna's personal judgments. *European Journal of Social Psychology* 1:327–38.

Wasserman, G. A., and Stern, D. N. 1978. An early manifestation of differential behavior toward children of the same and opposite sex. *Journal of Genetic Psychology* 133:129–37.

Wasz-Höckert, O.; Partanen, T.; Vuorenkoski, V.; Valanne, E.; and Michelsson, K. 1964. Effects of training and ability to identify preverbal vocalizations. *Developmental Medicine and Child Neurology* 6:393–96.

Weinberg, B., and Bennett, S. 1971. Speaker sex recognition of 5- and 6-year-old children's voices. *Journal of the Acoustical Society of America* 50:1210–13.

Weinraub, M., and Frankel, J. 1977. Sex differences in parent-infant interaction during free play, departure, and separation. *Child Development* 48:1240–49.

Weinraub, M., and Putney, E. 1978. The effects of height on infants' social responses to unfamiliar persons. *Child Development* 49:598–603.

Weisgerber, C. A. 1956. Accuracy in judging emotional expressions as related to college entrance test scores. *Journal of Social Psychology* 44:233–39.

———. 1957. Accuracy in judging emotional expressions as related to understanding of literature. *Journal of Social Psychology* 46:253–58.

Weitz, S., ed. 1974. *Nonverbal communication: Readings with commentary.* New York: Oxford University Press.

———. 1976. Sex differences in nonverbal communication. *Sex Roles* 2:175–184.

West, L. 1979. Women's intuition: An interdisciplinary analysis. Master's thesis, George Washington University.

Westbrook, M. 1974. Judgement of emotion: Attention versus accuracy. *British Journal of Social and Clinical Psychology* 13:383–89.

Whitcher, S. J., and Fisher, J. D. 1979. Multidimensional reaction to therapeutic touch in a hospital setting. *Journal of Personality and Social Psychology* 37:87–96.

White, G. L. 1981. Some correlates of romantic jealousy. *Journal of Personality* 49:129–47.

White, M. J. 1975. Interpersonal distance as affected by room size, status, and sex. *Journal of Social Psychology* 95:241–49.

Whiting, B., and Edwards, C. P. 1973. A cross-cultural analysis of sex differences in the behavior of children aged three through 11. *Journal of Social Psychology* 91:171–88.

Whiting, B. B., and Whiting, J.W.M. 1975. *Children of six cultures: A psychocultural analysis.* Cambridge: Harvard University Press.

Wiener, M.; Devoe, S.; Rubinow, S.; and Geller, J. 1972. Nonverbal behavior and nonverbal communication. *Psychological Review* 79:185–214.

Williams, D. G. 1973. So-called "nervous habits." *Journal of Psychology* 83:103–9.

Williams, J. E., and Best, D. L. 1977. Sex stereotypes and trait favorability on the Adjective Check List. *Educational and Psychological Measurement* 37:101–10.

Williams, S. J., and Willis, F. N. 1978. Interpersonal touch among preschool children at play. *Psychological Record* 28:501–8.

Williams, S. L., and Hicks, R. A. 1980. Sex, iride pigmentation, and the pupillary attributions of college students to happy and angry faces. *Bulletin of the Psychonomic Society* 16:67–68.

Willis, F. N., Jr. 1966. Initial speaking distance as a function of the speakers' relationship. *Psychonomic Science* 5:221–22.

Willis, F. N.; Carlson, R.; and Reeves, D. 1979. The development of personal space in primary school children. *Environmental Psychology and Nonverbal Behavior* 3:195–204.

Willis, F. N., Jr.; Gier, J. A.; and Smith, D. E. 1979. Stepping aside: Correlates of displacement in pedestrians. *Journal of Communication* 29(Autumn):34–39.

Willis, F. N., and Hofmann, G. E. 1975. Development of tactile patterns in relation to age, sex, and race. *Developmental Psychology* 11:866.

Willis, F. N., and Reeves, D. L. 1976. Touch interactions in junior high students in relation to sex and race. *Developmental Psychology* 12:91–92.

Willis, F. N.; Reeves, D. L.; and Buchanan, D. R. 1976. Interpersonal touch in high school relative to sex and race. *Perceptual and Motor Skills* 43:843–47.

Willis, F. N., and Rinck, C. M. 1983. A personal log method for investigating interpersonal touch. *Journal of Psychology* 113:119–22.

Willis, F. N.; Rinck, C. M.; and Dean, L. M. 1978. Interpersonal touch among adults in cafeteria lines. *Perceptual and Motor Skills* 47:1147–52.

Witryol, S. L., and Kaess, W. A. 1957. Sex differences in social memory tasks. *Journal of Abnormal and Social Psychology* 54:343–46.

Wittig, M. A., and Skolnick, P. 1978. Status versus warmth as determinants of sex differences in personal space. *Sex Roles* 4:493–503.

Wood, M. M. 1966. The influence of sex and knowledge of communication effectiveness on spontaneous speech. *Word* 22:112–37.

Woolfolk, A. 1978. Student learning and performance under varying conditions of teacher verbal and nonverbal evaluative communication. *Journal of Educational Psychology* 70:87–94.

Word, C. C.; Zanna, M. P.; and Cooper, J. 1974. The nonverbal mediation of self-fulfilling prophecies in interracial interaction. *Journal of Experimental Social Psychology* 10:109–20.

Yairi, E. 1981. Disfluencies of normally speaking two-year-old children. *Journal of Speech and Hearing Research* 24:490–95.

Yando, R.; Zigler, E.; and Gates, M. 1971. The influence of Negro and white teachers rated as effective or noneffective on the performance of Negro and white lower-class children. *Developmental Psychology* 5:290–99.

Yarmey, A. D. 1974. Proactive interference in short-term retention of human faces. *Canadian Journal of Psychology* 28:333–38.

———. 1979. The effects of attractiveness, feature saliency and liking on memory for faces. In *Love and attraction*. Ed. M. Cook and G. Wilson. Oxford: Pergamon.

Yin, R. K. 1969. Looking at upside-down faces. *Journal of Experimental Psychology* 81:141–45.

Young, A. W., and Ellis, H. D. 1976. An experimental investigation of developmental differences in ability to recognise faces presented to the left and right cerebral hemispheres. *Neuropsychologia* 14:495–98.

Young, F. M. 1947. The incidence of nervous habits observed in college students. *Journal of Personality* 15:309–20.

Young-Browne, G.; Rosenfeld, H. M.; and Horowitz, F. D. 1977. Infant discrimination of facial expressions. *Child Development* 48:555–62.

Zahn, G. L. 1973. Cognitive integration of verbal and vocal information in spoken sentences. *Journal of Experimental Social Psychology* 9:320–34.

———. 1975. Verbal-vocal integration as a function of sex and methodology. *Journal of Research in Personality* 9:226–39.

Zaidel, S. F., and Mehrabian, A. 1969. The ability to communicate and infer positive and negative attitudes facially and vocally. *Journal of Experimental Research in Personality* 3:233–41.

Zelazo, P. R. 1971. Smiling to social stimuli: Eliciting and conditioning effects. *Developmental Psychology* 4:32–42.

Zigler, E.; Levine, J.; and Gould, L. 1966. Cognitive processes in the development of children's appreciation of humor. *Child Development* 37:507–18.

Zimmerman, D. H., and West, C. 1975. Sex roles, interruptions and silences in conversation. In *Language and sex: Difference and dominance.* Ed. B. Thorne and N. Henley. Rowley, Mass.: Newbury House.

Zuckerman, M., and Allison, S. N. 1976. An objective measure of fear of success: Construction and validation. *Journal of Personality Assessment* 40:422–30.

Zuckerman, M.; DeFrank, R. S.; Hall, J. A.; Larrance, D. T.; and Rosenthal, R. 1979. Facial and vocal cues of deception and honesty. *Journal of Experimental Social Psychology* 15:378–96.

Zuckerman, M.; DeFrank, R. S.; Spiegel, N. H.; and Larrance, D. T. 1982. Masculinity-femininity and encoding of nonverbal cues. *Journal of Personality and Social Psychology* 42:548–56.

Zuckerman, M.; DePaulo, B. M.; and Rosenthal, R. 1981. Verbal and nonverbal communication of deception. In *Advances in experimental social psychology,* vol. 14. Ed. L. Berkowitz. New York: Academic Press.

Zuckerman, M.; Hall, J. A.; DeFrank, R. S.; and Rosenthal, R. 1976. Encoding and decoding of spontaneous and posed facial expressions. *Journal of Personality and Social Psychology* 34:966–77.

Zuckerman, M., and Larrance, D. T. 1979. Individual differences in perceived encoding and decoding abilities. In *Skill in nonverbal communication: Individual differences.* Ed. R. Rosenthal. Cambridge, Mass.: Oelgeschlager, Gunn & Hain.

Zuckerman, M.; Larrance, D. T.; Hall, J. A.; DeFrank, R. S.; and Rosenthal, R. 1979. Posed and spontaneous communication of emotion via facial and vocal cues. *Journal of Personality* 47:712–33.

Zuckerman, M.; Larrance, D. T.; Porac, J.F.A.; and Blanck, P. D. 1980. Effects of fear of success on intrinsic motivation, causal attribution, and choice behavior. *Journal of Personality and Social Psychology* 39:503–13.

Zuckerman, M.; Lipets, M. S.; Koivumaki, J. H.; and Rosenthal, R. 1975. Encoding and decoding nonverbal cues of emotion. *Journal of Personality and Social Psychology* 32:1068–76.

Zuckerman, M., and Przewuzman, S. J. 1979. Decoding and encoding facial expressions in preschool-age children. *Environmental Psychology and Nonverbal Behavior* 3:147–63.

Index

Judith A. Hall is assistant professor in the
Department of Social Medicine and Health Policy,
Harvard Medical School, and coauthor of Sensitivity to
Nonverbal Communication: The PONS Test *(also*
published by Johns Hopkins).